The Sixteenth Regiment Tennessee Volunteers

"Twenty-five Hours To Tragedy"

To Jim,
thanks for your
Support!

[signature]

(Author's Collection)

In memory of 1ˢᵗ Lieutenant William H. White and his brother Corporal John White

Company D

The History of

The

Sixteenth Tennessee Volunteer Infantry Regiment

In the American Civil War

~

A Consolidated Sesquicentennial Diary of the War

1861-1865

In Three Volumes

~

Volume II

"No hope of getting out alive."

September 1862 – December 1863

The History of the Sixteenth Tennessee Volunteer Infantry Regiment: Volume II "No hope of getting out alive."

Spring Hill, Tennessee

Printed in the United States of America

ISBN-13: 978-1480291249

ISBN-10: 1480291242

LCCN: 2012921870

BISAC: History / Military / United States

Cover photo courtesy of Robert Pratt

Acknowledgements: Tennessee State Library and Archives, The National Archives, The Library of Congress, Thomas K. Potter III, The Magness House Library, Neal Pistole, David Fraley, Stan Castles, Nancy Calhoun, Greg Biggs, Jim Brown, Tim Burgess, Andy Maloney, Ronald T. Clemmons, Gary Jolly and all who have supported me in this twenty-five year endeavor allowing use of photographs and other documents.

CONTENTS

Preface to the Series...10

Foreword...12

Introduction to Volume II...15

PREFACE
TO THE SERIES

The Sixteenth Tennessee Infantry is one of the most documented regiments of the southern Confederacy in the War Between the States. For this reason, and that I was fortunate enough to have ancestors that survived four years in this regiment through some of the hardest fought battles of the war, this regiment was selected to portray the everyday life of Confederate soldiers through one of the toughest struggles in American history. Included are photos, illustrations, maps and a day to day biography of the regiment as a whole. This will not only chronicle the story of the Sixteenth Regiment, but also be of invaluable aid to other researchers as to the lives of the men with whom the Sixteenth was brigaded with from the commencement of the war till its close. Considerable information will be had for those interested in the 8th Tennessee, 28th Tennessee, 51st Tennessee, 38th Tennessee, Donelson's Brigade, Wright's Brigade, Carter's Brigade as well as Cheatham's Division in the Army of Tennessee.

The Sixteenth Regiment participated in a much lesser chronicled, but equally intriguing West Virginia Campaign at the close of 1861. This campaign was vividly recalled by the men who endured it as a most trying struggle against illness and cold with a relatively uneventful conclusion. From there they are taken to the Atlantic coast of South Carolina and on to Mississippi for the actions around Corinth. By the autumn of 1862 they advance with Bragg and the Army to invade Kentucky and participate in the battle of Perryville with extremely heavy loss losing over fifty percent of their number engaged.

The close of 1862 found the regiment engaged in the Battle of Murfreesboro suffering an over fifty percent casualty rate once again.

Thence they moved on with the army where they quartered and fortified both Shelbyville and Tullahoma, Tennessee. Forced out of Tennessee in July of 1863 by the Federal army, the regiment participated in the Battle of Chickamauga and Missionary Ridge and was temporarily placed under Cleburne's command helping to form the rear guard of the army on their withdrawal to Dalton. From Dalton to Atlanta, the regiment served gallantly opposing Sherman's march, and fought with distinction during the battles of July 20th and 22nd at Atlanta. At Jonesboro, the regiment helped to save the Confederate right flank from disaster. Finally, following the fall of Atlanta, they were consolidated with two other regiments at Palmetto Station in September of 1864 due to dwindling numbers.

Under John Bell Hood, the Sixteenth advanced into Tennessee fighting at Franklin and Nashville and then participated in the rear guard actions back to the Tennessee River and on to Meridian, Mississippi in January 1865. In the last campaign of the war, they once again helped save the only escape route of the army fighting under the leadership of Joe Johnston at Bentonville—the final major battle of the war. Within weeks, the remnants of the regiment were surrendered at Greensboro, North Carolina. The long march home is also chronicled, and some of the hardships for them after their return home.

Lastly, this biography of the regiment is dedicated to my great-great-grandfather, First Lieutenant William H. White, and his brother Corporal John White, who served faithfully with the regiment through all of the engagements excepting the last at Bentonville. It is truly my hope that readers may greet these pages with as much enthusiasm as I had as I uncovered these revealing documents and memoirs that divulge the hardships and triumphs experienced by this regiment. These men truly deserve our respect and admiration.

FOREWORD

The history of the Sixteenth Tennessee has long been a passion of mine. When I learned as a young boy that my great-great-grandfather William H. White had served in the regiment, my interest focused on him and the battles that he had participated in. It was, however, many years before I was able to truly dig into his past and learn of the day to day activities and hardships that he and his comrades faced.

After a stint in the Marine Corps, I was finally able to do my own in depth research on the regiment. It became vividly clear to me—within a year or so of researching the regiment—that most of my knowledge of William H. White would be strictly from information obtained in his service records and pension applications. While in search of information about him, I continued to locate more memoirs, letters and documents pertaining to the regiment. Many of these documents contained in depth information about other members of the regiment, but due to the authors' proximity to Lieutenant White, he is unfortunately never mentioned by these first hand contributors.

Although I did find a photograph of him with the other members of his color guard at the unveiling of the Confederate Monument at Perryville in 1904, I found no written information concerning Lt. White outside of his personal documents that were on microfilm at the Tennessee State Library and Archives. Mostly due to this fact—what initially started out as a brief history of his life— eventually evolved into this book. As I read account after account of the men serving with him, it became clear to me that information specific to William was not that important.

I came to realize that he shared the same hardships, hunger, dehydration, soreness and battle fatigue that all of the other accounts of these veterans of the same regiment had. He laughed at the same Jeff Davis jokes, shared his coffee and rations, led them in battle, and likely wrote home to many widows to inform them of their husband's death. The stories that these men told—all of them belonging to the Sixteenth Regiment Tennessee Volunteers—*was in fact*—William's story of the war.

I had come across too many interesting characters and too many funny acts of youth in the military to keep these to myself. I nearly felt as if I would be doing an injustice to all these other men by not telling of *their* lives and stories—to tell their *collective* story. What follows is the story of *all* of the men of the Sixteenth Regiment Tennessee Volunteers. Their marches, their meals, their battles, the boredom, the filth, their enthusiasm, their gloom and nearly all the emotions that they experienced are laid down on these pages. Yet this is not the first attempt by an individual to tell the story of these brave and enduring men.

Thomas Head, an actual veteran of the regiment, wrote a book entitled <u>Campaigns and Battles of the Sixteenth Regiment Tennessee Volunteers</u>. Who better to tell the story than a veteran of the regiment? His book failed in no way covering the trials and hardships of the men as they performed their duties throughout the war; however, Head was captured at Kennesaw Mountain in 1864 and apparently relied on other books for much of the information concerning the regiment's activities for the remainder of the war. Some of these events were correctly related, while others were not. He was apparently the first to compile a list of the original members of companies and their initial commanders—but not due to his own failure— he left out many if not most all of the conscripts and other volunteers that joined the regiment during the course of the war. His story lacked only what time and research one-hundred plus years later could locate.

The pranks of soldiers, graphic accounts of wounds, day to day location and in-depth battle study will hopefully portray the most comprehensive and well rounded account of this regiment, and perhaps brigade, for many years to come, when yet another history will replace this one with more long lost accounts that can shed even greater light on the subject of these gallant and patriotic men. It is my hope that this regimental history certainly meets and hopefully exceeds the expectations of the most astute regimental historians as well as the arm chair generals that dab into Civil War history on occasion. I hope that as you read these pages, whether or not you had an ancestor in this particular regiment, you will gain a greater appreciation for the service of men on both sides of the battle line and find yourself truly amazed at the level of dedication that most all of these men proved over the course of our country's four year struggle.

INTRODUCTION TO VOLUME II

The first sixteen months of the Sixteenth Tennessee's service saw the men form individual companies into a regiment that was ten companies strong numbering about a thousand men. They were transferred to Western Virginia and saw action under Robert E. Lee in actions at Cheat Mountain. By December of 1861, the regiment and brigade were transferred to coastal duty south of Charleston, South Carolina. They remained there until the Battle of Shiloh was fought when they were immediately sent to Corinth, Mississippi. After participating in the skirmishes around that place, they withdrew with the army to Chattanooga in preparation for the Kentucky campaign ending their first sixteenth months of service.

This volume of their history explores their second stage of service. Those men who had survived their first sixteen months in the Confederate army through illness and skirmishes now encountered the most trying situation yet—full scale combat. The Battle of Perryville quickly enlightened the men as to what awaited them in future engagements. Having lost over fifty percent of their effective total, only the efforts of the Conscription Bureau could help to fill the vacancies caused by battle casualties in the Sixteenth Tennessee. Following the retreat from Kentucky and a brief lull in action at Tullahoma, the regiment joined the rest of the army at Murfreesboro. In less than three months they engaged in their second great battle and once again suffered over fifty percent casualties at the epicenter of the battle at "Hell's Half Acre." After withdrawing to Shelbyville and participating to a lesser degree in the Tullahoma Campaign, the army retreated to Chattanooga in July of 1863 under the leadership of a new brigade commander and regimental commander.

General Bragg engaged the Federals at Chickamauga in September, 1863 and won a signal victory with the Sixteenth

Tennessee suffering losses of over twenty percent. Bragg failed to follow up the army's success, and the Federal army occupied Chattanooga. The cracker lines opened up and supplied the Federals until they were strong enough to attempt a breakout of the besieged city. Cheatham's Division had been split up under Bragg's direction and there was ample dissatisfaction amongst the boys. After spending a month at Charleston, Tennessee guarding the bridge there, the brigade was marched back to Chattanooga in time to participate in the Battle of Missionary Ridge. There, they eventually fell under the temporary command of Brigadier General Lucius Polk of Cleburne's Division for the rear guard action protecting the army's retreat to Dalton. They ended 1863 in winter quarters at Dalton, Georgia preparing for what was to come—HELL.

Presently, the regiment and brigade had just departed Chattanooga for the commencement of the Kentucky Campaign. On August 31st they marched over Walden Ridge and descended into the valley four miles south of Pikeville. Unionists heavily infiltrated this place, and the boys longed to see their families so close by.

Chapter I

Off to Old Kentucky
1 September – 7 October 1862

Early on the morning of September 1st, Donelson's brigade raised their sore bodies and continued on a short march until they arrived at Pikeville, Tennessee. They halted there and lay around resting most of the day, but at six p.m., the brigade picked up and continued on toward Sparta. This night march was conducted on purpose as the heat was still intense enough to cause sunstroke. One soldier called Pikeville—occupied in the heart of the Sequatchie Valley—"...a dark spot of the world" as it was well recognized as a Union stronghold. They were happy to leave that night. The boys started the trek up the Cumberland Plateau and Little Mountain near dark and never stopped until they reached Cane Creek sixteen miles distant. Many of the men fell out of the march as the road ascending the mountain was so steep. They finally arrived near the creek at dawn on September 2nd and set up camp to rest thru the day and night.[1]

At 8 a.m. on the 3rd of September, they packed up and marched to Sparta and two miles beyond on the Gainesboro Road where they set up camp a little after 2 p.m.[2] Here, the army sat idle for the next two days. Just like when they were at Chattanooga, family members poured in from the surrounding counties to show

---

[1] (Womack, p. 58)(Etter, p. 15)
[2] (Womack, p. 58)

their support. James R. Thompson's father had come to see him off, and he wrote of the fare that they received one afternoon.

> There – many of our friends from White and adjoining counties came to see us. There was much rejoicing in our regiment. Our friends brought baskets and provisions and queensware and tablecloths. And a good lady by the name of Pollard arranged our dinner by spreading a nice white tablecloth on the grass and a full supply of nice white plates and a home-cooked dinner, which we enjoyed to the full extent.[3]

Others found themselves close enough to home to nearly get into some trouble. While many of the boys sought visitation by many friends and relatives, some of the more mischievous youngsters were on the lookout for good old Tennessee Applejack.[4]

> ... a comrade named Smartt and I started out to see if we could find just a bit of it. We would inquire of the natives and went to several distilleries and finally after going about eight miles we found it. We had two Yankee canteens apiece and had them filled and you never saw two happier fellows than we were when we started back to camp. We met some of Bragg's escort and the captain of the squad asked us if we had any liquor, and Smartt, fool-like, said we had some of the best apple brandy he ever saw, and right there is where Smartt made the mistake of his life for the Captain said, 'Well, boys, you'll have to pour it out.' That remark nearly broke my heart for I knew the jig was up, so we commenced to empty our canteens. As I emptied mine I stepped back through the soldiers, spilling the contents of one of mine on the ground. The other was under my coat and I saved that from devastation. Smartt got

---

[3] (Thompson, p. 8) The Mrs. Pollard referred to is believed to be Thursey or Nancy Pollard the mothers of either Thomas R. Pollard or Joseph M. Pollard of Company G. They were cousins, and both of them were from Frank's Ferry in White County.

[4] (Womack, p. 58)

rid of all that he had. The captain then said if we would go back with him where we got it we should have our money back, so Smartt went back with them and I stayed where we emptied our canteens. One of the cavalrymen asked me if I did not have some left. I told him to hush for if the captain should find it out it would be Katy with me so he went with the rest of the crowd. When Smartt got back we put ourselves in shape not to pour any of the rest on the ground and when we got back to camp about sundown Smartt[5] was cutting up so the Colonel was about to put him under guard but he did not and neither of us was punished for our trip.[6]

A number of boys had joined the Sixteenth while temporarily stationed at Chattanooga. Carroll Henderson Clark[7] had three buddies that would remain by his side for a long time to come that

---

[5] Private Ezekiel Smartt, of Company B, enlisted on May 23, 1861. He was sick at Bath Alum Springs in September 1861 and apparently rejoined the regiment right after Cheat Mountain. He was officially listed as Missing October 8, 1862 at Perryville and never returned to the regiment. It is likely he was observed by some other men of the regiment still alive and supposed captured and paroled; thus, he is listed as having deserted on January 1, 1863. He was 27 years old in 1863. There is an Ezekiel Smart listed in the 1850, 1860, 1880 and 1900 census in Grundy County that fits his age.

[6] (Carden, p. Apr. 5)

[7] Private Carroll Henderson Clark, of Company I, enlisted on May 20, 1861. He was promoted to 3rd Sergeant between July and September 1862. Clark was slightly wounded at Perryville on October 8, 1862. He was 22 years old in 1863. On July 22, 1864 at Atlanta, he was shot in the upper left forearm which broke the bone. Two days later Clark was admitted to Ocmulgee Hospital in Macon. He was later transferred to a hospital in Cuthbert, Georgia south of Columbus. He rejoined the regiment at Columbia, Tennessee during the retreat from Nashville. Clark was present as 2nd Lieutenant of Company F, 1st Consolidated Regiment Tennessee Volunteers at the final surrender on April 26, 1865 and paroled on May 1st at Greensboro, SC.

joined in August 1862: Jim Martin[8], George[9] and Math[10] McBride. Many of them had been too young to join up the previous spring and fall of 1861. Now, they found the proximity of the army very enticing; and with or without permission, they joined the ranks as the army passed.[11]

Naturally while at Sparta, many of the White County boys received bountiful supplies from family and friends in the neighborhood. A number of them received one or two day furloughs that lived in the neighboring counties. By the evening of the 5th, all the troops were to be back in the ranks, and on the clear, hot morning of September 6th, they broke camp again and marched seventeen miles in the direction of Gainesboro, Tennessee. All along the route through White and Putnam Counties, women and children lined the roadsides sharing their goodbyes with many of the boys that they would never see again. That night the Sixteenth camped on Knee Branch west of Cookeville.[12]

The morning of September 7th, they commenced the march at 5 a.m. and reached Gainesboro by 3 o'clock that afternoon. They

---

[8] Private James "Jim" Martin, of Company I, enlisted on August 20, 1862. He was elected 3rd Corporal only twenty days later. He was 18 years old in July 1863. Martin was present thru April of 1864 at which time his service records end. A James Martin, 24 years old and son of W. C. Martin, is found living in Van Buren County, TN in the 1870 census and again at age 77 in the same county in the 1920 census.

[9] Private George W. McBride, of Company I, enlisted on August 1, 1862. He was 18 years old in July 1863. He was present with the regiment at the final surrender on April 26, 1865 in Company F, 1st Consolidated Regiment Tennessee Volunteers and paroled on May 1, 1865 at Greensboro, NC.

[10] Private Mathew "Math" McBride, of Company I, enlisted on August 1, 1862. Math was 19 years old in July 1863. His last record is a clothing issue on September 20, 1864 with the regiment. A Matt McBride is listed in the 1880 census in Van Buren County with his wife Jane at age 35, and again in the 1900 and 1910 census in same county. His father was listed in the 1860 census as Daniel McBride. George was his brother.

[11] (Clark, p. #12)

[12] (Head T. A., p. 92)(Etter, p. 15)(Carden, p. Apr. 12)

continued two miles west of town to the Cumberland River and camped for the night.[13]

> A lot of us went down to the river to go in bathing, and I remember a circumstance that occurred while we were in the river. Some of our teamsters came down to water their mules and one of our boys asked permission of one of the teamsters to lead one of the mules into the water. There were several in the water at the time and the mule soon got into deep water and if there ever was a circus that mule certainly made one. It was but a little while till everybody was out on the bank and the soldier and the mule had the whole river to themselves. The soldier finally got away from the mule and we thought sure the animal would drown. Sometimes his head would come to the surface, then the other end would show up, then his feet were up, then he would disappear altogether but he finally quit his capers, stuck his nose out of the water, circled around a little and came ashore.[14]

The following morning, they retraced their steps four miles to the east and, taking off their shoes and rolling up their pants, they crossed the Cumberland River and marched up Jenning's Creek toward Tompkinsville. On the 9th, the march took them into Kentucky, and after twenty-three miles over rugged hills, they camped one mile south of Tompkinsville at 6 p.m. The following day the regiment remained in camps, and the boys were ordered to mend their worn and ragged clothing.[15]

On September 11th, they drew only half rations, departed at 10 a.m. and marched twelve miles toward Glasgow, Kentucky to encamp. The next day, they marched eighteen miles and arrived at Glasgow tired and hungry. The regiment stayed in the vicinity of Glasgow till the 15th only moving their camp one mile on the 14th. At noon on the 15th, they marched toward Munfordville fifteen miles

---

[13] (Womack, p. 58)
[14] (Carden, p. Apr. 12)
[15] (Tucker, p. 47) (Clark, p. #12) (Etter, p. 15)

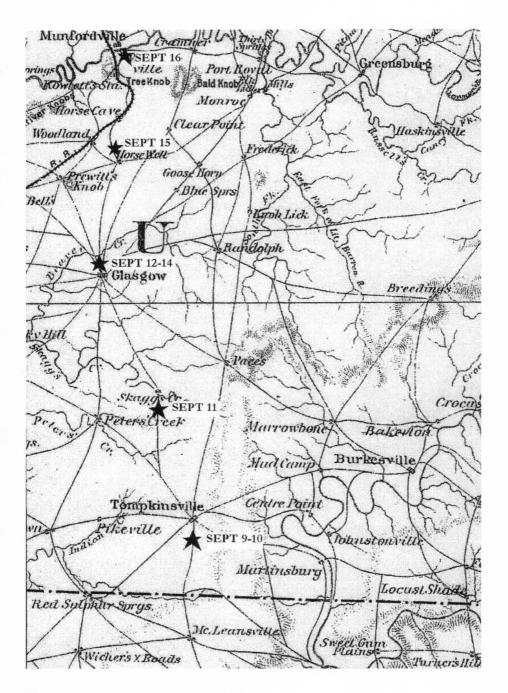

and halted to camp at dark. The following morning, they marched at daylight and stopped at 10 p.m. in position to invest the fort at that place.[16] That night, as Donelson's Brigade was arriving in line on the field, the rear guard of a leading brigade opened fire on Donelson and his staff as they rode ahead to determine their position on the field. Captain W. E. Lowe[17], A.I.G. for Donelson, was struck and killed by the volley. General Donelson's horse, as well as two or three other horses, was struck by the gunfire as well. That didn't end the excitement for the night however, as a sort of stampede took place throughout the army that night. Apparently, a team of horses got spooked pulling a wagon or caisson of some sort. Without a driver, the frightened horses ran headlong down the line of troops.[18]

> Everyone was asleep, I suppose, and such running and scrambling I never saw. I remember that I was so scared that I left my gun lying in the road and everybody seemed to be hunting a tree to get behind. I think a Yankee corporal's guard could have captured the whole outfit. I understood at the time that the panic ran through the whole army.[19]

Although the regiment had benefited from a small wave of new recruits in August from their counties of origin at home, few—now—seemed willing to join up. Back in McMinnville, Captain Womack had been temporarily detached to help recruit men from his old community. He had spent several days attempting to entice boys into joining the army to "defend their homes." Apparently, with little luck, he recorded in his diary that, "I am forced to the conclusion that but few men, now at home, can be induced to volunteer in the

---

[16] (Sullivan, p. 57)
[17] Captain Washington E. Lowe had served for a year in the 14th Tennessee Infantry and was serving on Brig. Gen. Donelson's staff as Assistant Inspector General when he was killed by friendly fire on September 16, 1862. He was 26 years old.
[18] (Tucker, p. 47) (Carden, p. Apr. 12)
[19] (Carden, p. Apr. 12)

service of their country. Many young men with whom I have met ought to be in the service, but their patriotism is blank."[20]

Back at Munfordville, the regiment was in position near the fort where they slept till daybreak when they were informed that the Yankees had surrendered at about 4 a.m. that morning. Four-thousand-five-hundred enemy soldiers were given up without the Sixteenth losing a single man, but the same could not be said for other Confederate troops. Upon Bragg's departure from Walden's Ridge back in Tennessee, General Buell, the commander of Federal forces in Nashville, had lost contact with the Confederate army. It had not been until their appearance at Gainesboro that Buell recognized a potential threat in his rear, and preparations were immediately made for a retrograde movement to prevent being cut off.[21] General Bragg had hoped to march rapidly to place his forces north of Green River at the Louisville and Nashville railroad before Buell could arrive there. On September 15th, Bragg had ordered Chalmers' Brigade and a detachment of cavalry with two pieces of artillery to Munfordville at the railroad for a reconnaissance in force. He was instructed to conduct a feint movement to determine the strength of the enemy. After arriving there, Chalmers apparently underestimated the number of troops garrisoning the works or misunderstood his orders. Moving into position, he assaulted the fort and was repulsed in a matter of minutes losing about four-hundred men in the process.[22]

Donelson's Brigade stayed at Munfordville all that day, and some of the boys took the time to go investigate the fort which they considered to be of very strong construction. That evening, they received orders to march to Bacon Creek eight miles away. After arriving there, they received orders to march back to Munfordville, and in a heavy rain, they made their way back. Tearing down rail fences, they built large fires and slept soundly through the rain all night. The next day the brigade was ordered back to Bacon Creek.

---

[20] (Womack, pp. 59-60)
[21] (Sullivan, p. 58) (Head T. A., p. 92)
[22] (Head T. A., pp. 92-93)

At daylight on September 19th, the brigade moved out once again for Munfordville and arrived there and stayed there all day and night. The afternoon of the 20th, the brigade received orders to march up the Louisville Pike and traveled about twenty-two miles before stopping.[23]

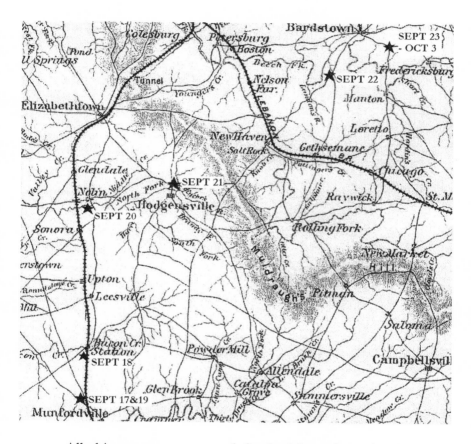

All this movement to and fro had been brought about by Bragg's failure to engage Buell at Munfordville. It had been Bragg's hope that Buell would come within striking distance or perhaps assail his forces, but by the 21st, it became clear that Buell's army was not

---

[23] (Tucker, p. 47) (Sullivan, p. 58)

only racing to Louisville but had a distance advantage as well. Bragg had—at this point—not only failed to bring on battle with Buell, but he had failed to cut off Buell from Louisville or make it to that city first. With this understood on September 21st, Bragg turned his army east. That day Donelson's Brigade marched twelve miles east and camped at Hodgenville.[24]

September 22nd, the brigade marched through New Haven and on to near Bardstown and halted after twenty-four miles. Here, they stayed the night until the next evening when they marched on through Bardstown and five miles down the Springfield Pike. The brigade and army remained encamped in this location for eleven days from September 23rd through the afternoon of October 4th. While here, the boys saw some of the captured Yankees from Munfordville who had been paroled and were heading back north. On the 26th, orders were read that called for a general inspection of arms and clothing at 9 a.m. the following morning. The regiment passed with everything in good order.[25]

Nothing else of consequence took place while the boys were camped outside of Bardstown other than company drill the last day of September and the first two days of October. It was clear that something was going to happen and likely very quickly. On the 2nd, orders were issued to be ready to move at a moment's notice. On October 4th, the orders arrived. That morning, they marched five miles to Frederickburg[26] and an additional ten miles passing through Springfield and encamped in a beautiful country. At 6 a.m. the morning of the 5th, they continued the march for twenty-seven miles and passed through Perryville and within three miles of Danville. The next morning, the brigade passed through Danville and arrived at Harrodsburg after marching thirteen miles. It was mid-afternoon

---

[24] (Head T. A., p. 93) (Tucker, p. 47)
[25] (Tucker, p. 47) (Sullivan, p. 58)
[26] Frederickburg is now known as Fredericktown.

of the 6th when they arrived, and the boys laid out their blankets to camp for the night.[27]

On October 7th, the brigade stayed in camps until about sunset. That same day Captain Womack returned to the regiment from his detached duty. At dusk, the division received orders to march to Perryville. The boys stepped off and began arriving at the hamlet about midnight. Most of the division spent the night in Perryville and east of it along Harrodsburg Road. Morning came too quickly for the footsore Confederates.

---

[27] (Sullivan, p. 59) (Tucker, p. 47)

Chapter II

The Battle of Perryville

Morning - 8 October 1862

As the pink hue of daybreak lit the eastern sky, the boys were woken from their restless slumber. It was a beautiful, clear October morning. Sporadic gunfire was already heard by 8 a.m. north and slightly west of Perryville and their division's current position. Cheatham's Division had been positioned the night before as far west as the city cemetery in which a portion of Maney's Brigade had slept amongst the tombstones. Stewart's and Donelson's Brigades were scattered across downtown Perryville with Donelson's Brigade the furthest east brigade. The men lay on their arms until as late as 10 a.m. that morning.[28]

Cannonading had been heard as early as sunrise, and as the morning progressed, the Federal batteries were occasionally responded to by Confederate guns. By about 9 a.m., it was reported that the Confederate skirmishers had been driven in, and a heavier volume of rifle fire was heard all along the front. Cheatham's Division was on the right of Polk's Corps, and about 10 a.m., Brigadier General Donelson was ordered to move his brigade to the right—east of town into the dry bed of Chaplin River. They halted on the road to Harrodsburg, and Donelson ordered the fence to be

---

[28] (Tucker, p. 47)

thrown down. The column then advanced about a half a mile down the bed of Chaplin River.[29]

About noon, Carnes' Battery, of Donelson's Brigade, was ordered forward to a ridgeline to engage the enemy front plainly visible at about 800 yards from the crest. Captain Carnes stated that it seemed that all the artillery on both sides seemed to open fire near the same time. Most of the fire was directed at Loomis' and Simonson's batteries. After sustaining their fire at four rounds a minute for over forty-five minutes, Carnes was ordered to withdraw his guns. The enemy guns had found their range. Carnes' guns—all 6 lb. Napoleons—were not accurate enough at that range. While no men were injured in this initial combat, Carnes lost three horses killed while engaged in the barrage. For two or so hours, Federal and Confederate guns had exchanged fire at an increasingly higher rate of fire.[30]

The regiment had followed in rear of the brigade battery and halted in defilade near the creek. They sat idly by for a considerable time. An occasional shell from an enemy battery would fly overhead or clip a treetop sending acorns raining to the ground during the cannonade. The day was beautiful with hardly a cloud in the sky, and the sun shone brightly as they sat amongst their comrades in conversation with many for the last time in the waist deep, tanned grass. They had meandered through the fields alongside Chaplin Creek a few hundred yards distant. Some of the boys took advantage of the creek to draw water for their canteens. Others just stared at the heavens, anxious of what awaited them.[31]

Earlier, Colonel Wharton's Cavalry had identified the Federal left flank. Continuing to arrive on the field, the Federals were pressing to extend their left flank to the east and north. Generals Polk and Cheatham had ridden to a point several hundred yards beyond the nearest Federal forces just west of Walker's Bend and in

---

[29] (Womack, p. 62) (Lindsley, p. 812)
[30] (Lindsley, p. 812) (Womack, p. 62)
[31] (Biggs, p. 141)

the vicinity of Wharton's cavalry. From their position, they saw the enemy advancing on the Benton Road from what would later be recognized as Starkweather's Heights. This force of the enemy was apparently in the act of deploying a battery of guns on an open knob.

Wharton had managed to delay the process with his troopers' nearby presence. Polk intended to take advantage of this Federal stumbling block. His intent was to move Cheatham's Division north immediately from its assembly area to an attack position due east of the enemy's most northern limit of deployment. Cheatham would assail the Federal left before they were prepared for the attack and route the enemy forces in their front effectively crushing the Federal left wing. Wharton was to send the 8th Texas Cavalry to brush the Federal skirmishers from a hilltop near by the attack position.[32] They would have to move quickly to take advantage of the situation. Couriers were immediately sent to Cheatham's Division—the lead brigade being Donelson's—with the Sixteenth Tennessee in the vanguard. Orders were then issued to make a double-quick march down the creek to the north. In moments, the boys were on the move and rapidly advancing along the creek with all their gear at the ready. A distance of about a mile brought them to a bottom a few hundred yards long with a steep ascent immediately on the west side of the creek.

It was nearly 2 p.m. when Captain Carnes was allowed to change position at his insistence to his commander. The battery had previously withdrawn to the cover of a depression. Soon after feeding their horses by the cover of the ridge, the battery was moved off to the north, and only minutes later, Donelson's Brigade was ordered to follow. Donelson's five Tennessee regiments were double-quicked about a mile north to a point near Walker's Bend and just a short distance from Chaplin River. Here, Carnes' Battery was attempting to gain the heights of a ridge on the north side of the bend. Seeing his difficulty in ascending the bluff and farm fence at

---

[32] (MacMurphy, p. Oct. 30) This hill was the first hilltop and finger descending from the ridgeline, only about 500 yards or so from the 'Open Knob.'

the top, the 8th and 51st Tennessee Regiments were temporarily detached by General Polk to render assistance in gaining the summit and provide support in Carnes' new position.[33]

This left Brigadier General Donelson with only three regiments for his command. The 15th, 16th and 38th Tennessee Regiments had just arrived at a position a hundred yards or less from Chaplin River. They stopped only long enough to pile away their blankets and knapsacks and any excess weight to render them unencumbered for battle. They moved through a narrow wood and crossed the creek. Now they faced a sixty foot nearly vertical ascent. This part of the bend had a high western wall that was covered in timber and undergrowth. To assume their attack position, the steep face of the bank had to be climbed.[34]

They quickly fell into line, and at the command, they began the fatiguing ascent up the nearly vertical rise from the creek bed. Grabbing at saplings and tree trunks, the boys pulled themselves slowly up the fifty-plus foot ascent; others were afforded the luxury of a "dug road" on the right of the regiment and took advantage of it. Primarily due to this, the Sixteenth was the first regiment to complete the climb.[35] Colonel Savage had taken advantage of the road as well. The road had been well beaten by the trampling of Wharton's men and the general staff of Polk and Cheatham. As Savage reached the top, he rode forward a couple hundred yards to a slight ridge running nearly north-south and surveyed the field to his front. As he looked west, he noted a distant battery of cannon deployed in a field.[36] Between his position and the battery, there was an open beech forest that descended and then rose back to another ridge line only three

---

[33] (Lindsley, p. 812) (Womack, p. 62)

[34] (Lindsley, p. 812) (Womack, p. 62) (Savage, p. 119)

[35] (Thompson, p. 9)

[36] This is believed to be Stone's battery and visible to Savage from the first finger at an elevation of 880 feet and seeing the distant battery at about 920 feet elevation with no obstructions other than the open forest.

hundred yards or less from his position by his own perception.[37] Near the guns but in the foreground, he noted a staked rail fence and beyond the battery was a wood.[38]

Captain J. J. Womack, commanding Company E, had just reached the top of the embankment. He apparently moved his men forward to the brow of the first finger and had his men lay down to await the remaining companies.[39] Womack took in the field as well.

> We now occupied ground about three hundred yards from where the enemy lay concealed in an enclosed wood[40], about one quarter of a mile in length north and south. At each extremity of this wood they had placed a battery. The one at the northern extremity, of 7 guns, that at the southern about the same.[41]

Savage peered over his left shoulder to the sight of the regiment finally arriving at the top of the creek bank and moving into the fields in his rear. To make room for the remaining regiments of the brigade and division, Lieutenant Colonel Donnell advanced the

---

[37] Savage's account was written in the late 1890's and not printed until 1903. His recollection was made when he was near 85 years old. The actual distance was about 750 yards, but the terrain plays tricks on the eyes at Perryville. The undulating terrain tends to play with perception regarding distance.

[38] (Savage, p. 120)

[39] (Womack, p. 62) Womack stated, "… and quietly [we] formed in line of battle behind the top of the hill, lying, till the whole line would have time to cross over and form."

[40] This 'enclosed wood,' referred to, was an open beech forest that allowed a visual for some distance through the trees and to the finger of land west of their position. The batteries that fronted the men appear to have been that of Parson's on their right-front, and Bush's and Stone's on the distant hill primarily to their front.

[41] Ibid. Womack, obviously from a different vantage point, was able to see a second battery, unlike Savage. The one on the southern end was the combination of Stone and Bush. It is believed this second battery was Parsons' that was in the act of unlimbering on the Open Knob.

regiment to the defilade slope of the finger upon which Colonel Savage sat on his war horse 'George.' The sound of distant gunfire had grown sharper as Federal skirmishers of the 98th Ohio and 33rd Ohio engaged the men of Hardee's wing to the west-south-west over 800 yards away.

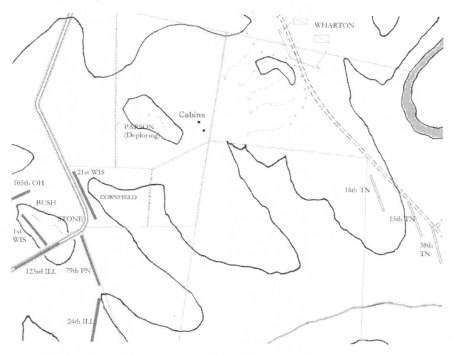

The Federal soldiers—on this part of the field—had only just begun to deploy. General Rousseau and McCook had overseen the initial troop placement before noon. After giving instructions to Rousseau, McCook immediately left for Buell's headquarters. Rousseau extended the position east and north and awaited the arrival of his last brigade commanded by Colonel Starkweather. Upon McCook's return, Rousseau and Jackson were ordered to deploy further to the east, onto a commanding ridge that was to be anchored by Parsons' battery. This location would later become known as the "Open Knob." The battery was advanced first, and following not far behind, the 123rd Illinois and 105th Ohio—of

Terrill's Brigade—advanced to provide support for the guns. Unbeknownst to McCook who had moved off to the right of his line after issuing the orders—less than 1,000 yards east— Cheatham was busy massing his division at Walker's Bend.

While in motion to execute this order, the skirmishers of the 98th Ohio, of Webster's Brigade, became hotly engaged in their front with troops of Hardee's wing. Jackson, hearing the firing, sent a courier to rush Terrill on. It seems that there was a lack of urgency on the part of the Federal left to gain their positions, but at the same time, it was McCook's thought that the action that was developing was at the Federal center. Although Colonel Leonard Harris and Colonel William Lytle had pretty much solidified their positions, Colonel John Starkweather had been cut off by Jackson's Division as they moved to Perryville. With his brigade having just arrived on the field, his guns—commanded by Captains Stone and Bush—had just been unlimbered and his infantry support was being placed in position. Thus, the first two brigades to be assailed on the left were the last to be positioned and in fact were still deploying as the Sixteenth Tennessee stepped off in the advance. Parsons had not finished unlimbering all of his guns. The 105th Ohio had been stopped in support to the north of the Benton Road in column. The 123rd Illinois was marching with its right in front in the direction of Parsons' guns.[42]

Having already conferred with Cheatham at a location north of the "dug road," Donelson received orders to commence the advance toward the extreme left of the Federal positions. From their vantage point—a hill top about five hundred yards east of the Open Knob—Generals Polk and Cheatham had certainly seen the approach of a Federal battery[43] and their halt on the knob. This point was recognized by Cheatham to currently be the extreme left flank of the Federal Army. This point had to be taken quickly. Couriers were immediately sent south to Donelson with positive

---

[42] (Oldershaw, p. 1059)

[43] This battery would have been that of Parsons caught in the act of unlimbering.

orders to seize the guns and take the knob. As Colonel Savage sat mounted peering intently to his front, Brigadier General Donelson appeared on his right trotting toward him from the heights north of his position. In a few moments, Donelson rode up to the colonel stating, "Colonel, I am ordered to attack." Savage sat motionless—still peering at the distant battery. Donelson—staring directly at Savage—repeated that he was ordered to attack. Savage still did not reply. Leaning forward in his saddle and raising his voice, he exclaimed, "Colonel, I am ordered to attack the enemy!" Savage finally responded, "General, I see no enemy to attack except that battery over there in the field. Do you mean, sir, that you want the Sixteenth to charge that battery?" The general replied in the affirmative. Turning toward the general, he said, "General, I will obey your orders but if the Sixteenth is to charge that battery you must give the order." The general rose up in his stirrups staring Savage in the eyes and shouted "Charge!"[44]

The captains called the companies to their feet, and the men rose adjusting their gear. Weapons were loaded, and the regiment was aligned. The 15th Tennessee formed to the left rear of the Sixteenth—and beyond them—the 38th Tennessee. Savage had already surveyed the field in his front.

> There was running up from Chaplain Creek a long hollow about half way between the battery and where the regiment was in line. I thought as soon as I moved into that hollow I would be out of reach of the battery and that I could come up on the other side within sixty or seventy yards of the battery. I

---

[44] (Savage, p. 120) Savage wrote: "I believed that the battery was supported by a strong line of infantry concealed by a fence, and a forest not more than eighty yards in its rear, and that it had been placed in the field as a decoy to invite a charge. I believed that a charge would end in my death and the defeat and ruin of my regiment, and while I had often disobeyed Donelson's orders, for which he had court-martialed me, I could think of no military principles that would authorize me to disobey such an order in the face of the enemy and at the beginning of such a battle."

was in no hurry; got in front of my regiment and said, "Forward, march!"[45]

Presently, the regiment was in line and facing west on the eastern military crest of the first finger that gently sloped off to the south towards Doctor's Creek. The 15th Tennessee was aligned in echelon to the left of the Sixteenth, while the 38th Tennessee would advance in rear of and a hundred yards or more behind that regiment. The battery that appeared on the horizon from Cheatham's vantage point was indeed Parsons' Battery, but from Donelson's position, the only visible battery was that of Stone and Bush—also on an open hilltop. Whether Donelson had been present with Cheatham and was directly issued the orders is not known, but by the time he arrived at his brigade attack position several hundred yards away, the terrain may have played tricks with his perception of the battlefield. Donelson had probably not misconstrued this order, but after returning to his brigade, he mistakenly recognized Bush and Stone's batteries as the intended target which sat upon a hilltop in the open as well. This was later referred to as Starkweather's Heights some 400 yards in rear and south-west of Parsons' guns. He would later admit that he did not have the proper direction.[46]

Savage, leery of Donelson's intent, had purposefully forced him to give the command to advance in full view of the regiment. Their relationship had not only been strained by political views and seniority but also the six month old court-martial in which Savage

---

[45] (Ibid.) This paragraph likely explains that the hollow that Savage refers to, is not the valley that accommodates the tributary running into Doctor's Creek running westerly to easterly, but more likely the draw or "hollow" that separated the first and second fingers running north-south. If his advance was on Harris' Battery, as others suggest, his advance would have been over 1,800 yards and have very gradually ascended the valley which accommodates the tributary to Doctor's Creek lengthwise from end to end rather than traverse its width. His mention of the hollow running into Chaplin Creek was apparently this first draw.

[46] (Noe, p. 199)

had been acquitted. Savage truly regarded Donelson as a personal enemy. The boys in the ranks were eager for a fight. Other than their brief engagements at Cheat Mountain in Virginia and skirmishing in front of Corinth, they had missed the full scale combat that many of their counterparts had experienced at Shiloh. Colonel Savage rode "George" to the front and at his command, the regiment commenced the advance.

It was shortly after 2:00 p.m. when the colonel had the regiment step off.[47] With the intention of turning the Federal left flank, the brigade would have been deployed in an echelon. The Sixteenth was in the advance on the right, followed by the 15th Tennessee and eventually the 38th Tennessee that was distant as 250 yards to their left rear. They commenced the descent of the first finger directly toward the battery that Savage had observed far in the distance. Occasionally, they were slowed to push over split rail fences and conform to the terrain spotted with trees as they advanced, but they moved steadily forward.[48] As they neared the bottom of the hollow—still taking no fire, but hearing the sound of gunfire to the south-west—a courier came dashing down to Savage from the heights to his right-rear. Savage halted the regiment just as they reached the security of the hollow in complete defilade.[49]

As the Sixteenth stepped off descending the western slope of the finger, Generals Cheatham and Polk had observed their advance from an elevation to the regiment's right-rear—quite possibly near the location that would soon accommodate Turner's Mississippi Battery. Marching in line as they approached the hollow, it became evident that perhaps a miscommunication had taken place. It was recognized by Cheatham and Polk that Savage's advance was to the left of the desired point of contact. The intent was for Donelson's brigade to assail the extreme left flank of the Federal army which was recognized by Cheatham as the position occupied by Parsons' Battery. Although Savage wasn't advancing to the center of the

---

[47] (Hooper, p. Oct. 8)
[48] (Head T. A., p. 96)
[49] (Savage, p. 120)

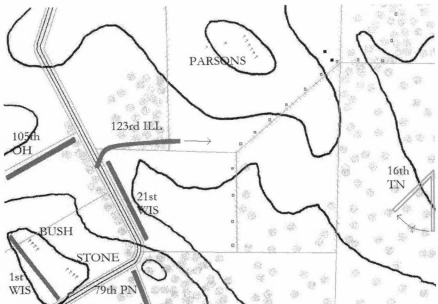

Union line, he was several degrees south of the intended axis of advance. Apparently, Donelson had not correctly interpreted the order, as their initial advance was directing them to the left of Parsons and straight to the guns of Stone and Bush. Having halted his men in the hollow with no cannon or small arms fire directed on his men to this point, Savage was informed that, "...the enemy that General Cheatham wanted attacked was in the woods at the head of the hollow at the right."[50] Indeed, only about four or five hundred yards away, Parsons' guns—still being positioned—sat at the head of this hollow on the open knob. Evidently, both Cheatham and Polk accompanied at least one other staff officer to the vicinity of the Sixteenth Tennessee.[51]

---

[50] (Savage, p. 120)

[51] (Hooper, p. Oct. 8) Hooper stated that they advanced to within three to four hundred yards of the enemy position, "...when General Cheatham give command to charge-General Polk also told us to let the Yanks know what Tennessee steel was made for..." It seems that although Cheatham did not directly relay the new orders to Savage personally, he and Polk both

Savage continued, "I halted the regiment, ordered my color bearers to the front and ordered the regiment to dress on them so as to march in the new direction indicated by Cheatham's order."[52] Thus, the original direction of march was corrected from westerly to a north-westerly route. J. C. Biles, a member of the color guard that day recalled, "...the regiment moved as if to charge the battery and was halted after moving a short distance, and was formed in line of battle at right angles to the line when marching to charge the battery in the field."[53]

The color guard[54] and guides stepped out of line and dressed for the new direction of march. The regiment was quickly formed on the colors. In the security of their defilade position, they now faced the head of the hollow and the hill top upon which Parsons' Battery was positioned and the 123rd Illinois and the 105th Ohio were just about to deploy onto. Still fully three hundred plus yards from their objective, Savage prepared for his advance and remarked on the lack of action by Bush and Stone's batteries, stating:

> I was in no hurry, for outside of Cheatham's aide and Donelson there was no Confederate in sight. There was no reason why the battery should not have fired upon the regiment while it was in line, except that a fire would pass through the line and only do little damage. Marching in the

made their appearance with at least a portion of the regiment. As Hooper served in company A, he would have been in line of battle on the extreme right of the regiment, the direction from which the generals would have approached.

[52] (Savage, p. 120)

[53] (Ibid.) This new direction of march literally put the regiment facing a nearly right angle to their previous direction of march.

[54] The original color guard for the regiment that day consisted of Ensign W. T. Mayberry, and four color guards—J. C. Biles, H. L. Moffit, Jasper Roberts and John McConnell.

new direction indicated by Cheatham's aide, I was soon in an open beech forest on the top of the hill.[55]

The new line of advance led the regiment obliquely up the eastern slope of the second finger. As they moved forward, the left flank reached the apex of the finger then the center of the regiment and eventually the right flank, but this movement was not fluid and disciplined.

Parsons' Battery had just been placed on the knoll and was still in the act of unlimbering the last of its guns when General Terrill, the brigade commander for the Federal left flank, gave orders for the 105th Ohio to advance to a position north of Benton Road in reserve. Within minutes, Terrill and Jackson heard the crackling of gunfire in the hollow to their right front. The advance of Donelson's Brigade had been detected by the light skirmisher screen of Terrill's Brigade that had preceded Parsons' advance. The detached troops nearest the knob had withdrawn without firing, but skirmishers of Starkweather and Harris were firing at long range at the visible troops of the 15th and 38th Tennessee Regiments in the edge of the woods and open fields of the valley to the Sixteenth's left.[56]

The 105th Ohio was immediately ordered, along with the 123rd Illinois, to rapidly advance further east to the support of Parsons' lone battery of eight guns. The 105th Ohio was to advance to protect the extreme Federal left, while the 123rd Illinois advanced to the right of Parsons in order to cover the Beech woods to their right front. Unbeknownst to them, the new recruits of the 123rd Illinois were about to confront Savage's men only moments away as they crested the hill.[57]

---

[55] (Ibid.) Just as the battery was visible to Savage, he and his men were equally visible to the battery, and urgent messages were sent on the Federal side to push infantry forward to contest this advance.
[56] (Anderson)
[57] (Oldershaw, p. 1059)

"The whole line of battle was expected to keep in line on the forward movement, but some of the boys seemingly anxious to close in on the enemy raised the yell & rushed forward which caused our regiment to get far in advance of our main line..."
Private C. H. Clark

"Victory" for our motto was shouted all along our line, and fearlessly and gallantly we charged them."   Captain J. J. Womack

As the Sixteenth neared the top of the finger, they identified the enemy presence, not all at once, but from left to right as they reached the military crest. For the Federals, the green 123rd Illinois was the advance regiment and was being hurried into the fields south of Parsons' guns to meet the advance of the Sixteenth Tennessee. The Assistant Adjutant General of Terrill's Brigade stated that as the 123rd was rushing into the field, "... the rebels at the time could be seen within 200 yards advancing to occupy the same ground."[58]

When the Sixteenth reached the apex of the finger—the batteries of Stone and Bush—that they had originally oriented to assail—were now on their left flank.   Parsons' battery was still deploying on the knob a short distance to their right-front. The 123rd Illinois had just arrived and was deploying to their direct front behind a staked and rider fence. The 105th Ohio was out of sight on the northern side of the knob and crossing Benton Road. Their time had come; the Sixteenth Tennessee was now to show their fighting prowess on the field of battle. Colonel Savage was riding in front of the right of the regiment. He knew something was about to happen, but the shock of what did happen was forever burned into his memory. The left of the regiment had reached the edge of the wood and commenced their advance into the field while the right was just cresting the top of the finger. Much of their line formation had disintegrated as they rushed to the top and the boys immediately opened a heavy fire on the 123rd Illinois from about 200 yards.[59]

---

[58] (Anderson, p. 1063)
[59] (Savage, p. 120) (Thompson, p. 9)

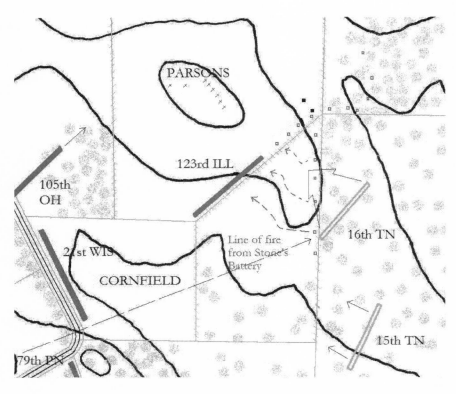

The 123rd Illinois[60] had been put in an unfortunate situation. They had advanced with their right in front. This meant that as they deployed into line behind the fence to face the enemy, the regiment found its rear rank facing front toward the Confederates. The Sixteenth's minie balls were finding their mark. Crowded and confused, the 123rd loaded and fired on the Sixteenth as best they could. This newly recruited—and hardly drilled—regiment found itself in a trying situation with men falling fast. To their momentary relief, the guns of Stone's Battery—300 yards to their right—fired a volley of grapeshot into the left flank of the Sixteenth. About the same time, Parsons' right most guns were ordered to be turned on

---

[60] This regiment, mustered into service on September 6th, had not conducted any battalion drills as of yet and likely, very little company drill.

the Sixteenth's right flank by General Terrill—shocked by the sudden appearance of the Confederate force.[61]

This initial charge of canister shot blasted down the length of the line from left to right punching holes through the rank and file. Savage's war horse—'George'—took a direct hit to the head at that very moment. His head snapped quickly to the right, and the animal's front legs momentarily gave out. The grapeshot had entered under his left eye and passed through his head exiting on the right. 'George' momentarily staggered under the colonel's weight, but at length, he regained his footing. The war-horse was disabled but not killed. Savage dismounted from his lame mount and threw his bridle over a snag of a tree with enemy bullets snapping past his body. Looking left, he saw the carnage wreaked by this first blast of shot. Near a dozen men lay motionless and maimed while others reeled in agony on the ground.[62]

Stone and Bush had held their fire for the approach of the Sixteenth, but seeing the regiment appear over the finger in a new direction, they were certainly thrilled to have a much more favorable target that enabled them to fire down the length of the regimental line with enfilading shots inflicting much higher casualties than previously possible.[63] Savage immediately drew his Remington pistol and ordered the regiment forward. Although this took them closer to the guns, it would hopefully get them to a semi-defilade position.[64]

The right of the regiment had still been under cover of the ridgeline, but the sudden sprint toward the top of the ridge threw the

---

[61] (Anderson, p. 1063)

[62] (Savage, p. 121)

[63] Savage noted in his memoirs that he supposed the battery had not fired on his men as they had advanced directly toward it due to the minimal damage that would be inflicted, with his flank fully exposed, after the change of direction it was a much more inviting target at closer range.

[64] (Savage, p. 121) Savage actually stated that he, "…ordered the regiment forward to get out of range of the battery." He hoped to close on the enemy infantry so that their artillery could not be used against him.

regimental line out of order. Tom Hooper, on the right flank, stated in his diary, "...we raised the yell and charged with few obstacles; got in 1 ½ or 200 yards where we turned loose on them."[65] Turned loose—they did; the right of the regiment took deliberate aim on the left flank of the 123rd Illinois as well as Parsons' right guns as they attempted to load and fire. Nearer the middle of the regimental line, R. C. Carden, of company E recalled, "We had just got to the top of a small hill when we saw the enemy rise to their feet and then business began, and things were hot for a time."[66] Carden had observed the advance of the 123rd Illinois to support the right flank of Parsons' Battery and had been ordered to advance upon the appearance of Savage's men ascending the hill.[67] In their debacle at the fence, the 123rd Illinois' officers tried to steady the men and encourage them to load and fire in the midst of a shower of balls from the Sixteenth.[68] Pvt. James R. Thompson, of company A, wrote, "We were perhaps two hundred yards from the enemy when we were ordered to open fire, which we did with effect on the enemy, judging from the piles of dead which were before us after firing a few rounds."[69]

Apparently, the Sixteenth had commenced an abrupt sprint into action as each portion of the regiment reached the crest and the enemy came into view. In the Sixteenth's rush to close on the enemy, Colonel Savage continued, "Descending the hill some forty or fifty yards, we were fired on by the main line of the Yankee army, not more than fifty or sixty yards distant, concealed behind a rail fence which was a prolongation of the fence enclosing the field in which the battery was situated."[70] The regiment was now oriented in a north-westerly direction with its left resting in a shallow draw fronting nearly west and its center arcing in a northward orientation. Only fifty or more yards away from the Sixteenth's center, the 123rd

---

[65] (Hooper, p. 76)

[66] (Carden, p. Apr. 12)

[67] (Oldershaw, p. 1059)

[68] (Anderson, p. 1063)

[69] (Thompson, p. 9)

[70] (Savage, p. 121) This was the 123rd Illinois and Parsons' Battery.

Illinois was still trying to make sense of their situation and how to correct it. In front of the Sixteenth's right wing, the guns of Parsons' Battery were blasting canister into their ranks. The right wing now focused its fire primarily on the gunners of Parsons' battery.

In what would later become a great point of contention, Captain Womack of Company E wrote, "Donaldson's brigade either executed orders too promptly, or else other commands not hastily enough, in consequence of which this brigade, and the 16th regiment especially, was exposed to a most terrific fire from both the above batteries and at the same time an opening line of infantry."[71] Struck by fire from several directions, the regiment pushed forward. "'Victory' for our motto was shouted all along our line, and fearlessly and gallantly we charged them."[72]

Federal generals Terrill and Jackson had immediately ordered Parsons' guns to be turned on the Confederate advance, and all but two of his eight guns were oriented to the right—facing the Sixteenth's right flank—and commenced a terrible storm of grapeshot and canister.[73] At the same time, Bush and Stone were pouring their volleys of grape on the Sixteenth's left flank and center.[74] In the initial minutes of combat and their first true general engagement, the Sixteenth displayed a willingness to accomplish the mission no matter what the cost as their comrades fell killed and maimed all around them.

The majority of eyewitness accounts of this engagement refer to three specific charges made by the Sixteenth Regiment on this

---

[71] (Womack, p. 63) Savage died believing that Donelson and Cheatham were guilty of a war crime by sending his regiment "solitary and alone" into the fight.

[72] Ibid.

[73] (Anderson, p. 1063)

[74] (Hooper, p. Oct. 8) Hooper stated, "We were at this time and had been for some time in about fifty to one hundred yards of a battery of 8 or 9 pieces on our right and our left wing with another firing down on our center; all heavily supported by infantry."

wing of the enemy—each with more success. The first charge was their rush toward the fence and the 123rd Illinois. Lieutenant Jesse Walling, of company E on the right-center of the regiment stated, "We charged in a right oblique course and were met by the grape and canister shot of these guns, which killed many of our men..." Parsons' had wasted no time in turning his guns unleashing relentless blasts of canister on the right wing of the Sixteenth.

As the center of the regiment raced toward the fence, the 123rd Illinois had just arrived there and delivered a staggering volley. Walling related, "All at once the enemy raised up from behind a rail fence, pouring a deadly fire into us and killing great numbers of our men. We fell back a short distance..."[75] After coming under a galling fire from rifles in their front and batteries to their left and right, the men were forced back to the edge of the beech forest. On the extreme left with Company B, Pvt. Carden witnessed the carnage wreaked by cannon fire from Stone and Bush almost as if in slow motion. As he loaded his rifle, a man standing directly in front of him was struck him in the breast by canister shot; the impact was so quick that he stated, "... I saw the white flesh before it bled."[76] Captain Womack, near the center-right of the regiment wrote, "...we were compelled, after the most stubborn resistance possibly to be made, to fall back, not without however, having first dislodged the enemy from his stronghold and chosen ground."[77]

Slowly the Sixteenth fell back forty or fifty yards to the cover of trees near the eastern slope of the finger. Anxious to exploit this initial repulse, Terrill ordered the raw 123rd Illinois to charge the enemy with fixed bayonets. As the 123rd commenced their run toward the Sixteenth, their organization fell apart. In their charge, they struck the farm fence that hindered the movement, and at the same time the Sixteenth delivered a devastating volley of musketry. Completely routed, they turned and ran back over the field amongst a scattering of Savage's men as well as their own that lay reeling in

[75] (Savage, p. 127)
[76] (Carden, p. Apr. 12)
[77] (Womack, p. 63)

agony and crawling for safety. They continued their retreat to the fence where they had fired their initial volley.[78]

Thus in only a matter of minutes, both regiments had met face to face in mortal combat only for both to fall back to regroup. Although the shock and rage of battle had become painfully evident to the men of the Sixteenth, Major Winchester—out of view of the combat—recorded a more romantic commentary of the battle, "…the rattle of small arms was terrific and unceasing – a thrilling accompaniment to the deep bass of the thundering artillery as it filled earth, air and heaven with its startling reverberations."[79] The first of the walking wounded started their weary journey to the cover of Walker's Bend and the hell of the field hospitals.

There were two small cabins[80] situated down the hill and on the right flank of Parsons' Battery fronting the right flank of the Sixteenth regiment. When routed from in front of the Sixteenth, a portion of the 123rd Illinois had run for the cover of the cabins and fence which continued west into a field and south along the ridgeline the Sixteenth occupied. Colonel Savage knew that to *act* was critical at this point. Savage wrote:

> There was a fence and a field on my right running up to two cabins at the line of the enemy's forces. There were skirmish lines along this fence which fired on our rear as we advanced.

---

[78] (Oldershaw, p. 1059)

[79] (Winchester, p. 76)

[80] These cabins are only referred to by men in the Sixteenth. They were not large, commanding structures. Some of this reevaluation is based on the supposition that the two cabins were not part of the Widow Gibson Farm, but on the eastern slope of the Open Knob. There used to be two clumps of trees near one another in the heart of which were slight depressions, indicative of former structures. The stands of trees have been cut down since. The northern cluster was cut after November 2004, and the southern stand of trees was cut after September, 2006. Evidence can be seen of these clusters on Google Earth.

The Sixteenth had no protection except a few trees in the forest. I ordered a charge.[81]

Amidst the roar and din of battle, Savage commanded the men forward, and the captains of companies rose with sabers in hand to cheer their men into the fray again. Captain Womack recalled, "With our numbers now much weakened we rallied and charged them a second time..."[82]

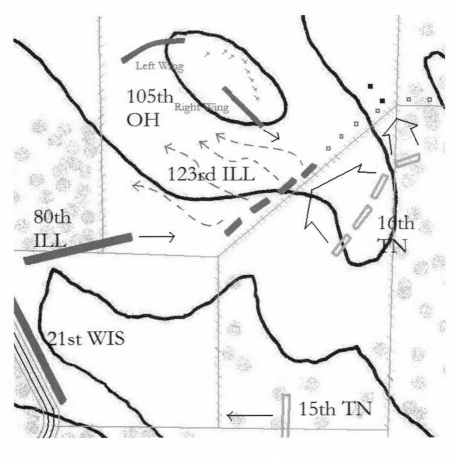

[81] (Savage, p. 121)
[82] (Womack, p. 63)

The men dug deep, and with another yell, the regiment rose from behind the trees and rushed forward. Struck by enfilading fire on both flanks by the batteries and the infantry lying in the field to their front, their numbers diminished with every step. The artillerymen were firing their guns at a rate of two to three times a minute. At this range—nearly point blank on the right and perfect range of four hundred yards on their left—practically every blast of canister tore holes through the Sixteenth's line. The dirt flew in droves as the ground was plowed by concentrations of canister balls. The minie balls tore into the earth and shattered limbs and splinters onto the combatants. Private Thompson rushed forward and dove to take cover behind a small stump. As he rested his gun atop the stump to aim and fire, friendly fire plowed into the stump barely missing him. With balls whizzing past his ears, Private Clark— witnessing the slaughter—later wrote, "I had no hope of getting out alive. Such trials as that has a tendency to temporarily derange the minds of some, at least it was the case with me."[83] The bullets zipped past the boys clipping their clothes and equipment with every step. Private John Smaller—just a boy—had joined the regiment on the march to Kentucky. As he rushed forward to the fence, he was stuck down and killed instantly. George Sparkman had been hit as they commenced the charge. Crawling to the cover of a tree, grapeshot found its mark, and Sparkman slumped over—dead.[84]

But in the midst of the bloodshed, the Sixteenth pushed on causing the enemy troops at the fence to die in place or give way. Pvt. Thompson stated, "...we went forward with a rush. The enemy fell back and we crossed the fence they were behind amid hundreds of their slain."[85] Colonel Savage watched as his men shot many of the retreating enemy fleeing from the cabins and fence.[86] The 123rd Illinois broke in confusion rushing in rear of Parsons' guns. As they attempted to follow up their recently won success, the Sixteenth

---

[83] (Clark, p. #14)
[84] (Clark, p. #15)
[85] (Thompson, p. 9)
[86] (Savage, p. 122) The remnants of the 123rd Illinois broke and ran in rear of Parsons' guns.

pushed forward to gain the rear of the battery. Suddenly, they were met by more galling infantry fire combined with the grape and canister on their flanks.

This additional rifle fire raked into the Sixteenth's right flank. The right wing of the 105th Ohio had reached the field to protect the left flank of Parsons' battery. Terrill—seeing the advancing Confederates—ordered Major Perkins of the 105th to stop their advance at all hazards. It was apparent that they were, "…determined to charge through the left of the One hundred and twenty-third Illinois Volunteers and cut off the battery." Major Perkins led the advance and opened fire as they neared Savage's right flank.[87] At about the same time, the 80th Illinois and Garrard's Detachment arrived in the field on the Sixteenth's left flank.

Albion Tourgee recalled the advance of the 105th Ohio led by Major Perkins.

Our left companies, the right of our line as we stood faced to the rear, overlapped the battery. General Jackson fell just as we advanced. Some of our men fell to the rear to pass the group that knelt about him. The left was refused, because of the overlapping of the enemy's line and the conformation of the ground. Those whose guns were loaded fired; the others made haste to load. Men fell, sometimes with a groan, sometimes without a sound. It was slow work loading and firing with the old muzzle-loaders. The air seemed full of flashing ramrods. One and another staggered wounded to the rear. The line-officers went back and forth encouraging, directing. We stood alone, a thin line of blue, in the open field. The enemy were mostly under cover. On our right the nearest force was along the wooded ridge to which the rest of our brigade had retired. To the rear, near half a mile, was Starkweather with his veterans. Then we first heard the rebel

---

[87] (Hall)

yell we were to hear so often afterwards. The gray line burst from the wood and rushed up the slope.[88]

"Forward!" cried Terrill. "Do not let them get the guns!"

His face was flushed with agony at the thought of losing the battery of which he was so proud.

"Charge!" commanded the major, whose horse having been shot, was on foot with the left companies. There was a clang of bayonets. The left companies surged forward to the front of the battery. Cumings, of ours, fired the two right guns, double-shotted with canister, full in the faces of the enemy, then almost at the muzzles of the pieces, and with his few remaining men dashed through our ranks to the rear under cover of the smoke. We would have cheered them but were too busy with our own work to give more than a flash of the eye to their gallantry. When it lifted, the enemy had faltered, half-way down the slope. Our fire was too hot for them to stand. They fell slowly back and began firing again.[89]

This second charge had punished the defenders worse than the Sixteenth's first assault but not without the regiment suffering more staggering losses. The 105th Ohio had stymied the Sixteenth's second

---

[88] This is the reference to the Sixteenth's charge on the 123rd Illinois that had withdrawn some distance and had skirmishers firing on the right-rear of the Sixteenth as they advanced. Colonel Hall of the 105th Ohio stated that, "At the moment of coming into position on the left and rear of Parsons' battery it was apparent that the enemy were determined to charge through the left of the One hundred and twenty-third Illinois Volunteers and cut off the battery."

[89] (Tourgee, pp. 121-22) This was the charge led by Major Perkins with a wing of the regiment which stymied Savage's attack leaving his right wing at the cabins and left along the fence and trees as stated by Colonel Hall as well. Maney's Brigade was not yet engaged. Tourgee was apparently not with the wing that then attempted to flank Savage's right. This was almost immediately repulsed by the sudden arrival of Maney's brigade on their flank.

assault by hitting them hard on their right combined with the arrival of the 80[90] Illinois on their left.[90] As the gunfire reached another crescendo, the Sixteenth wavered and fell back again a short distance to the cover of the fence, trees and the recently won cabins. By now the regiment had been engaged in their firefight nearly thirty minutes.

Unbeknownst to the Sixteenth, they may have likely inflicted a serious blow to the Federal army at this point. The Assistant Adjutant General of Terrill's Brigade later reported that when the six guns of Parsons' battery were turned to the right to engage the Confederates at close range, General Jackson was struck down at Terrill's side.[91] At least three soldiers of the Sixteenth suggested that the regiment had likely shot down General Jackson. Jesse Walling witnessed one likely candidate.

> One of the bravest men I have ever seen was one of the enemy, who stood upon his fine brass gun, waving his hat over his head after all his comrades had fled. But he too fell in this brave act. I could not hear distinctly his words as he stood there waving his hat.[92]

Pvt. Clark recorded, "We were in forty yards of the enemy & they were falling fast. I hurriedly glanced to the right & left to see if the main line was engaged."[93] To his surprise, and to the other men

---

[90] (Anderson, p. 1063)

[91] (Anderson) The A.A.G. of Terrill's brigade stated in his report, "Six of his guns were brought to bear upon the enemy and drove them back. At this instant General Jackson was shot dead."

[92] (Savage, p. 128) This was more likely an officer in charge of one of the sections, as the gunners had not abandoned their pieces at this point, but Tourgee, of the 105th Ohio, wrote: "When the Thousand came up, the right of the brigade had fallen back, and the enemy, checked by the hot fire which greeted them, had halted in the edge of the wood along the fence below. The battery stood alone upon the crest of the hill, half its guns silenced, its men and horses being cut down by the fire of the enemy. It was said the order to withdraw the battery had been given. Even then it was too late."

[93] (Clark, p. #14)

of the regiment, the Sixteenth was the only visible Confederate unit engaged. Lieutenant Walling noted, "I was in the center of the regiment, and noticed that we were not supported either to the right or to the left."[94] Engaged to their front and using cover of the Beech forest without advancing, the 15th Tennessee had veered far to the left engaging the skirmishers of the 79th Pennsylvania over 200 yards away and was still not in true supporting distance of the Sixteenth. Worse, the 38th Tennessee lagged far behind them.[95]

Still without any real support, Savage recognized how critical the situation was for his regiment—also how important the position they occupied was. He felt they had to hold his position to retain an advantage over the enemy on this part of the field. The hell at the cabins was vividly recalled by Colonel Savage.

> The right of the regiment was at the two cabins. There was a battery in the line of battle to the right, about thirty or forty yards from these cabins, between which cabins there was an entry, or space, of ten or fifteen feet. The battery opened fire on us, killing many men, and at the same time a fire of small arms from the line of battle was directed upon these cabins. The battery fired obliquely into this space. I stood between the two cabins, would watch the gunner ram home the charge, and say, "Lie low, boys; he is going to fire," and step for protection close to the cabin nearest the battery.[96]

The hesitation at the fence was short lived. Mustering all their courage, the regiment rallied and held their ground firing deliberately

---

[94] (Savage, p. 127) To the left and rear of the regiment, the 15th Tennessee had advanced and was receiving skirmish fire as well as canister fire from Stone's Battery and the shots that flew over the Sixteenth from Parsons' guns.
[95] The 38th Tennessee was the last regiment to step off for Donelson's Brigade. They were also the furthest left regiment, but as they corrected their advance near the hollow, they would come up between the 15th and 16th regiments in due time.
[96] (Savage, p. 122)

at the 80th Illinois and Garrard's Detachment as they filed through the fields in their front at double-quick.

Captain Womack noted that they were directly in front of the guns on the northern extremity of the Federal line. This again indicated that Parsons' Battery fronted them on the right.[97] Colonel Savage recalled, "The battle was furious, the men loading and firing as rapidly as possible, falling back and again charging up to the fence."[98] As the boys fought to hold their ground, Private Andrew Mercer, of Company C, cried, "Boys, let's take the battery," and started off at a sprint toward the cannons.

Unseen by Pvt. Mercer, the wing of the 105th Ohio—that had been ordered to the support of the 123rd Illinois—had commenced a move to outflank the Sixteenth's right. Colonel Savage continued:

> At this time I saw a force to my right and in my rear. I countermanded Mercer's order, but he had gone some five or six steps towards the battery to a tree. Seeing that he was not supported, he hugged the tree closely for a short space of time and returned to the cabin without being wounded.[99]

At the same time Savage was at the cabins identifying the threat that was flanking their right and rear, Lieutenant Colonel D. M. Donnell appeared in his presence.[100] With the enemy force rushing to outflank them, Savage gave orders to his Lieutenant Colonel.[101]

> ...Donnell, came to me and said: "Colonel, order a retreat. We are losing all our men and are not supported." I replied: "Protect your men by those trees and that fence and I will

---

[97] (Womack, p. 63)
[98] (Savage, p. 122)
[99] Ibid.
[100] (Thompson, p. 9) "Colonel Donelson [*Lt. Col. Donnell*] appeared on the right where I was and a flanking party had started around us on our right with their guns at right shoulder shift."
[101] (Anderson) This force could have been the right wing of the 105th Ohio or a portion of the 80th Indiana—perhaps a combination of both.

54

protect this wing by these cabins. We are ordered to fight. To order a retreat at the beginning of a battle is not war. We must hold this position until supported, and it is the duty of our commanding officers to bring us support.[102]

Unbeknownst to Colonel Savage at this time, General Cheatham had already ordered up the brigade of Brigadier General Maney; however, it had taken longer than anticipated to align his brigade in the proper position—one far enough north so that it would not overlap Savage's regiment in its advance.

"After proceeding several hundred yards through the woods in the course I had first taken, I was informed General Donelson had become hotly engaged and was in great need of reinforcements. The action seemed but a short distance to my front and appeared to be fiercely waged, both with infantry and artillery."

Brigadier General George Maney[103]

Maney's Brigade consisted of five infantry regiments: the 1st, 6th, 9th and 27th Tennessee Regiments and the 41st Georgia. As few as ten minutes into Savage's initial engagement, it is likely that Maney had already received orders to move his assistance, but the terrain would delay the brigade's advance for nearly twenty minutes. Marcus B. Toney, of the 1st Tennessee Infantry regiment in Maney's Brigade, recalled:

About three o'clock we were in line of battle on our extreme right and in a valley of the Chaplin River two and one-half miles from Perryville. There had been some skirmishing before our arrival, and about three o'clock the musketry and cannonading became quite brisk, the shells falling around us as we climbed the fence in battle line. We crossed Chaplin River, ascended a high bluff, and when we reached the height Colonel

---

[102] (Savage, p. 123) In hindsight, it is almost possible to hypothesize that Savage was nearly willing to lose his regiment or his life to make his belief that Donelson wanted to ruin his regiment or kill him come true.
[103] (Maney)

Savage's Sixteenth Regiment was hotly engaged with the enemy.[104]

While the Sixteenth had engaged the enemy at the fence and driven the enemy back inflicting heavy casualties on the Federal troops of Parsons' Battery and the 123rd Illinois, Maney had been moving into position attempting to form on Savage's right with the 1st, 27th, 9th and 6th Tennessee and 41st Georgia Infantry Regiments in a single line from left to right.

Captain Thomas Malone, serving on General Maney's staff, reveals a detailed account of Maney's movements and dispositions that afternoon. Malone wrote, "…we advanced across an open field, under a rather sharp fire of the enemy's skirmishers, to the foot of a wooded hill, where it became evident that the enemy's line still flanked ours, and we must march by the right flank, taking ground to the right."[105] Maney had conducted a personal reconnaissance of the field to his front.

> … I ascertained by a personal reconnaissance the position of the enemy. Facing my approach and slightly to the right of General Donelson's command was a strong battery placed on a hilltop[106] in an open field and less than 120 yards from the nearest edge of the woods, in which I was. The battery was actively engaged, partly on Donelson's command at short range[107] and partly in firing into the woods through which I was approaching. General Stewart's Brigade, which was to form between General Donelson's and mine, had not yet arrived, but my instructions as well as the immediate assistance

---

[104] (Toney) From their location east of the first finger, the Sixteenth was likely fewer than 500 yards to their front on the second finger to the west.

[105] (Malone)

[106] Clearly indicative of Parsons' Battery.

[107] This substantiates the claims of Savage and all of the eyewitnesses from the regiment. They are engaged with the battery at less than 40 yards. Even G. L. Mac Murphy of the 8th Texas Cavalry claims that they were no more than 30 yards apart.

needed by General Donelson's command committed me to engagement without delay and my preparations to attack the battery were made forthwith.[108]

Marcus Toney wrote, "To uncover from Colonel Savage we had to move by the right flank, and while executing this move some of our men were wounded. When we uncovered we again moved by the left flank."[109]

Approaching the objective in line, Maney had realized his force was at least partially in rear of Savage's regiment. He had his two left regiments (the 1st and 27th Tennessee) march by the right flank in column a few hundred yards and halt facing to the left again; this placed the two in a second line. The brigade then steadily moved forward till reaching a high staked and rider fence. After being ordered to form the 1st and 27th Regiments in this position, Captain Malone continued:

> While I was thus placing these two regiments, I heard a heavy fire of musketry and artillery break out near the head of the column. ...I saw the 41st Georgia and the 6th and 9th Tennessee Regiments lying on the ground, engaged in a bitter fight with the line of the enemy on the edge of the hill in their front, which line was supported by Parson's Battery...[110]

Unbeknownst to Maney, his timely arrival had single-handedly stymied the Federal counterattack on the Sixteenth's right flank. The arrival of these three regiments flanked the portions of the 105th Ohio (and/or 80th Illinois) attempting to gain Savage's rear and forced the Federal soldiers to break and run back over the open knob giving much needed relief to the Sixteenth Tennessee.[111] Although

---

[108] (Maney)
[109] (Toney)
[110] (Malone)
[111] (Womack, p. 63) (Anderson) Anderson wrote, "A heavy force of the enemy was now seen advancing on both of our flanks."

relieved of the threat on their right, the Sixteenth was still heavily engaged to their front and left.

Private Thompson—with the Sixteenth—recalled, "When the flanking party was driven back, it opened the way for our artillery, which was put in use with vigor."[112] Turner's Confederate Battery had hurriedly been positioned on a knoll about five-hundred yards east of the open knob that Parson occupied. Captain Malone, with the 1st Tennessee, corroborated this.

It seemed to me that our men could not have maintained our position at all but for the fact that old Turner – the best artilleryman, but the poorest drilled man in the army – was imperatively demanding the attention of Parson's guns. He thundered with his, little 6-pound howitzers right over the heads of our men, and with grape was making it very hot for Parson's and his infantry support.[113]

At that time the Sixteenth still found itself fighting for dear life, attempting desperately to hold their position while Maney's Brigade hesitated at the rail fence a hundred or more yards to their right and rear.[114] General Maney found himself in a dilemma. Three of his five regiments were at the base of the knob occupied by Parson's Battery and supported by the 105th Ohio. Maney knew he had to act; he had sufficient force. This hesitation at the fence was only going to decrease his chances of seizing the guns as enemy fire was poured into his men. Maney, still mounted, rode along his brigade front inspiring his men for the uphill push. In only minutes, they would conduct their assault.

Meanwhile, Colonel Savage, while holding his position at the cabins, fell seriously wounded. As the men hugged the earth and crowded for cover around and about the old cabins, rifle fire and

---

[112] (Thompson, p. 10)
[113] (Malone)
[114] (Anderson) Anderson stated, "They moved up to within 100 yards of our line without discharging a musket. They then opened a deadly fire."

grapeshot were constantly poured into the wooden structures causing splinters and bullets alike to ricochet dangerously. Savage stood by the cabin nearest the battery directing his men when a deafening blast of double canister was fired from less than forty yards away on his position. Smoke fully engulfed the men, and in an instant, a wooden sabot from a canister shot ricocheted off of the opposite cabin and struck him in the body. As he staggered and fell, a minie ball passed through his calf. Seriously stunned by the velocity of the wooden projectile, he crawled to the protection of the cabin.[115] With Savage down, the command temporarily devolved upon the shoulders of Lieutenant Colonel Donnell.

In the moments following Savage's wounding and in the midst of combat, the Sixteenth continued what it had quickly come to know. Initiative must have been instilled at the lowest levels if not just their simple realization that only silencing the enemy would spare their lives. Private Thompson was one of this number.

There was a battery just to our right side. When the flanking party was driven back, I thought it should be silenced or captured. There were two little log cabins just behind the enemy line that we had captured and a fence running about north and south. I jumped over this little fence and started toward the battery. I came to a small shade tree and rested my gun against it. I commenced firing at the cannoneers. A ball from down the fence tore through my hat and hair. About this time Alvin Simpson, one of our company, came and rested his gun against the six or seven inch tree and fired. A ball from the same direction that had clipped so close to me, split his hat on the side about four inches.[116]

---

[115] (Savage, p. 122)
[116] (Thompson, p. 10)

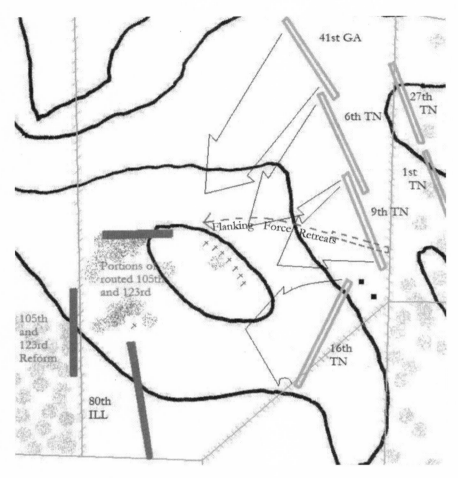

Although Maney's men had not yet begun their advance from the fence, the well aimed fire of Savage's men combined with Maney's regiments at the fence had already inflicted serious casualties on the gunners of Parson's Battery as well as their infantry support combined with the fire of Turner's guns. In fact, Turners' guns had been place so as to effectively graze the remaining infantry support of the 105th Ohio forcing them to withdraw from the forward slope and crest of the Open Knob leaving only a few infantrymen and a small number of effective artillerymen to man the battered and bullet riddled cannons. Lieutenant Parsons tried in vain in to rally his men to withdraw the guns but found his attempt futile as the infantry and artillerymen raced for cover in their rear.[117]

At this moment and almost in unison with the three regiments of Maney's Brigade, the Sixteenth gathered their strength and—with a blood curdling yell—made a third exhausted push towards Parsons' guns. Captain Womack related that [we], "...formed and charged for a third time, but our forces were so diminished by this time that I am not at all sure we would have been able to drive them from their guns had it not been for the timely arrival of reinforcements on our right."[118] Parson's Battery consisted of eight cannon, and with the distribution of space between these guns, the battery stretched the full distance of over one hundred yards. The right most guns of the battery were trained on the Sixteenth Tennessee with the left guns focusing on Maney's and Turner's threat to their direct front. Simultaneously, the Sixteenth had commenced their final push on this position as Maney's men surged up the hill.

Captain Womack, referring to Maney's men, continued, "...they appeared in time to gain the day, although they scarcely fired a gun themselves. But their appearance on the field struck terror to the already retreating enemy..."[119] Even Captain Malone with Maney's Brigade admitted, "We did not fire a shot from the time the charge began until the enemy's whole line of battle was in flight, and then, shooting deliberately, the butchery was something awful."[120] Lieutenant Walling recalled, "The third time we went over the fence, driving the enemy before us, capturing the cannon."[121] At least at Parson's right most guns, the fight was already over as the Sixteenth

---

[117] (Anderson) "In spite of the efforts of the officers most of our men broke and fell back in great confusion. Lieutenant Parsons at the time was placing his seventh gun into position, when every man at the piece deserted him."

[118] (Womack, p. 63) Maney's Brigade.

[119] Ibid.

[120] (Malone)

[121] (Savage, p. 127)

charged headlong toward them. Colonel Savage noted that, "The men at the battery had been killed or wounded or had fled before Maney's Brigade appeared in the field to my right, some hundred or more yards distant."[122] He continued, "I said to Colonel Donnell: 'I am unfit for duty. Take charge. Go to the battery. It belongs to the Sixteenth.'"[123]

Lieutenant Walling felt sure that, "The Sixteenth was engaged with the enemy for at least thirty minutes when General Maney's men appeared to our right as we were running the enemy across the field."[124] Private Thompson, regarding the rout of the Federal troops from their position, wrote, "...the enemy finally yielded this line and fell back a few hundred yards to a lane."[125] The Sixteenth's stand at the fence and cabins had undoubtedly ensured the successful rout of the Federal General Jackson's flank. Had Savage retired the Sixteenth in the face of the enemy without holding their position and sustaining their fire, Maney—although possibly successful—would have faced three regiments of infantry and the full force of Parsons' guns.

In regards to the mass casualties Captain Malone witnessed as he passed the guns of Parson's Battery, he later wrote, "...what struck me at the time, and strikes me now, is the fatal accuracy of the fire of the 41st, 6th and 9th while the enemy were lying down. It seemed to me that one-third of them were lying dead on the line which they had been holding so gallantly."[126] Clearly, much of the carnage witnessed by Captain Malone was in fact inflicted by the rifles of the Sixteenth. Even Private Hooper, in his diary, wrote that,

---

[122] Although this was certainly stretching the truth, the Sixteenth was aware that they had already severely crippled the defenders of the Open Knob when Maney arrived to their right within one hundred yards.

[123] (Savage, p. 122) Savage wanted as much credit for the capture of Parsons' guns as did anyone. He encouraged the men to seize it with Maney's men.

[124] (Savage, p. 127)

[125] (Thompson, p. 10) The lane referred to is Benton Road.

[126] (Malone)

"We with our assistance now taken the battery on our right, but before this I think we had killed nearly all their horses and a great many of their men."[127]   Lieutenant Walling had witnessed the slaughter of the men of the 105th Ohio as well and simply stated, "Their dead and wounded lay thick behind the fence and over the field."[128]

With this rout, the survivors of Parson's guns and the remnants of the 105th Ohio, 123rd Illinois and 80th Illinois with Garrard's detachment fled back toward the cornfield and lane due west of their former position. Here, the 21st Wisconsin laid in wait for the rushing surge of victorious troops of Savage's and Maney's commands. They would not have to wait long.[129] As the Federals retreated to the west the Sixteenth followed rapidly in pursuit. Although running to the rear, the fight was not out of the fleeing enemy yet. Private Clark stated that they would load as they ran, and then whirl back and shoot. While passing the little cabins on the hill, Clark was stuck just above his right hip and fell to the ground. Jim Martin was about the only uninjured man near him at the time. Martin asked him if he could assist him from the field. Clark's response was that he would make it off, but for Martin to, "… go on & kill all of them!"[130] They continued to move on with Maney's men as they crested the hill and the 38th Tennessee—finally and belatedly—joined in the attack on their left flank.[131] Davis Biggs, a member of the Thirty-Eighth Tennessee, recalled, "Soon we advanced through a field where the grapeshot and shrapnel were rattling against the cornstalks, which had been cut and shocked up, also thinning our ranks." Biggs continued, "Going through this field, the 38th got somewhat mixed with the 16th, Col. John H. Savage's

---

[127] (Hooper, p. 76) Hooper made his entry the day after the battle.
[128] (Savage, p. 127)
[129] (Anderson) "He was then ordered by General Terrill to withdraw his battery. He succeeded in bringing away but one gun, four caissons, and two limbers, the horses being killed or disabled."
[130] (Clark, p. #15)
[131] Ibid.

regiment… After passing this field, we struck a rock fence diagonally, each pushing off a few rocks to make climbing easier."[132]

The Sixteenth's advance toward the lane and through the cornfield had bunched the regiment together dramatically. Their earlier line frontage of about 120 yards would likely now be reduced to less than 60 yards due to the casualties already received and the lack of a true line formation as they poured in mass across the field into the face of more heavy fire. Lieutenant Denny Cummings was struck in the mouth by a shot—breaking his jaw. His head snapped to the side and a dozen or more teeth flew from his mouth—he crumpled to the ground thought to be mortally wounded.[133] As they poured across the field, the boys found themselves intermingled with the 38th Tennessee crowding their left and the 9th Tennessee infringing on their right, but nonetheless, they continued their steady advance toward the 21st Wisconsin and remnants of the 105th Ohio and 123rd Illinois which were supported by the 1st Wisconsin holding higher ground in their rear all the time taking heavy frontal fire from Bush and Stone's Batteries.[134]

As the boys ran across the field leaping over dead and wounded Federals, they reached the cornfield where the Twenty-first Wisconsin lay in wait. Sgt. Mead Holmes, Jr., of said regiment, recorded in a letter dated October 9, 1862:

They lay in a cornfield, and the rebels came on within twenty feet, when the orders were given to "Fire and charge." But no order was heard. They saw the rebels were on them, and fired as well as they could.[135]

---

[132] (Biggs, p. 1412) Apparently, Savage had commanded the regiment to fix bayonets prior to the charge. Biggs noted that Savage called them 'bagonets.'

[133] (Clark, p. #15) Cummings actually recovered from his wounds and rejoined the regiment in time to participate in the Battle of Chickamauga.

[134] (Hall)

[135] (Holmes, pp. 92-96)

Captain Womack recalled that when the survivors of the Federal defense fell back about three hundred yards from the open knob and Parson's guns, their defense at this lane, "…was very slight compared with that of their first."[136] The badgers, blinded by the corn and stragglers passing in their front to the rear had effectually blocked their ability to conduct a solid defense of the lane and field. With practically two brigades advancing on their position, most of the regiment began to fall back in disorder.

The walking wounded from the Sixteenth's initial engagement at the fence and cabins tried to steadily make their way back to the regimental aid station located near Walker's Bend. Private Clark was horrified at the scene as he walked hunched over and grabbing his side to the rear. Buddies lay motionless and pale with only the glistening scarlet blood coloring their bodies, clothing, leaves and the ground around them.[137]

> "I watched with a confidence assured but with an intensity of anxiety which I never expect to experience again. The advancing column as they passed upon the wood within which the enemy stood sheltered, and from which they were pouring volley after volley upon our uncovered lines for three long hours, or until night closed the scene the conflict raged."

George Winchester, Q.M., Donelson's Brigade[138]

Faced with Maney's entire Brigade and at least the 16th and 38th Tennessee Regiments of Donelson's Brigade in their front, the

---

[136] (Womack, p. 63) J. R. Thompson added, "And the enemy finally yielded this line and fell back a few hundred yards to a lane." This was Benton Road.

[137] (Clark, p. #15) George W. Winchester, Quarter Master of Donelson's Brigade, wrote in his diary, "… I passed an overhanging bluff near a stream which had been selected as the temporary hospital and here were seen the first bitter fruits of this unnatural fratricidal strife. Here they were borne from the field on litters, in wagons & carts, and upon the arms of their friends, and here was administered such relief as the poor skill of men can apply to suffering humanity…" (Winchester, p. 76)

[138] (Winchester, p. 77)

Wisconsin troops made what slight resistance they could and poured up the hill in their rear to the support of the guns of Bush and Stone. As the Confederates rushed through the field, they received more heavy fire from the retreating Wisconsin troops and theses Federal batteries. The infantry support of the 1st Wisconsin was firing over the heads of the 21st Wisconsin running from the cornfield below.

At the Benton Road following the rout of the 21st Wisconsin, the Sixteenth Tennessee—in tandem with the 9th Tennessee crowding their right and the 38th Tennessee on their left—paused to catch their breath and at least partially reform in the defilade free of Stone's guns. The rush—across the field and into the adjacent cornfield where the 21st Wisconsin had laid in wait—helped to diminish the ranks with more shots of grape and canister from Stone's commanding position. Although a light volley of musketry from the 21st Wisconsin had dropped a few men, the attackers were still confident following the collapse of Terrill's men on the open knob.

Beyond the 38th Tennessee to the Sixteenth's left, the 15th Tennessee had pushed beyond some remnants of Garrard's men and on to a close combat with the 79th Pennsylvania. The 38th Tennessee pushed ahead on their flank and helped to force the Pennsylvania troops from their initial position and back about a hundred yards. The Sixteenth and 9th Tennessee replenished their cartridge boxes from dead and wounded of both sides without orders from field officers and continued up the eastern slope of what became known as Starkweather's Heights. As they neared the crest of the slope, Stone's gunners again began a terrific cannonade firing double shots of canister that furrowed the ground and threw up dirt and rocks on the attacking force. Some of the men were struck and nearly shredded by the point blank blasts while others were temporarily incapacitated by spent canister balls that had ricocheted off the ground and swept them off their feet. Many recovered momentarily and regained their feet rushing to catch up to their comrades— bloodied but not unbowed.

By this time, nearly every Confederate regiment on the right had had lost at least one color bearer or more as well as other members of their color guards. The same was so with the Sixteenth regiment. Private W. T. Mayberry had been designated the regimental color bearer following the resignation of P. H. McBride earlier in April. In this battle he had undoubtedly carried the colors in the front of the regiment as they had assaulted the 123rd Illinois and Garrard's men, but at some point he had been struck down by the heavy fire directed at the colors of the regiment. Seriously wounded, he melted to the ground, and as in every other regiment, a courageous soul would grab the colors and lead the regiment on. William H. White had been with the regiment since its organization.

Serving in Company D, he was originally elected corporal, but he was now serving as a private. As Mayberry slumped to the ground, White rushed to seize the colors and bore them to the front.[139]

Nearing the top of the hill where Stone's Battery was planted, little unit cohesion could be noted. In the midst of combat with missiles zipping in every direction, the boys concentrated on the enemy more and their command organization less. Nearly all of Maney's Brigade had meshed into a gray clad mob that rushed in waves to the breaking point at the crest of the hill and in the face of the battery. Time and again, the 6th and 9th Tennessee Regiments with the Sixteenth at their side reached the crest to receive a withering fire and concussion of artillery in their very faces.

The 1st Tennessee had approached the hill from the north and pushed on to the brink of Bush's guns—shooting down the gunners as they ran to the rear. At least Bush's guns were momentarily captured, but a sudden and heavy fire was thrown into the Confederate ranks from the tree line south of Benton Road combined with shots from Stone's guns. The 79th Pennsylvania had withdrawn to a point along the heavy brush and trees that allowed them to completely cover the ground in front of Stone and Bush's batteries.

On the left, Donelson's three regiments had meshed together also—their right—with those regiments of Maney's left. In their front, the 79th Pennsylvania and 24th Illinois poured incessant fire into their ranks as they fought their way forward. Here, the fight grew desperate with the Confederates of Donelson and Maney's brigades pushing forward only to be forced slowly back. It became a seesaw battle. At least the 15th and 38th Tennessee[140] benefited from the cover of some trees south of Benton Road, but portions of the 38th Tennessee with the Sixteenth and all of Maney's men had to sprint from a wood at the foot of the hill by Benton Road across a

---

[139] (Service Records.)(Pension Application.)
[140] (Service Records.) Colonel John C. Carter was wounded and had his horse killed beneath him in the attempt to seize the heights.

shocked up corn field to the mouth of the guns and heavy infantry support. Private Thompson recalled, "The battle now raged with terror and the slaughter was terrible."[141]

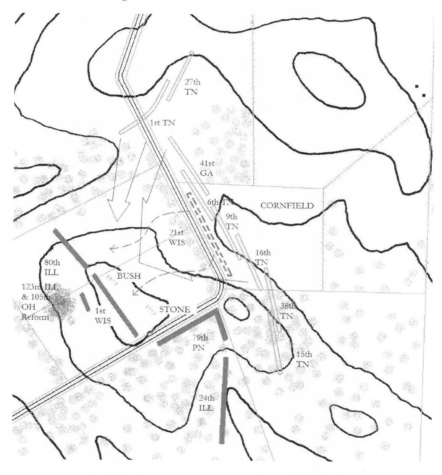

The combined forces of the 15th, 38th, 16th, 9th and 6th Tennessee Regiments forced their way into the cornfield atop Starkweather's Heights and caused the gunners of Stone's Battery to give way. But combined fire from the 79th Pennsylvania in a thicket

---

[141] (Thompson, p. 10)

south of Benton Road, and a heavy fire of canister from Bush's guns drove the boys back again and again. They relentlessly pressed the Federal line, but having already sustained heavy losses, both Maney and Donelson's brigades found themselves losing the momentum that had brought about such success so far.

General Cheatham had given instructions to General Stewart before Donelson's advance to maintain a proper supporting distance. But, there was a problem. Brigades would normally maintain a supporting distance of six hundred to eight hundred yards. Here on the undulating terrain north of Perryville, Donelson's men had become heavily engaged only five hundred yards from their attack position. Advancing his brigade would bring them under fire without being able to engage the enemy in his front due to friendly forces. Thus receiving no additional orders, Stewart remained idle at the attack position at Walker's Bend. Although Stewart undoubtedly heard the heavy fire in his front when the Sixteenth became engaged, he was reluctant to advance to their support; additionally, he had certainly been informed by the division commander of Maney's movement north to the advance. Finally—as Donelson's men had disappeared over the second finger which signaled Terrill's collapse—Stewart began to advance his brigade in one long line. He still didn't commit them but advanced to maintain supporting distance.

By now it was about 4 p.m.. Major General Cheatham had been observing Maney and Donelson pound away at Stone and Bush's batteries at Starkweather's Heights with little success and finally ordered Stewart into the fray. Stewart's Brigade advanced through the same obstacles of trees, underbrush and fences through which Maney and Donelson had passed. Now, they were not the only obstacles; the fields and fences were strewn with dead and wounded. But still, there was only the sight of what *had* happened until they crested the second finger.

To their front only about four hundred yards away, the brigade came into full view of the guns of Bush and Stone obstinately defending the heights. The sights and sounds of battle became crisp and sharp as the minies snapped past them occasionally finding their mark with a loud 'thud!' As they advanced toward and through the cornfield, they observed the wrecked and destroyed caissons and limbers of Parsons' guns. Turner's battery had also advanced to the open knob to their right and rear and was raining plunging fire into the Federal lines atop the distant hill in the front.

As Stewart's Brigade was arriving east of the cornfield, officers of Donelson's Brigade recognized Stewart coming to the relief. The ones that weren't presently focused on the enemy began to call their men to rally points for a brief move to the rear to rest and replenish their cartridge boxes. While large numbers of men from the various regiments rallied on their commands, others were swept up by Stewart's men advancing across Benton Road and up the hill. Never shifting their focus from the enemy, men from all three of Donelson's regiments—and much of Maney's brigade—surged forward as Stewart's right flank intermingled with both the Sixteenth and 9th Tennessee Regiments.

Although officially disengaged, a 'majority' of men from these regiments—slowly but forcefully—pushed on to the crest finally forcing the enemy from the eminence about 4:30 p.m.. Tom Hooper of Company A was one of this number from the Sixteenth. He had already been 'scalped' on the side of the head earlier in the engagement near the open knob, and now he found himself pushing forward in the midst of many men he didn't even recognize. It wasn't even a concern to him. As many others, he was focused on defeating the enemy. It was him or them, and he was determined it wouldn't be him.[142] Reaching the summit still under fire, the hodgepodge of Johnnies seized the remaining guns that Stone was unable to withdraw under a hail of Confederate rifle fire. To their left, the 24th Illinois and 79th Pennsylvania had been steadily forced back by the center of Stewart's Brigade. This relentless push was assisted by the remnants of Donelson's men—unaware they had been relieved. The 15th and 38th Tennessee had helped to press the

[142] (Hooper, p. Oct. 8)

two Federal regiments from the killing ground north of the bend in Benton Road. It was nearly 5 p.m. when Hooper received yet another wound. He had been knocked down at least five times up to this point. Crossing the field on the heights, he was struck in the jaw—knocking him down again. He sat up feeling as if he had just been hit with a hammer; he instinctively put his hands to his face. He was bleeding like a "stuck hog," and initially feared he might bleed out. Eventually he gained his feet and started to stumble to the rear. Surprisingly, he met the Sixteenth marching in line toward him and the front lines only a short distance to his rear.

The boys that had rallied and fallen back to replenish their ammunition had about thirty minutes to rest up and hit a canteen of water. Roles hadn't been called, but a heads-up muster had unquestionably taken place. Of the 378 men that went into action at the start of the fight, their ranks were now deceivingly short. Probably less than 140 men now filled the ranks. This number was in fact deceptive however. Perhaps as many as 80 to 100 men had not been aware of the relieving force and had forged on in the action much like Hooper. The remaining number lay in the regiment's aid station near the front or the division hospital at the Goodknight House in the rear. Others were still making their way to the rear or lying motionless—bleeding away their life's blood on the field. Still, more of them—whether in the ranks now or fighting alongside the relief—were destined to catch a minie or receive a second wound… or be killed outright in battle.

As Hooper headed to the rear, he—as many others did— took an opportunity to supplement his wardrobe. Although he took a pair of shoes off a dead Yankee, he admitted that he would not have done it had he not been, "…in great need of them." He also managed to pick up a cup and a canteen. Passing a small peach orchard, he wished he had the strength to gather a bunch up, but lacking the energy, he pressed on toward the field hospital.[143] He retraced his footsteps past the fences and cabins where the regiment

---

[143] (Hooper, p. Oct. 8)

had been so heavily engaged. As he walked, he scanned the field for his comrades. He recognized several wounded but saw none killed. Finally, he made it to the aid station, but the doctors were too busy dressing more serious wounds. With a couple of wounded buddies he ran into along the way, they made their way in search of the division hospital.[144]

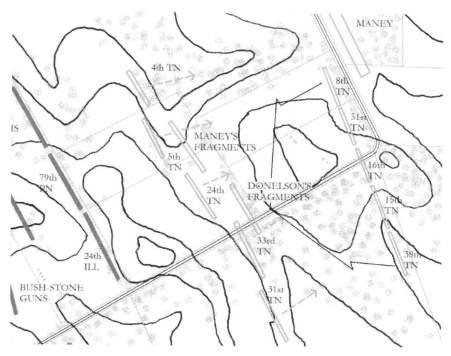

By 5:15, Donelson's Brigade was marched back into the fight. By now, the 8th and 51st Tennessee Regiments[145] had rejoined the

---

[144] Ibid.

[145] The 8th and 51st Regiment's are believed to have possibly been engaged earlier in the fight. They likely advanced from the position occupied by Carnes' Battery that was on the north side of Wilson Creek, north of Starkweather's Heights. From there, the two regiments had likely advanced on the right of Maney's Brigade and had been lightly engaged in the attempts to seize the heights.

brigade. They were pushed forward to exploit the Federal withdrawal from Starkweather's heights caused by Stewart and the remnants of Donelson's and Maney's Brigades. The Federals had withdrawn to a position just as strong about a half mile west of their original position. Advancing within firing range, the brigade once again engaged the remaining organized resistance of the 79th Pennsylvania, 24th Illinois and 1st Wisconsin with portions of other regiments of Terrill's and Starkweather's brigades.

The day had slipped away quickly in light of the earlier combat, and although severely pressing the newly established Federal lines, the Confederate's momentum on the right had slowed to a crawl. Shortly after 6 p.m. and just before the sun began to set, Donelson' men and the Sixteenth were withdrawn to the vicinity of Benton Road west of the Open Knob. Skirmishers were left well forward, and the brigade rapidly began reorganizing and conducting headcounts. Although the action had ended for the day on the Confederate right, Liddell's Brigade pushed forward on the division's left shortly after sunset. Within twenty minutes it had nearly become too dark to see, but with the Sixteenth anxiously listening, Liddell pushed forward with loud crashes of musketry and routed a host of Federal troops in his front effectually seizing Harris' battery west of the Widow Gibson's Farm. Cheers rang out all along the front and the boys felt confident of success. They now set to the task of recovering the wounded and began preparations for the morrow's actions.

Unaware of the location of the division hospital, Hooper and his comrades walked a mile, then boarded a wagon and traveled two to three more miles before giving up. He finally managed to find Army headquarters and spent the night with the headquarters staff. All throughout the evening, the wounded streamed back to the rear in search of aid.[146]

Reverend Joseph Cross, of the 2nd Tennessee, had spent the early afternoon with Dr. Quintard of the 1st Tennessee. Before his

---

[146] (Hooper, p. Oct. 8)

services were needed elsewhere, he observed the initial combat from some heights. "The crash of artillery was deafening. The roar of the musketry was like the voice of the stormy sea. The fierce missiles went screaming and whistling past me every moment, and fell around me like a fiery tempest." He was engrossed by the scene in his front, but when the wounded started streaming back to the rear in search of aid, he was asked to help attend to them.[147]

Cross was shocked at the sights he saw at the hospital. One young artilleryman arrived with his legs crushed by a solid shot. Another man had a hole through his body, "…which would admit a man's arm; yet, strange to say, he lives a full hour." Another was carried to the growing line of casualties whose face was so smeared with blood and brains that he, "…presents no semblance of the 'human face divine.'"

> Some are shot through the breast, through the lungs; others through the arm, the hand, the shoulder. One has lost a little finger or a big toe; another is minus a nose, or has had one of this ears cut away; while a third will need a new set of teeth, and has parted perhaps with a piece of his tongue.[148]

His clothing soaked with blood, Cross continued to aid the wounded, and sometime about dark, a young soldier of the Sixteenth came under his care with his shoulder "shattered." He informed the reverend that Colonel Savage—with who Cross had become quite good friends—was badly wounded and trying to make his way to the hospital. After tending to the boy's wound, he mounted his horse and went off to aid the wounded colonel. Riding a couple of miles, he came upon a group of Yankee prisoners being moved to the rear. Not far behind, the colonel riding upon his war horse 'George' trailed slowly along. Greeting the reverend, the colonel stated that he had all of his wounded off the field and was now retiring himself. Cross asked if he was badly hurt, and the colonel replied, "Not much, I think—shot through the calf of the leg; no bones broken; but poor

---

[147] (Cross, p. 61)
[148] (Cross, pp. 61-2)

old George has had a ball through his head, and I have to ride slowly." At that, Cross saw that the horse's head was leaking blood like a broken bucket. 'George' stammered under the colonel's weight, and the reverend begged Savage to exchange horses. The colonel declined his offer stating, "Old George has a good constitution—I think he will hold out with me." Thirty minutes later, they arrived at the surgeon's quarters, and Cross helped the colonel dismount. Pulling Savage's boot off, a pool of blood poured out. His wound was dressed, and he remounted 'George' ignoring the reverend's pleas. They continued two miles further and stopped at an abandoned house where the reverend placed Savage in an old straw bed.[149]

Others had wandered back to the aid stations and division hospital. Finding their way, they were laid under the large trees that surrounded the Goodknight House. Wounded men occupied the house, its outbuildings and the whole of the yard. Major George Winchester, the acting brigade quartermaster, recalled:

> I returned about 9 o'clock to the principal hospital to witness a scene revolting to humanity – the house, yard, and every available space upon an acre of ground were covered with the wounded – The night was quiet, and the moon shone as calmly and as placidly down as if nature looked with approving smile upon the terrible drama which had just been enacted. I soon found myself in the midst of the dead and dying, of every stage of suffering and death.[150]

Mart Gribble[151] was one of many who had made it to the hospital. Gribble had been shot in the face and the leg and suffered greatly from the pain. After being placed under a tree in an apple orchard near the house, he was considered seriously wounded and could not be moved. Bob Ware, one of Gribble's company, was also seriously

---

[149] (Cross, pp. 62-3)
[150] (Winchester, 1862-63)
[151] Martin VanBuren Gribble was a private in Company D. His wound damaged the bone in his leg and he was practically immobilized.

wounded—but in the mouth. He had been struck by a ball that broke his jaw, passed through his neck, and stopped just before exiting the back of his neck.[152] In fact, over fifty percent of the entire regiment that had been engaged in action were wounded or killed on the field. But not all the men of the regiment had been engaged. Sergeant Major Tom Potter, of the Sixteenth, had collected a detail for the brigade before the battle. Each regiment of the brigade had provided fourteen privates and one non-commissioned officer to provide details for the ordinance and ambulance corps. These men were to assist in resupplying the brigade with ammunition during the action and assist wounded off the field. The Sixteenth was the only regiment to supply a commissioned officer in charge of the detail.[153]

The ranks that had been filled that morning with devoted and courageous young men and boys were now depleted severely. While one company had not suffered a single man killed on the field, others had as many as twelve killed outright. The boys were shocked as they consolidated with the rest of the regiment. While some went in search of brothers on the field, others helped to assist the wounded to the rear as the full moon rose almost immediately after dusk. Private White, who had seized the colors upon the wounding of Ensign Mayberry, remembered the full moon shining brightly and casting shadows of the massive trees, and the pitiful cries of the wounded as he prayed for his fallen comrades. The night passed slowly and hauntingly by. Captain Womack finished his diary entry for the day with these memorable lines.

> When the broad face moon began to shed her silvery beams on the faces of the dead and dying, the field presented a most horrible spectacle indeed; and the shrieks and groans of the wounded constantly pointed to where another brave and gallant fellow had sacrificed his all on the altar of liberty.[154]

---

[152] (Yeary, p. 286)
[153] (Potter, 1861-1865, p. 82)
[154] (Womack, p. 64)

Chapter III

Kentucky to Tullahoma

9 October – 31 October 1862

The next morning, 'George' was still alive—standing in a pool of his own congealed blood.   Once again, the colonel mounted him and rode eight miles further to Harrodsburg.   There, Savage was taken in by a Mrs. Keller who, "...nursed him as if he had been a brother."[155]   The regiment, under the guidance of Lieutenant Colonel Donnell, was gathered up and withdrawn with the rest of Cheatham's Division early that morning near dawn.   On the road to Harrodsburg, they continued to pick up stragglers and meet walking wounded comrades all along the route.

At the division hospital near Perryville, the wounded were informed very early of the intent to withdraw.   All who could walk would have to find their way to Harrodsburg where the army would organize.   Those incapable of walking or being moved must be left behind.   This included Mart Gribble, Bob Ware and John Gribble, all of Company D.   Will White, of the same company—although suffering from a nasty and painful thigh wound caused by a canister shot—hobbled up, and like many of his Confederate counterparts, he did all in his power to make the trek rather than fall into Yankee hands.

Many of the more slightly wounded, and some who were not wounded at all, were designated to remain behind to care for their

---

[155] (Cross, pp. 62-3)

comrades. The long columns of infantry passed on toward Harrodsburg—evacuating the field for which they had so nobly fought and died for less than twelve hours earlier. Still not aware that they were soon to retreat from Kentucky, many of the boys saw this withdrawal as only a temporary move. Some of the wounded that could be moved to Harrodsburg were sent by ambulance, cart, cannon limber, or whatever transportation the boys could acquire.

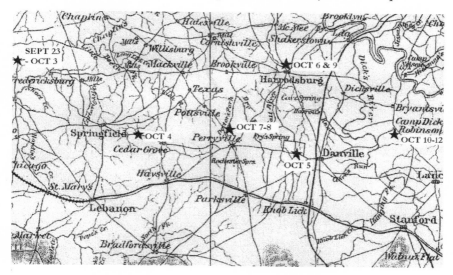

Private Clark was one of many sent to the Harrodsburg Courthouse that day. As the Confederate Army surprisingly marched on about eight miles further to Camp Dick Robinson, many boys found themselves unable to keep up or continue at all. A good number of the more seriously wounded stayed behind at the courthouse that night. Clark stated that nine of his buddies died during the course of the evening.[156] Tom Hooper was more fortunate; he got permission to hop on the regimental sutler wagon and was able to move on with the army.[157] By the time Hooper caught up with the division, they were going into camp near a small river four miles below Camp Dick Robinson. That evening,

---

[156] (Clark, p. #15)
[157] (Hooper, p. Oct. 9)

Reverend Cross went with an ambulance to pick up Colonel Savage at Mrs. Keller's in Harrodsburg, but upon arriving, he was informed that the stubborn colonel had once again remounted his injured steed and continued on in the direction of the main body of the army.[158]

The number of wounded was so great that over the next few days as the Federal troopers captured the boys in the hospitals and scoured the field, they sent many of the more seriously wounded as far as Lebanon, Kentucky—seventeen miles from Perryville.[159] On the 10th of October after sitting for nearly thirty-six hours in a pool of his own blood with blood soaked, dirty bandages on his face and leg, Mart Gribble was approached by Bob Ware. Bob, seeing Mart's weak condition, suggested that he should try to get up and move from his exposed position. Mart expressed that he couldn't get up in the state he was in. Bob left for a few minutes and came back with John Gribble and some make-shift crutches—a plow handle and a stick. He recommended to Mart that they should go across the battlefield in search of friends or a safer location.

As they wandered aimlessly near a little house, they found their captain—John G. Lamberth—lying dead by a log. Mart was exhausted, he could go no further; he sat on the log by his captain with a distant stare. Bob urged Mart to get up and continue on, but dehydration and his wounds would not allow it. Bob and John wished him the best and continued on across the field.[160]

As Mart sat staring at the corpse of his beloved captain, he heard a distant rumble approaching at a feverish pitch. Looking up,

---

[158] (Cross, 1864, p. 64)

[159] (Confederate Veteran, pp. V. 29, p. 197) Confederate wounded of Donelson's Brigade at Lebanon, Kentucky on October 24, 1862 in the Male Academy. Sgt. S. D. Boggry, Co. G, 15th Tenn., Sgt. John Golden, Co. C, 15th Tenn., B. A. Ware, Co. D, 16th Tenn., M. V. Gribble, Co. D, 16th Tenn., J. S. Boon, Co. H, 8th Tenn., B. F. Scudder, Co. F, 16th Tenn., with nurses: J. S. Brown, Co. H, 38th Tenn., W. A. Kimball, Co. H, 8th Tenn., B. E. Tilman, Co. C, 51st Tenn.

[160] (Yeary, p. 286)

he saw a group of five Yankee cavalrymen galloping at full speed toward him over Confederate corpses strewn across the field. They came to a halt within feet of him. One of the men asked, "What are you doing here?"

I replied that I was just sitting on the log.

"Have you been here since the battle?"

"No sir, I belong over at the hospital."

"To which side do you belong?"

"The Confederate."

"Who is that lying there?"

"My Captain."

"What kind of a man was he?"

"He was a good man and his name was Lambert."

They said that he might have been a good man, but was fighting for a bad cause.

Another said, "Who's coat is that you have on?"

"It is mine, I suppose."

"No sir, that is our uniform coat." And it was—but it was all I had.

One of them said to me, "Pull it off, sir."

"Well if I must, I will," and began pulling it off.

Another of the bunch said, "No, you will not pull it off."

So they got up a quarrel among themselves, and the one who took my part drove them all away from me. But I was sure in my mind that they would come back and kill me.[161]

By the end of the day, Mart had been picked up by the Federal ambulance corps and was in route to the Male Academy at Lebanon, Kentucky with Bob Ware who had also been apprehended a distance away. Others suffered longer, more agonizing waits. Private George Parks, of Company H, had been seriously wounded in the left leg by a ball that had broken the bone. He had been placed in a stable and hardly attended to for days after the battle. His clothing was mostly shot away during the fight, and his leg wound suffered horribly. Flies had swarmed on the wound and his leg swelled tremendously. Soon maggots had infested the hole, and although they ate quite well—they may well have saved him by eating away the decomposed flesh. He was eventually moved to Harrodsburg and paroled early in January by the Federal Provost Marshall. His service was done. Incapable of performing the duties of a soldier, he made his way back home many months later.[162]

When Tom Hooper finally caught up with the regiment at Camp Dick Robinson on the morning of the 10th, he was shocked at what he saw. It appeared to him that the whole of the regiment was little bigger than his company had been at the war's commencement. He learned of all the killed and wounded in the company writing in his diary, "God bless their souls in Heaven."[163] It was October 12th when all rumors as to what the army was doing were answered. The next day they were on the retreat out of Kentucky. The Sixteenth Tennessee had left its mark on the bloody field of Perryville leaving dozens of men slain on the field and dozens more to perish in the stink and filth of hospitals. They had also established themselves as a hard fighting, dedicated unit.

---

[161] (Yeary, pp. 286-87)
[162] (Confederate Veteran, pp. V. 29, p. 197) (Tennessee Veteran Questionaires, V. 4, pp. 1688-89) (Compiled Service Records)
[163] (Hooper, p. Oct. 10)

So conspicuous was the part of Cheatham's brigades, that when General Bragg issued his general order authorizing the several commands engaged at the battle of Perryville to inscribe the name of that field on their colors, he said: "the corps of Cheatham's division, which made the gallant and desperate charge resulting in the capture of three of the enemy's batteries, will, in addition to the name, place the cross-cannon inverted.[164]

General Polk later remarked on the conduct of Donelson's, Maney's and Stewart's Brigades.

This charge of these three brigades was one of the most heroic and brilliant movements of the war. Considering the disparity of the number of the troops engaged, the strength of the enemy's position, the murderous character of the fire under which they had to advance, the steadiness with which they endured the havoc which was being made in their ranks, their knowledge that they were without any supporting force, the firmness with which they moved upon the enemy's masses of infantry and artillery, it will compare favorably with the most brilliant achievements of historic valor.[165]

Donelson's Brigade had suffered severely, but the Sixteenth Tennessee had lost far more than their share. The regiment's total losses were more than half of the number lost by the entire brigade. The boys had won a signal victory—both tactically and mentally. This hard earned victory would become one of many of their strategic losses. The sheer number of the Federal troops was overwhelming, and their hard won victory would be in vain. Although they had bloodied the nose of the Federal army and perhaps instilled amongst the Federals a new found respect for Confederate fighting abilities, it would not be enough to call this Kentucky foray a victory. Soon enough, the boys found themselves in a pursued retreat in a nearly dreamlike state. Few remembered

---

[164] (Evans C. A., p. 52)
[165] (Finley C. L., p. 248)

many details of the retreat or wanted too. At least they were headed back to Tennessee.

The Confederate Army commenced the movement on the 13th with the Federals harassing the rear of their columns the whole time. The army marched non-stop until reaching a point near the residence of Dick Nailer late on the evening of the 14th. The march was taken up again by 3 a.m. on the morning of October 15th. By evening, the boys had reached the north bank of Rock-Castle River where they went into bivouac with heavy skirmishing at the rear of the column. The morning of October 16th dawned cloudy and warm, and Cheatham's Division acted as rear-guard of the army. The boys had just passed about two miles south of Wildcat Creek when the rear of the division was pressed very hard by their Federal pursuers. The regiment and brigade were ordered back to the creek to remain until morning, but by the time the regiment arrived, the 8th Texas Cavalry had driven the enemy back. General Cheatham had gone to the rear of the column with the brigade. The regiment's rations had finally been depleted. The supply trains were still far in the advance, and the boy's stomachs growled for bread. Late that night, they finally received a few ounces of fresh, unsalted beef that they roasted over the coals of small fires they had built.[166] General Cheatham had always done all in his power to ensure the comfort of his men, but control of the rations was out of his hands this far in the rear. When a hungry Texan saw nearly a dozen ears of corn hanging from his horse's saddle, the Texan said to the general, "Old man (addressing Cheatham), I will give you a dollar apiece for those ears of corn."

"Do you know whom you are talking to?"

The soldier said "No, and I don't care a damn, but I will do what I said I would about that corn."

---

[166] (Womack, p. 61)

The general smiled, untied his corn, and threw it to the hungry men who scuffled over it as very hungry hogs would have done.[167]

At five a.m. the morning of the 17th, the brigade stepped off as rear guard and passed through London by eleven a.m. and continued six miles to a "little muddy creek." The brigade halted there after they caught up with the supply trains to cook some scant rations. The boys had not eaten anything since the small ration of beef the night before. On the following morning, they woke to the first frost of the season and left the creek at eleven a.m. They marched eighteen miles to Barboursville and arrived there at night. With the drastic temperature change, Captain Womack admitted, "Here we reduced to the necessity of camping in an open field and of burning plank and rail fences to make fires, which we did without much mercy." By seven a.m. on the 19th, they stepped off and marched along the Cumberland River until crossing at Cumberland Ford where they camped for the night.[168] The Federal pursuit had stopped days earlier, but now the harassment of Federal bushwhackers had become an incessant annoyance. During this movement through the mountains, the cowards stole pock shots at the column as it passed through the valley below. Finally, "… a general officer, without halting, ordered some picked cavalrymen to surround the nest of skulkers; and this order was so effectually obeyed that five of the wretches apologized by permitting themselves to be hanged near the roadside."[169]

The 20th of October, the regiment and brigade continued on the march for twenty miles and encamped two miles beyond Cumberland Gap. Private Carden recalled suffering more from hunger on this retreat than any other time during the war. One day during the march, Carden and a comrade had stopped to rest by the roadside when their Assistant Surgeon[170] went riding by on his horse.

---

[167] (Blackburn)
[168] (Womack, pp. 65-66)
[169] (Lindsley, p. 814)
[170] Assistant Surgeon Charles K. Mauzy.

Carden asked if he could spare anything to eat. "He reached down in his haversack and gave me a biscuit which I divided with my comrade, and I think to this day how good that biscuit tasted."[171] On the 21st, they continued the march for three miles and camped on Powell River and still received only quarter rations. The next day they marched twenty miles through Tazewell, Tennessee. After crossing Clinch River, the boys went into camp. The 23rd of October they marched thirteen miles to Maynardville and three miles beyond when they stopped to camp at the Owler Farm. Finally, on the morning of the 24th, the army continued on for thirteen miles and halted about five miles north of the Knoxville. After arriving in close proximity of the city, sufficient amounts of food were distributed to satisfy their appetites. Here, on the outskirts of Knoxville, the army remained encamped until the morning of the 29th.

The first snowfall had come on the 26th and amounted to five inches, but the boys were still clothed in their campaign attire which consisted of just their drawers, a hat, jacket, pair of pants and brogans. They weren't prepared for an early winter. On the 27th, many of the wounded who had traveled with the army were sent into Knoxville for care at the hospitals there. Lossen Keiff, John Van Hooser and W. T. Moore were among the number that was sent into the city. These men were almost immediately embarked on trains for trips to hospitals in the vicinity of Chattanooga. The following day, details were arranged to return home to gather winter clothing. Captain Womack wrote in his diary that their friends back home were a "...much more reliable source" for clothing and noted that the government was still "...rather poorly supplied." Sergeant R. G. Webb was detailed to gather clothing for Company E[172] while Lieutenant "Fayett" Hayes was detailed for Company H. Before leaving, Fayett was given a letter to deliver to Private Roysdon Etter's wife who was the sister of C. M. Rutledge of the same company.[173]

---

[171] (Carden, p. Apr. 12)
[172] (Womack, pp. 67-68)
[173] (Sullivan, pp. 68-69)

Knoxville, Tenn. October 28, 1862

Mrs. S. A. Etter,

Dear Sister, I once more seat myself to drop you a few lines. Thinking you would like to hear from Roisson and me. I can't tell you much about Roisson. I left him the 10 of this month at Harisbaurgh, Ky. He got wounded in the head and the ball went in at his cheake and ranged thru the back of his jaw and was taken out between his shoulders. He didn't appear to be suffering much. When I left him he said he was going home as soon as he got able to travel. I think he will be able to travel in a short time. I suppose you have heard all about the battle and if not Fayett can tell you more than I can write. I didn't get hurt myself but very little and was glad to get off as well as I did. There is but 17 men in our company.[174] The rest was killed and wounded. Isaac Cunningham hasn't been heard of yet. Fayett is coming home after clothing. You needn't pester yourself about sending me any and if you do you must spend the money I sent you for them and not try to make them yourself. It is getting late and I must close. These few lines leave me well. You must write to me soon. So no more - only remaining your brother until death.

C. M. Rutledge[175]

Being so close to the city, some of the officers were allowed to go into Knoxville to get newspapers and other comfort items.

---

[174] This number suggests that the company went into action with 35 effective men—as eighteen men were listed on the official casualty report.

[175] Interestingly, Etter is not on the official report of casualties of the Sixteenth Tennessee, and neither is Rutledge who clearly states that, "I didn't get hurt myself but very little and was glad to get off as well as I did." This is another of many indications that wounds that did not require surgeon's treatment were merely treated by the men themselves. He was likely "scalped" or grazed by a bullet during the fight—enough to bleed.

Yankee articles regarding the fight at Perryville had been published in northern newspapers, and by now they had been republished all across the Confederacy in southern papers. The boys gathered around in groups to hear what the Yankee papers had printed. One correspondent that had been on the field after the battle reported a grisly scene.

His battery [Stone's] was worked with fine effect, as was that of Captain Bush, and with their supports of infantry they retained their position till the very last. Bloody was their fight, and hundreds were left on the field in their front. In Captain Stone's front I this morning saw four dead rebels who had been killed by a single shot. The top of the head of the first was taken off, the entire head of the second was gone, the breast of the third was torn open, and the ball passed through the abdomen of the fourth. All had fallen in a heap, killed instantly...

I have been over a part of the battle field and with Capt. Williams have counted what rebels I *saw* dead on the field. On our left and in front of where Starkweather fought, and Maney and Donelson's rebel brigades attacked, I *saw* and counted 211 dead. At the hospital, near the cross roads, there are two more who I saw dead and eight wounded. At Gen. Cheatham's hospital[176] there are fifty-two dead and five hundred wounded. In a pen in front of where Harris fought, there are eighteen dead...

The First Tennessee lost two hundred killed and wounded, and on the retreat the Sixth, Sixteenth, and Thirty-first Tennessee regiments reported themselves cut up entirely. The first Confederate brigade was destroyed if their own stories are to be believed...

The correspondent falsely reported that Brigadier General George Maney had been killed in the fight; however, he did report finding

---

[176] The Goodknight House.

Confederate officers on the Confederate right and found, "...a captain and a first lieutenant lying unburied on our left." All the boys—by then—were aware that Captain Lamberth and Lieutenant Spurlock had been killed there on the field and probably supposed this report to be in reference to them. [177]

While here, 2nd Sergeant J. L. Davis took the time to write a brief casualty report to be delivered by the man appointed to gather clothing for Company F back in Putnam County. The local paper later printed the note in its entirety.

To The Friends At Home, Putnam County, Tenn.

Report of the killed and wounded of Co. F. Sixteenth Regiment Tennessee Volunteers, on the 8th day of October, 1862, at the battle of Perryville, Ky.

Capt. J. B. Vance, shot in the head, mortally wounded.
2nd Lieut. W. W. Baldwin, shot in the thigh, flesh wound.
3rd Lieut. D. G. Pointer, shot in the body and died next morning.
Orderly Sergt. Jo. Bullington, shot dead on the field.
4th Sergt. J. P. Mayberry, shot in the arm, pretty bad flesh wound.
5th Sergt. H. L. P. Pearson, slightly wounded on the hip, flesh wound.
Private M. M. Anderson, killed dead on the field, shot through head.
F. M. Amonett, slightly wounded in mouth.
Samuel Benson, badly wounded in the shoulder by bomb.
O. E. Boyd, wounded in the left arm, flesh wound.
C. T. Bledsoe, slightly wounded on right arm.
John Choat, wounded on the hip, flesh wound.
W. F. Grimsley, shot through the groin and out at the hip.
H. J. Hughes, badly wounded in the mouth and shoulder.
M. J. Nichols, badly wounded in both legs, flesh wound.
J. L. Ollison, shot through both legs, flesh wound.

[177] (The Louisville Daily Journal, 1862)

J. J. Richardson, mortally wounded in the breast.

B. F. Scudders, mortally wounded in the breast.

T. C. Thompson, mortally wounded in the groin and died since.

P. M. Wassom, mortally wounded in the thigh, and leg was cut off since.

Corporal John Bullington, middle finger shot nearly off.

Corporal Crockett Clark, missing; don't know what has become of him.

W. H. Sullins, missing, was not hurt when seen last.

I. M. West and G. B Jaquess missing. These two belonged to the Infirmary Corps, carrying off the wounded. They are taken by the enemy, I reckon. This is true a list as I can make at this time.

J. L. Davis, 2nd Sergt. Commanding Co. F, 16th Regt. Tennessee Vols.

Show this to the friends of the old Cookeville company. I will give a true account of the killed in the Sixteenth Regiment as I can. We lost 42 killed dead on the field, and in killed and wounded in all we lost 200 and came out with 198. Several of them that were wounded are nearly well. Loss Pearson is nearly well. I have not heard of any of them since we left the battlefield. J. L. Davis.[178]

Davis listed an additional six men that were not reported in the official casualty report submitted to Richmond. F. M. Amonett and C. T. Bledsoe were in fact wounded. Crockett Clark, I. M. West and G. B. Jaquess were captured, but apparently, W. H. Sullins had run for the hills and made his way back to Tennessee to hide out the remainder of the war.

By now, it was clear just how much damage had been done to the numerical strength of the Sixteenth. Company A had gone into the fight with an impressive eighty-four men and reported an official

---

[178] (Davis, 1862) F. M. Amonett, C. T. Bledsoe, Corporal Crockett Clark, W. H. Sullins, I. M. West and G. B. Jaquess are not listed on the official casualty report. Two were slightly wounded and four missing. This is only one company that had discrepancies, and it is likely that all of the companies had more casualties than officially reported.

loss of thirty men but only managed to muster sixteen men fit for service the following morning.[179] Company C had forty men in line at the beginning of the fight but had only twelve able for duty now.[180] Captain Womack stated that 50% of his company (E), "...was wounded, but not a man killed upon the field..." He reported twenty-five on the official casualty report, thus the company must have gone into the fight with approximately fifty men.[181] With these dramatically thinned ranks, the army received orders to march on the morning of the 29th.

By 2 p.m., the army had commenced the short march into Knoxville and boarded trains bound for Chattanooga at 6 p.m. The regiment traveled all night by rail and arrived in Chattanooga around 11 a.m. on the morning of October 30th. There, they waited until 2 p.m. for another train that was headed to Bridgeport, Alabama. The train arrived there at 10 p.m., and the boys went into camp near the Tennessee River. Captain Womack had been made aware that most of the wounded had been transported by rail to area hospitals in the days prior and took a chance at finding his wounded brother—but to no avail.[182]

The following morning, the boys learned that the bridge had not been completed, thus, they had to carry all of the regiment's baggage four hundred yards to the river to be transported by ferry.

---

[179] (Savage, p. 127) This numerical difference doesn't account for 38 men. Perhaps a larger number of men came from Company A for the infirmary/ordinance corps detail that Sgt. Maj. Potter had gathered for the brigade prior to the battle. Then again, it may account for men that were wounded, but not seriously enough to be treated at the hospital.

[180] (Evans C. A., p. 520) Company C reported 22 casualties. This still does not account for eight men that were most likely very slightly wounded.

[181] (Womack, p. 63) The numerical strengths of the companies varied greatly. The largest company—from the very beginning—was Company A. The smallest companies appear to be Company D and G with each going into the fight with about 30 men. Company D had lost a large number of men to P. H. McBride's cavalry company in April of that year. The average strength per company had been 40 effective men.

[182] (Womack, p. 68)

Once across, the same routine was conducted on the north side of the river. The train finally arrived at 5 p.m., and the boys hopped aboard the cars once again bound for Tullahoma. Five hours later, they arrived there and slept the remainder of the night in the cars.[183] Their excursion had been almost exactly two months long and very costly, but they knew they were veterans now—that had been tried in the most hellish of combat. The soldiers dreamed the night away in anticipation of soon reuniting with their loved ones.

---

[183] Ibid.

Chapter IV

Tullahoma to Murfreesboro and the LaVergne Expedition

1 November – 30 December 1862

Early in the morning on a clear and cool November 1st, the boys disembarked the trains, gathered their camp equipage and pitched the few tents that they still had. Their bivouac was established about a quarter mile west of the town near the old Tullahoma graveyard. Greeting them there were the recruiting officers that had missed the campaign and "about" one-hundred and eighty new recruits from their counties of origin. Many of the boys were younger brothers, cousins or neighbors of the now Veteran Sixteenth soldiers. The next few weeks were to be spent training and drilling the new soldiers and turning them into troops that the Sixteenth would be proud of. The only problem was that the vast majority of the boys had not been home since their enlistment over eighteen months earlier. Immediately, it became apparent that most of the men and officers were experiencing "great anxiety" as they were now so near to their homes. Captain Womack even noted that,

"…this protracted absence, a thing the soldiers did not expect at the time of their enlistment, was ripening to a source of frequent desertions, and was annoying indeed."[184]

J. R. Thompson had been appointed to gather winter clothing for the men of Company A. He and the other detailed men had traveled with the regiment to Tullahoma, but now had to go afoot up to forty or more miles to their neighborhoods to gather sufficient clothing for the boys. The men were given instructions and then set off towards their homes.[185] Donelson's Brigade and the vast majority of the army remained stationary in these camps through the 21st of November. On the 3rd of the month, Captain Womack discharged J. R. Skelton for being physically unfit for service. The same day he filled out a furlough for his company, "On account of the constant clamor about going home…" The furlough was not approved, but, Lt. Col. Donnell—who had commanded the regiment since Colonel Savage's wounding at Perryville—assured him and the rest of the men that they would be furloughed as soon as possible.

The first of the furloughs was granted on the 5th of November. Small groups of men from each company were granted leaves of absence for five day increments. Apparently, each company selected five men for furlough, and upon their return, another five men could take leave. The first five from Captain Womack's company included Lieut. B. P. Green, Sgt. A. M. Mason, Cpl. J. W. Bratcher, Michael Mauzy and Luke Purser.[186] Some men were reluctant to wait for their furloughs and took short leaves without permission. The boys didn't want to wait for something that might not happen, thus they went absent long enough to get outfitted for the winter and see their loved ones. J. R. Thompson recalled that there was, "…no trouble about it. I was relieved of collecting their goods."[187]

---

[184] (Womack, p. 69)
[185] (Thompson, p. 10)
[186] (Womack, p. 69)
[187] (Thompson, p. 10)

Through November 21st nothing of much consequence took place. The new recruits were certainly drilled by the noncommissioned officers while the remainder of the men lived a relatively comfortable camp life. Visitors frequented the camps and often brought delicious pies and other eatables to the thrill of all of the boys. Occasionally a comrade who had been wounded would return to his company and be poked fun of for his hospital stay by the clown's of his outfit. An inseparable esprit de corps had formed between the veterans of the Sixteenth, and the recruits looked at them with a want and need for acceptance. The boys shared their stories with the recruits. They listened attentively and tried to suppress their emotions of fear, exhilaration and wonder. Certainly, some asked too many questions and were quickly put in their place, while others tried to be disinterested or matter of fact regarding the hellacious stories that were regularly told. Other veterans taught different things to the new bloods.

R. C. Carden had been twice elected to corporal—and twice he was reduced to the ranks for his youthful antics. Carden found himself within fourteen miles of his home while situated in Tullahoma. "Our adjutant liked a drink of applejack quite well and as there was a still near my home I would get a pass frequently. I suppose our Colonel did not know anything about it, so I would run up home, visit the folks and lay in a jug of brandy."[188] One evening Carden learned that one of his partners had a brother in law—a preacher nonetheless—that lived within five miles of their camp. The preacher had a stash of liquor and had been selling it to the nearby soldiers. Carden and his buddies didn't want to buy the liquor; why should they buy it when they could just trick the preacher? They soon devised a plan. Carden, C. G. Lance and a few other boys went to the preacher's house with one of them acting the role of an officer. When the preacher admitted he had liquor for sale, the 'officer' informed him that they had to confiscate the liquor and take him to camp as well. "If you ever heard any begging – that preacher did it." The boys suggested to the 'officer' that if he

---

[188] Regimental Adjutant – Lieutenant John R. Paine.

promised not to sell anymore they could "let him off." Needless to say, the preacher promised, and the boys took off with the preacher's liquor.

On the way back to camp the boys "commenced to store it away," and by the time they reached their bivouac, Carden admitted that they were a "lively set." Carden couldn't stop at that. It was a cold, frosty night, and he thought it would be fun to catch a dog with a fishhook that belonged to an old man in his company. He baited the hook with a piece of meat and hid a distance off holding on to the string. The dog failed to bite for some time until one of their crowd became a little too 'boisterous' on the company grounds. A company officer was about to throw the fellow in the guard house, so Charlie Lance took off to go help out when—in the darkness—he fell into a freshly dug well. Carden heard the fall and broke out into laughter. He knew the old man that owned the dog would hear him laughing, "…so I jumped up to run just as the dog got the bait in his mouth and I dragged him a little distance when the fish hook tore loose and the dog got away."[189] He had learned how to break the monotony of camp life and was teaching it to the new recruits.

During this stay at Tullahoma, a small shipment of Whitworth rifles had arrived at the army. To ascertain who should receive the arms, General Bragg instituted a target practice and competition. The best shots of each company competed with the best shots of the other regiments and brigades in the army. The supply was very limited so only a small number of men would receive the prized rifles that were accurate at over a thousand yards. J. D. Phillips, of Company A, proved to be one of the finest shooters in the army and claimed his prize after defeating many others in the competition. From this point forward, Phillips was used as the sharpshooter for the Sixteenth.[190]

As the army had returned to middle Tennessee, it had now found itself somewhat better supplied. More tents were now issued

---

[189] (Carden, p. Apr. 19)
[190] (Head T. A., p. 100)

to the troops, a luxury that had escaped the boys for over two months. Some of the officers had their wives or families sew them new uniforms of gray jean. Food and equipage appeared to be in quantity, but the burden of clothing the army still fell—to the largest degree—on folks from home and Relief Societies that had been established for the comfort of the common soldiers. The issue of recruiting was never completed, and on the 13th of November, Lieut. J. K. P. Webb was detailed to recruit back in Warren County for fourteen days. The following day, the regiment furloughed another bunch of soldiers for five days that included W. C. Womack, Sr., H. A. Van Hooser, John L. Tanner and David Bonner. At least the officers got paid here, and Captain Womack settled a debt for dental work completed by A. F. Claywell in 1860. On the 15th, Captain Womack took his own leave of absence and returned to camp with his brother J. B. Womack on the afternoon of the 20th. The next day, Cheatham's Division received orders to move out at daylight with three days of rations.[191]

On a clear and cool November 22nd, Donelson's brigade stepped off as the Van Guard of the army at 10 a.m. After crossing Little Duck River, they camped at Manchester. That night, Captain Womack and Lieut. B. P. Green spent the night at Mrs. Joanna Briney's Boarding House which had been formerly owned by the captain. The next morning they marched at 11 a.m. two miles north of Beech Grove and camped on Garretson's Fork. At 8 a.m. on the 24th, the boys continued the march and arrived at Murfreesboro by 4 p.m. They continued north, up the Nashville Railroad and pitched tents for the night on the "margin of a little creek." Two days later, the brigade was moved east across the railroad and camped near the Nashville Turnpike. They were informed that they would probably spend the winter at this location. On the 27th, cannonading was heard in the direction of LaVergne, and it was learned that the Federals had, "…entered the village, burned it, and retired." November 28th through December 4th the regiment stayed in camp. James R. Thompson recalled that the camp was visited, "…daily by

---

[191] (Womack, pp. 70-71)

friends from home and many of the Tennessee soldiers were indebted to home folks for good clothing." Some attended field services conducted by Reverend Cross. Captain Womack was so affected by one of his sermons that he wrote a long letter home to his wife. He also went to the office of the "Rebel Banner"—a newspaper dedicated to the soldiers and their experiences that was circulated throughout the army.[192]

The evening of the 4th, the regiment received orders to cook three days of rations and be prepared to move out in the morning. At dawn, instructions were given to Generals Donelson and Preston Smith—whose brigade had just been added to Cheatham's Division. They were ordered to conduct a reconnaissance toward LaVergne. The morning was especially cold, and by 10 a.m., a heavy snow began to fall. At 11 a.m., the two brigades commenced their expedition amongst "...hooping and yelling equaled only by a victorious army after a flying enemy..." The snow died away about noon, and the brigades arrived at LaVergne at dark. The snow had fallen two inches, and the boys stopped in a wood.

> But the most delightful hour came with darkness of night, finding us halting in the woods without axes, the ground beautifully covered with snow and blankets by no means plentiful. Here we had a fine time raking and clawing away the snow, clearing up ground upon which to spread our blankets for the night. As my Regt. was thrown out in front of the main command, we chanced to halt near a small lot that, fortunately for us had been fenced with cedar rails, and never did I see them burn more freely in my life. So we spent a merry night in the suburbs of the famous LaVergne.[193]

The next morning, December 6th, the regiment advanced three miles up the Nashville Pike. During the movement, Carden and his buddy—Mose Messick—saw a group of men at a house about three hundred yards away. They decided to go see what the fuss was about

---

[192] (Womack, pp. 72-73) (Thompson, p. 10)
[193] (Womack, p. 73)

and discovered a citizen selling apples out of a window of the house. The man was selling apples 50 cents for a dozen. Neither Carden nor Messick had any money, so after standing there for a few minutes, Messick cried out, "Look here, ain't you going to give me my change back at all?" The man replied that he didn't know he owed him any change, and with Carden as a witness that Messick had given the man five dollars, the man handed Mose four dollars and fifty cents. Mose then gave Carden part of the money and he bought a dozen apples.[194] The regiment was not engaged at all during the day and returned to their camp of the previous night at sunset. The cavalry had managed to capture a significant foraging party of the enemy, but the main force of the Federals was not engaged.

At noon on December 7th, the brigades marched back to Murfreesboro and arrived at about sunset going into their camps. The 8th through the 24th, the weather remained cold, and the boys stayed in camp, huddling around fires and conducted drill. On the 9th, Captain Womack presided over a court-martial for a man in company D for abandoning his post while on outpost duty. The man was found guilty and sentenced to 105 hours of hard labor with the forfeiture of one month's pay. In the absence of Colonel Savage, Lieutenant Colonel Donnell, Major Coffee and the most senior captains, Captain Womack conducted dress parade for the regiment that same evening. On the 12th, brigade drill was conducted—which was the first that the regiment had participated in. The next day, President Davis arrived and reviewed the Army of Tennessee. "It was truly an imposing scene, and a time of rejoicing throughout the army and surrounding country, the Ladies, old men, children and negroes turning out enmass to see their esteemed president and the army." The regiment was paid on December 20th, and three days later, Colonel Savage returned to the regiment. His wounds had healed sufficiently to return to the army, but he did not yet assume command of the boys. Many of the boys had worked hard to make their lives more comfortable in camp. The same was so for Captain

---

[194] (Carden, p. Apr. 19)

Womack. He spent the day constructing a brick chimney for his tent. "It drew finely, and made my tent as comfortable as a stove."[195]

Christmas day dawned warm and cloudy. The boys had now spent their second Christmas in the army. Captain Womack recorded his thoughts in his diary.

> Another Christmas is passed and gone! How differently spent from that of sixty one! That I passed in Charleston and fort Sumpter, where I was delighted and pleased; this I have spent in my tent by the fire near Murfreesboro, attending to many of the daily duties of the soldier. May the coming Christmas in sixty three find our now distracted and unhappy country reposing in the lap of an infantile and glorious peace.[196]

Doubtless, most all of the boys felt the same way. The only consolation this Christmas was that they were close enough to home to be visited by family. The next morning was warm and rainy. The boys learned that the Federals had moved out of Nashville in force with their cavalry in the advance between Murfreesboro and LaVergne. On Saturday the 27th, heavy skirmishing was heard as the Federals advanced five miles south of LaVergne to Stewart's Creek. That afternoon, the army moved out of camp and took up positions a short distance north of Murfreesboro. All of the army's wagons were packed and sent to the rear that night. Sunday morning Cheatham's Division formed line on the south side of Stone's River while Maney's Brigade skirmished with the Federals on the north side of the river. They stacked arms at 9 a.m. and remained in camp as the reserve.[197]

Monday the 29th dawned rainy and cold. Orders came early for the division to cross the river and form a reserve line of battle in rear of Chalmers' Brigade. They occupied an elevation just north and west of the river and about 300 yards southwest of Mrs. James

---

[195] (Womack, pp. 73-76)
[196] (Womack, p. 76)
[197] (Womack, p. 77) (Donelson, p. 710)

residence. Donelson's Brigade stretched from the railroad that ran along the river on the east to a point just beyond Wilkinson Pike to the west. The regiments were aligned with the Sixteenth Tennessee anchoring the extreme right of the brigade with two companies extending beyond the railroad to the river. The Fifty-first Tennessee was aligned to the left of the Sixteenth and the Eighth Tennessee to their left. The left of the brigade was anchored by the Thirty-Eighth Tennessee. Beyond the Thirty-Eighth regiment, Stewart's Brigade was in line from just beyond Wilkinson Pike further west. They spent the day with a moderate barrage of artillery fired in their direction but none of the boys were injured. An officer described the weather on Tuesday as "rainy, cold and disagreeable." Although the regiment remained in the reserve line all day, they were kept alert by the heavy amount of skirmishing in their front. Colonel Savage had assumed command of the men, but Lieut. Colonel Donnell had been suffering from a skin ailment for some time and being unable to attend to his duties, Captain Lucien N. Savage was acting Lieutenant Colonel of the regiment. Additionally, Major P. H. Coffee had yet to recover from his wounds so Captain Womack filled his role as acting Major of the regiment. When darkness fell that evening, Donelson was ordered forward to relieve Chalmers' Brigade in the front line. Word came down the line and the boys picked up and moved forward with only their rifles and full loads of ammunition. After reaching the line, Chalmers' men retired to rest up and get a bite to eat. Prior to dawn, Chalmers' Brigade returned to their original position and relieved Donelson's men from the front line.[198]

The night had passed slowly—especially for the newly recruited soldiers. Fear of the unknown certainly consumed many of their minds. The horrible stories told by the veterans of the field at Perryville. Likewise, the veterans of the regiment—knowledgeable of the horrors of war—sat pondering the hell that lay ahead. Making their way back to the reserve line at 4 a.m., the boys had laid down in hopes of one last wink of sleep before the coming storm.

---

[198] (Womack, pp. 77-78) (Donelson, p. 710)

This photograph of **Colonel John H. Savage** was taken in the late 1850s while he was serving as a congressman from Tennessee and is the closest to his wartime likeness. Savage was very well respected by both officers and men of the Tennessee brigade and Cheatham's Division.

COLONEL D. M. DONNELL.

Colonel David M. Donnell was Colonel Savage's replacement. Donnell was a strict disciplinarian and a teacher by profession – but very popular among the men. Engraving is from Thomas Head's regimental history.

Captain James M. Parks of Company H was mortally wounded on September 19, 1863 at the Battle of Chickamauga while rallying his men in the left wing of the regiment. Engraving is from Head's regimental history.

CAPTAIN L. N. SAVAGE.

Captain Lucien N. Savage was the only brother of Colonel Savage. He commanded Company A from the war's commencement until his death from wounds received at Murfreesboro. He was serving in the capacity as acting lieutenant colonel when he was struck down by an enemy ball. He lingered for 132 days with a bullet lodged against his spine until finally succumbing on March 12, 1863. Engraving is from Head's history.

Captain J. H. L. Duncan was commander of Company B but served much of his time on detached duty. Often, he was ill suffering from diarrhea and chronic rheumatism. He was medically discharged on August 10, 1863 after spending the last twelve months in and out of hospitals.

Private Pleasant M. Wassom of Captain Dillard's Company enlisted on June 9, 1861 at Camp Trousdale. He was severely wounded at the Battle of Perryville on October 8, 1862 and left behind. His left leg was amputated due to the wound. Wassom was captured at Harrodsburg, Kentucky on October 10, 1862, sent to Camp Douglass and later transported to the General Hospital at Petersburg, Virginia where he was furloughed on April 14, 1863 for 40 days. He rejoined the regiment on April 23, 1863 and was immediately put on sick furlough. He never returned to duty. Photo is courtesy of Carlisle Barracks.

Private George W. Kennedy enlisted at McMinnville on February 20, 1863 at 18 years of age. He was assigned to Company B and was present with the regiment until he was reported "missing in battle at mouth of Chickamauga Creek" on November 24, 1863. Kennedy was captured by Federal forces on November 27, 1863 at Dowdy's Ferry and sent to Rock Island, Illinois on December 11, 1863. He was released on May 23, 1865 and returned to his home in Manchester, Coffee County, Tennessee. This wartime image was made sometime between March and November 1863. It was likely taken at Chattanooga in July or August 1863. Photo is Public Domain.

Private James Lycurgus D. Smith enlisted in Company D on September 1, 1862 at Pikeville, Tennessee. He was severely wounded on December 31, 1862 at Murfreesboro and sent to a hospital. He was paid for his service on July 1, 1863 and was never returned to duty. Photo is courtesy of Nancy Calhoun.

Brigadier General Lucius Polk, of Cleburne's Division, temporarily gave direction to Wright's Brigade at during the actions at Missionary Ridge on November 24 & 25, 1863.

Private Henry Clay Eastham enlisted in Company A on May 18, 1861. In May and June of 1862 he was absent acting as a Sutler. He was reported as having deserted in December of 1862. Photo is courtesy of Perryville Battlefield.

2nd Lieutenant Cicero Spurlock, of Company C, was killed in action on October 8, 1862 at the Battle of Perryville, Kentucky at 24 years of age. This photo was taken while enrolled at Cumberland University in 1861. Photo is courtesy of David Fraley.

LIEUTENANT-COLONEL T. B. MURRAY.

Lieutenant Colonel Thomas B. Murray was not reelected in May of 1862 at the reorganization and was released from service on May 17, 1862. He returned to McMinnville and organized the 22nd Tennessee Infantry Battalion – also known as Murray's Battalion. It was assigned to Wright's Brigade alongside the 16th Tennessee in February of 1863. By the summer of 1863, the battalion had been consolidated with the 38th Tennessee Infantry Regiment. Engraving is from Thomas Head's regimental history.

113

Private Hiram Taylor "Pomp" Kersy enlisted in Company A on May 18, 1861. He was absent without leave for 15 days in January or February of 1863. Pomp was listed as having deserted in March of 1863, but he had returned and was present with the regiment in July of 1863. He finally deserted for good on August 4, 1863. Although he deserted the regular army, he didn't quit waging his private war on the Federal army and its sympathizers. He soon became recognized as a fearful Confederate Guerilla and operated around Smithville in DeKalb County. He was born in 1841 and died on July 23, 1864 at the hands of Federal troops at Short Mountain. He and six other men were killed, stripped and thrown into an oxcart and hauled through Mechanicsville. Photo is Courtesy of SCV website.

Private Lewis Shockley transferred from the 35th Tennessee to Company I of the 16th Tennessee on February 23, 1863. He is dressed in a captain's frock coat – a rank he never attained. He deserted the army on April 29, 1863. Photo is courtesy of Ronnie Mangrum.

Brigadier General Marcus J. Wright was promoted to brigade command over Colonel Savage in February of 1863. His combat command capacity was questionable at best. In February of 1864 he was transferred to Post duty at Macon, Georgia after serving in his position only one year. His ability to command a brigade was questioned by the men at Chickamauga and Missionary Ridge. Engraving is from Head's regimental history.

(Courtesy Texas Division of the United Daughters of the Confederacy)

The Flag of Company E, 16th Tennessee was captured by the 3rd Ohio Cavalry on November 24, 1863 south of Ooltewah, Tennessee. The brigade wagon train was en route from Charleston to Missionary Ridge when it was forced to take a detour toward Ringgold, Georgia. The flag and General M. J. Wright's uniform coat were put on display in Ohio on December 13, 1863. The flag was made of silk and had had nine – five pointed stars on a blue field with two red stripes and one white. The dimensions were 96 inches on the fly by 48 inches on the staff. A gold metallic fringe rings the fly sides of the flag. The flag reads:

WARREN GUARDS!
VICTORY_{OR}DEATH

Lieutenant General Joseph Eggleston Johnston's appointment to the command of the Army of Tennessee in December of 1863 was cheered by the men. "What 'Old Joe' didn't know about handling an army wasn't worth much." Photo is courtesy of the National Archives.

The four surviving members of the regimental color guard from the Battle of Perryville at the unveiling of the Confederate Monument on May 19, 1904. William H. White—the color bearer—stands on the left. J. C. Biles stands behind John McConnell (left) and H. L. Moffitt. All the members of the color guard were wounded that day. A fifth guard—Jasper Roberts—was mortally wounded in the battle.

Chapter V

The Battle of Murfreesboro

31 December 1862 – 4 January 1863

The Morning dawned cold and cloudy. Earlier in the night, Brigadier General Donelson had received orders from Major General Cheatham that the army was conducting a "vigorous and persistent attack at daylight." Donelson was directed to, "conform the movements" of his brigade to Chalmers' who was in his front. He was instructed to maintain a close supporting distance of about 600 yards and be prepared to support Chalmers on order. Donelson's Brigade organization had changed slightly since Perryville. His command still included the 8th, 16th, 38th and 51st Tennessee regiments, but the 15th Tennessee had been placed on Provost Guard duty in Tullahoma and apparently was dropped from the brigade. Two days earlier the 84th Tennessee had been added to his command. Owing to the rawness and small size of the 84th Tennessee[199]—commanded by Colonel Sidney S. Stanton—the regiment was ordered to support Captain Carnes' battery that was still the brigade artillery support.[200]

---

[199] The 84th Tennessee was later consolidated with the 28th Tennessee Infantry Regiment in March of 1863.
[200] (Donelson, p. 710)

The boys checked and rechecked their weapons, filled their canteens and prepared for the days operations. The rattle of bayonets and clanking of cups and canteens reverberated through the cold morning air. At the crack of dawn rolling musketry was heard far off to the left. Gradually, the sharp crack of the fire grew nearer and nearer until Chalmers' men advanced from the front lines into the fray around 9 a.m. At about 10 a.m., Donelson received orders to advance his brigade and shouts came down the line to fall in and dress ranks. The whole brigade advanced in line—except the 84th Tennessee that remained as guard for Carnes' Battery. During their advance, they witnessed Chalmers' Brigade assault the enemy positions and disappear into the sulfuric smoke as it billowed across the field. Solid shots from Yankee artillery flew through the air and plowed into the ground throwing up fountains of earth that showered the boys. Finally they reached the front line from which Chalmers' men had advanced and again hunkered down to watch the contest in their front.[201]

The regiment and brigade had only been in their position a few minutes when General Chalmers received a severe wound that caused his command to waver and break. The greater part broke in confusion and streamed to the rear in total disorder. Donelson immediately ordered his 1st Tennessee Brigade forward, and the Sixteenth rose to their feet and commenced a steady advance under heavier hostile artillery fire. It was not quite 11 a.m. when the brigade commenced the advance. Shot and shell flew everywhere. General Donelson's horse reared up in pain as it was struck by grapeshot. At about the same time, Colonel Savage advanced with the regiment—while mounted—toward the broken regiments of Chalmers' Brigade that streamed to the rear. Just then, a fleeing soldier was flattened by a cannon ball very near the colonel. Savage's horse was so alarmed by the sound of the impact that it, "made desperate efforts to throw him." The regiment actually halted momentarily to see the outcome as the colonel's horse reared and bucked over and over. Savage was unable to calm his new mount, so

---

[201] (Donelson, p. 710)

he dismounted the animal and continued the advance on foot for the remainder of the fight.[202]

Captain John Bradford—brigade inspector and acting assistant adjutant general to General Donelson—rode to Colonel Savage's position and directed him to advance along the railroad with two companies on its right and the remaining eight companies to its left. As the brigade neared the Cowan House which had been burned in the days previous to the fight, it found serious obstructions of the walls of the house and outbuildings and a picket fence that caused the brigade to split and lose unit cohesion. The 51st Tennessee bore the brunt of the obstruction, and it split in two while seven companies advanced to the left and the remaining three companies advanced to the right of the structure. When the balance of the brigade had cleared the house—its focus was more on the enemy than its alignment. The 51st, 8th and 38th Tennessee regiments continued forward but veered to the left slightly and became completely disjointed from the whole of the Sixteenth and the three right companies of the 51st Tennessee.[203] The brigade became intermingled here with a large number of men from Chalmers' command that were seeking refuge behind the house and outbuildings of the Cowan place. These obstructions forced the other seven companies of the 51st Tennessee to follow in rear of the 8th Tennessee as they passed the burnt structure.

The advance was made "…under a shower of shot and shell of almost every description."[204] When General Donelson reached a location near the Cowan House, his horse was struck by another shot which caused it to stagger and whinny. Bleeding from two wounds, the horse managed to maintain the general's weight and continued into the fight. Savage now advanced on foot at the right front of his regiment. After passing the Cowan House, the Sixteenth passed into a corn stalk-field, and with no sign of the rolling musketry slowing, they arrived at the edge of a cotton field. All this time as the

---

[202] (Donelson, p. 711) (Savage, p. 139)
[203] (Savage, Report of Col. John H. Savage, Sixteenth Tennessee Infantry, p. 713)
[204] (Donelson, p. 711)

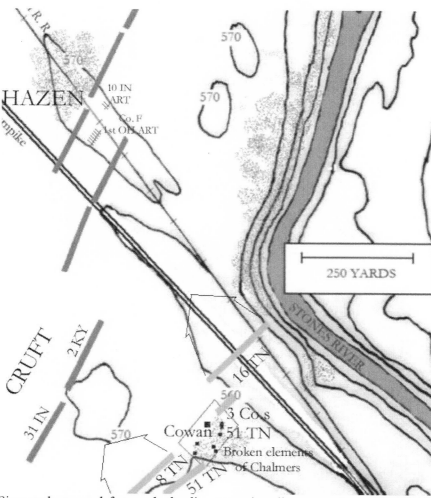

Sixteenth moved forward, the line occasionally stepped over dead or dying men that were wounded in some of the most horrific ways. Oddly, this incessant fire that was directed toward them failed to create many casualties in the initial advance, but not all of the men were so lucky. Hardin S. Lane was one of the new recruits in the regiment. As he marched alongside his comrades, a spherical case shot exploded in front of and above the regiment raining shrapnel down amongst the boys. Hardin had no time to react, and the nature of his wound caused him to immediately drop in a heap. Perhaps the same explosion had knocked P. H. Cantrell unconscious. He was quickly picked up and carried to the rear. In the face of this concentrated fire, the new recruits were marching directly into the fight with an assured confidence that was steadfastly maintained by the veterans of the Sixteenth.[205]

While the majority of the brigade had advanced to a wood and thicket to the left of Nashville Pike, the Sixteenth and companies A, D and F of the 51st Tennessee saw themselves advance into open fields with no protection whatsoever. Only the two right companies of the Sixteenth had any protection that was provided by a thin skirt of trees that bordered the bank of the river on their extreme right. The left eight companies were the first to be engaged by a strong force of Yankee infantry at less than 150 yards to their direct front. Chalmers' men had managed to force the Yankee line back to a thick cedar thicket a short distance to their front. Federal Colonel W. H. Blake of the 9th Indiana recalled the scene in his front as he relieved the 41st Ohio that had expended its ammunition following the repulse of Chalmers' Brigade. He had just formed his regiment between the Nashville Pike and the railroad.

At this time a brigade of the enemy's infantry advanced from their rifle-pits, and marched obliquely in the direction of my position. Although at long range, I at once opened fire on them, which thinned their ranks as they continued to approach. As they drew nearer, one of the regiments moved to the front, and advanced at the charge step upon my position. My men poured upon them a galling and deliberate fire that halted them within 75 yards of our line, where they lay down, covered somewhat by the cotton furrows, and opened fire on us, from which we suffered. Their colors had been struck down three

---

[205] (Donelson, p. 711) (Thompson, p. 11) (Daily News Journal, 1992) (Cantrell, Vivid Experiences in Prison)

times during their advance, and every field officer of the regiment was killed.[206]

The Yankee force consisted of Hascall's and Hazen's Brigades and was supported by two batteries of artillery. Just as the right companies of the Sixteenth cleared an eastward bend in the river and approached the cotton field, a heavy fire was poured into them from a line of infantry, "…extending to the right as far as I could see."[207] This first massive volley of rifle fire took a horrible toll on the Sixteenth from left to right. Captain D. C. Spurlock was instantly killed while leading his men into the field. The same volley had probably dropped W. T. Mayberry to his knees. Mayberry was carrying the regimental colors, and unable to continue, he passed the flagstaff on to Private John S. Womack who bore the colors only to slump to the ground wounded. The boys would kneel and fire, reload, advance a few paces and kneel to fire again. Some had instinctively dropped to a prone position using the cotton furrows for cover and commenced firing. Captain Womack watched the Federal line as it slowly emerged from the cedars, "…keeping up and incessant fire."[208]

---

[206] (Blake, p. 552) Colonel Blake reported that, "The regiment was the Sixteenth Louisiana, Colonel Fisk of General Chalmers' brigade, composed of the Ninth and Tenth Mississippi and Sixteenth Louisiana. These facts were obtained from prisoners and burial parties that evening, and, I presume, are reliable." A note at the bottom of the page states that, "The Sixteenth and Twenty-fifth Louisiana regiments (consolidated) were in D. W. Adams' brigade." The report states this all happened before 11 A.M. – That would mean that the unit could not have been the 16th Louisiana as they didn't assault till after 2 P.M. and the mentions of the 9th and 10th Mississippi were likely portions of Chalmers' men that were being led by Savage as was the 39th N.C. and Col. Blythe's Mississippi regiment with the three companies of the 51st Tennessee. In fact, Colonel Savage was the only officer in the Sixteenth to escape being wounded that day.
[207] (Savage, Report of Col. John H. Savage, Sixteenth Tennessee Infantry, p. 717)
[208] (Savage, Report of Col. John H. Savage, Sixteenth Tennessee Infantry, p. 717) (Womack, p. 78)

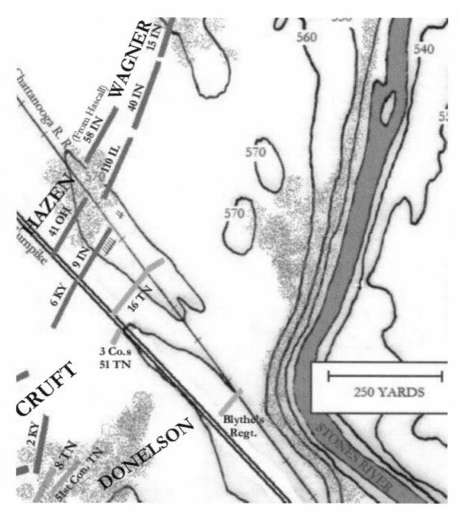

WAGNER
15 IN
40 IN
Chattanooga R. R.
(from Hascall)
58 IN
110 IL
HAZEN
41 OH
Turnpike
9 IN
6 KY
16 TN
3 Co.s
51 TN
CRUFT
2 KY
8 TN
51st Con. TN
DONELSON
Blythe's Regt.
560
540
5:
570
570
5:
250 YARDS
STONES RIVER

It wasn't long before Hazen's Federal brigade began receiving strong support on its left—to the right of the Sixteenth. Wagner's Federal Brigade had closed up with Hazen's left. It was then that Captain Womack recalled, "...the contest became most severe." Volley after volley was fired at the Sixteenth from the Yankee line across, "...an unobstructed plain of about one hundred yards; we lying and shooting, they standing." The 58th Indiana of Hascall's Brigade was directly in front of the left of the Sixteenth and emptying their cartridge boxes into the ranks of the regiment at a frightful pace. Private James Kirby was lying down amongst the men of Company E. He was leaning on his left elbow and had just capped the nipple of his rifle when a ball smashed into his left shoulder twisting him around. The ball had crashed through his cartridge box strap and clothing and plowed through his flesh and muscle and lodged under his left shoulder blade. The boys fell dead and wounded at a feverish pace. Now, Colonel Savage—that had been advancing with the right of the regiment—realized that the remainder of the brigade was no longer supporting him on his left. Worse, if he continued to advance, his entire right would be left open. He knew that the enemy could easily outflank and enfilade his lines on either side. Savage quickly gave orders for the boys to halt and fire—an order that was redundant under the circumstances—as the boys could hardly advance in the face of such a murderous fire. Minute by minute, more of the boys were struck by grapeshot, minie balls and shell. They took aim killing the gunners of the batteries and the batteries' horses—dropping them in clusters.[209]

In the cotton field between Nashville pike and extending across the railroad, the Sixteenth exchanged fire with the Federal troops in the "Round Forest" for over an hour engaging the 58th Indiana, 41st Ohio, 110th Illinois, 9th Indiana and 40th Indiana Regiments that continually rotated to the front. During this exchange, Captain Lucien Savage—acting lieutenant colonel—was struck down by an enemy ball at his brother's side. He had not sought the shelter of a wooden fence that the men had been instructed to use as cover, but he remained by Colonel Savage's side for the entire fight up to this time. While standing by his brother's side, Colonel Savage heard the unmistakable deep "thud" of a ball punching into flesh, and turning toward his brother, he saw him laid out, motionless on the ground. The colonel tended momentarily to his brother with assurances, but the wound was fearful and both he and Lucien knew it. The ball had been fired from a .58 caliber

---

[209] (Womack, p. 78) (Buell, p. 481) (Kirbey) (Savage, Report of Col. John H. Savage, Sixteenth Tennessee Infantry, p. 717)

Springfield and struck Lucien in his mid-torso lodging against his spine. With balls buzzing past his head, Savage assisted Lucien to a slightly safer location so that the infirmary corps could carry his brother from the field. Lucien had been ordered to take cover behind a staked fence that ran along the regiment's front, but the captain refused to do so while his brother colonel stood erect, encouraging his men along the firing line. When Savage returned to the firing line only yards away, he found that his acting major— Captain J. J. Womack—had been struck by a bullet in the arm that had horribly broken the bone. Womack gathered his limp, useless arm with his good one and with assistance was borne from the field in his blood soaked frock coat. Lieutenant Jesse Walling was directing the men of Company E just to the left of the railroad tracks when a minie ball smashed into his upper arm—passed through his body breaking his shoulder blade—and knocked him to the ground. Six foot-six inch tall W. R. Nunley—known as "Big Riley" to the boys—had just had his index finger shot away when he saw Walling fall. Nunley ran to Jesse, scooped him up in his arms and carried him nearly 400 yards under heavy fire to the cover of the river bank where a body of wounded men had collected. When he arrived at a fence row by the river, "Big Riley" pinned Walling to the ground as two others ran a silk handkerchief on the end of a ramrod through the Lieutenant's wound and out through his back. By now it was noon.[210]

At about 12:15, a staff member of General Donelson delivered an urgent message to Savage. Lieutenant General Polk had informed him that the brigade would be reinforced in a short time. Colonel Savage was ordered to, "…hold his position at all hazards." Savage likely took this order as another attempt at his life. But the necessity of the situation required strict obedience to orders. The colonel described the scene in his front.

> There were batteries to the right and left of the railroad which literally swept the ground. The men maintained the fight

---

[210] (Savage, Report of Col. John H. Savage, Sixteenth Tennessee Infantry) (Womack, p. 78) (Nunley) (Head T. A., p. 292)

against superior numbers with great spirit and obstinacy. The left companies being very near and without protection, sustained a heavy loss. Thirty men were left dead upon the spot where they halted, dressed in perfect line of battle.[211]

As the Sixteenth lay prone in the fields firing at the line of battle in the cedar brake to their front, an apparently disoriented regiment—the 39th North Carolina of Walthall's Brigade—approached Savage's position. The lieutenant colonel of the regiment offered his assistance to Savage. Savage's most immediate threat was the long line of enemy infantry extending to his right, so he ordered the lieutenant colonel to move his line of battle to the Sixteenth's right. As the 39th North Carolina moved into position, the lieutenant colonel was shot down and carried from the field, but Captain A. W. Bell assumed command and pushed the force into line on the Sixteenth's right. Savage recalled that, "...then a furious battle ensued between the Sixteenth and Hazen's and Wagner's brigade

---

[211] (Savage, Report of Col. John H. Savage, Sixteenth Tennessee Infantry) "Donelson's regular aides were his son-in-law and his son. They were not upon the field; he says in his report that they were absent by leave. Captain Rice, a distinguished lawyer of Nashville, attended him as a volunteer aide. Rice told me that when he and Donelson came over the hill in that part of the field in which the Sixteenth Regiment was fighting, "the regiment was engaged with the forces coming up the river from Round Forest;" and that Donelson, seeing a lot of men lying upon the ground between the railroad and the turnpike, near where the Hazen Monument now stands, called his attention to them, and said "Look there. Those men are skulkers. Go and order them to join Colonel Savage, who is fighting down the river." Rice says he galloped over to where the men were lying and found them all dead, dressed in perfect line of battle, that he galloped back and said, "General, these men are not skulkers. They are dead men." He said the general shook all over and the tears ran down his cheeks." (From Life of Savage, page 143.) Captain J. L. Rice was a volunteer aide-de-camp and former member of the 20th Tennessee who had been relieved.

supporting these batteries, assisted by such help as other parts of the left wing were in condition to give."[212]

The help from the left was sporadic. The left wing faced the threat and occasional advance of portions of Hazen's and Hascall's Brigades. Although the three companies of the 51st Tennessee supplemented the left half of the regiment, these eleven companies combined were barely sufficient to prevent the enemy's advance. On the left, two guns of Battery F, 1st Ohio—that had been blasting their charges in the face of the left of the regiment—were abandoned. In fact, they had become unserviceable due to combat damage. The battery lost only one man killed and six wounded, but they lost sixteen horses killed or disabled in this position. Even the battery commander's horse was killed beneath him. While Savage thought that his men had silenced the battery, it only withdrew the serviceable guns long enough to resupply their ammunition which had nearly run out. Apparently, Savage considered ordering his conglomeration of men forward now, but at that moment he was informed of a large body of the enemy advancing up the river about 150 yards to his right and rear.[213]

Colonel Wagner—who was commanding the 2nd Brigade of Federal General Thomas J. Wood's Division—had noticed the advance of the 39th North Carolina into the skirt of woods along the river to the Sixteenth's right. He immediately ordered the 15th Indiana and 57th Indiana to flush this force away from the woods. As they advanced toward the Sixteenth's right-rear, Savage noticed a body of Confederate infantry collected near the railroad in his rear. It was a portion of Blythe's Mississippi Regiment[214] and the three companies of the 51st Tennessee. Savage sent word for them to join

---

[212] (Savage, Report of Col. John H. Savage, Sixteenth Tennessee Infantry, p. 717) (Savage, The Life of John H. Savage, p. 140)

[213] (The War of the Rebellion: A Compilation of the Official Records of the Union and Confederate Armies., Vol. 20, Pt. I, p. 522) (Savage, Report of Col. John H. Savage, Sixteenth Tennessee Infantry, p. 717)

[214] Blythe's regiment was later designated the 44th Mississippi Infantry Regiment.

him on his right, while Horace McGuire—the regimental bugler—was sent across the railroad to order Private Wright S. Hackett to bring the eight companies to the right of the railroad in order to support their attack on the enemy columns advancing in their rear. Hackett had served as an officer in the regiment's first year in the

army. Now, all the officers in the left eight companies were killed or disabled. Hackett took charge of the body of men and they quickly raced across the railroad bed under a continuous fire of the enemy. Companies A and D, in conjunction with Blythe's Regiment and the companies of the 51st Tennessee, advanced to meet the Federal regiments. The 15th and 57th Indiana had pressed the 39th North Carolina back when this demi-brigade[215]—commanded by Colonel Savage—met the two Federal regiments and forced them to retire. This success was short lived, for as the Sixteenth and its assistance advanced and pressed back the Indiana regiments, the 10th Indiana Battery opened with heavy blasts of canister supported by hellish, continuous rifle fire of the 40th Indiana. The boys were stopped in their tracks and recoiled under a barrage of fire that caused them to immediately withdraw.[216]   W. H. Head of Company I was lying in reserve in rear of and supporting Blythe's Regiment between the railroad and the Nashville Pike when the artillery opened. They had just taken cover behind a tiny breastwork of rails from a fence. Just then—a spherical case shot exploded right above them wounding Head and four or five others. 2nd Sergeant David Miller of Company H lay prone near the railroad tracks at a point the boys would later refer to as the "dead angle." Here—fire raked the line as they attempted to load and fire. Miller was in the act of loading when a bullet grazed his head and crashed into his shoulder. A second ball then plowed across his neck leaving him doused in his own blood.[217]

Colonel Savage knew his men could not defeat this vastly superior force but was determined not to surrender this position. The colonel immediately ordered his command to form a skirmish line that stretched about 400 yards with nearly half of this line oriented to the right and the other half fronting the "Round Forrest." Here, the fire of the enemy failed to slacken. The only consolation was that they had slightly increased their distance from the enemy lines. The furthest right companies also had protection of the skirt of woods near the river. In this position, the regiment continued to lose men. 4th Sergeant James R. Thompson had been on the right for the

---

[215] By now, the force under Savage's direction included the 16th Tennessee, 39th North Carolina, the majority of Blythe's Mississippi Regiment and three companies of the 51st Tennessee. This force probably numbered no less than 700 men.

[216] (Wagner, p. 494) (Savage, Report of Col. John H. Savage, Sixteenth Tennessee Infantry) (Savage, The Life of John H. Savage, p. 140)

[217] (Confederate Pension Applications)

entire fight. Company A reached a skirt of open woods not far from the river bank. Here, Thompson used the cover of a tree to load and fire at the enemy in his front. Lieutenant R. B. Anderson was standing next to the tree and holding Thompson's ramrod when another enemy rifle ball found its mark. Anderson spun and dropped to the ground leaving the regiment without a single commissioned officer other than Colonel Savage. J. L. Patton was on the firing line right beside Lee Patterson when he saw Patterson get struck by a ball in the center of his forehead that killed him instantly. While some men fell to never rise again, others—like P. H. Cantrell who had been knocked out by the explosion of a shell in the advance and carried to the rear—gained their senses and rejoined the regiment to fight the remainder of the battle. The regiment's casualties continued to mount as they waited nearly an hour for the anticipated support.[218]

Finally, the long overdue reinforcements arrived in rear of Savage's position. In fact, Jackson's Brigade was the first to arrive about thirty minutes earlier but had been given the wrong axis of advance. His brigade went to the left of the Cowan House and retraced the steps taken by the majority of Donelson's Brigade hours earlier. By now it was after 1 p.m. when General John Adams arrived and informed Savage that he was there to relieve him. As Adams prepared his brigade for the advance, Savage quickly sent word to the firing line to withdraw to the bend of the river. Still under a heavy and constant fire, the boys ran bent over towards the cover of the trees at the river. Savage stated that Adams' Brigade advanced, "…in gallant style, but only for a short distance, when it broke and fled in confusion." Prior to Adams' advance, the 10th Indiana Battery had retired to resupply their ammunition. When Federal Colonel George Wagner saw the approach of Adams' men, he chose to strike first—rather than be assailed by the Confederate troops without his artillery support. While the majority of the troops of Hazen's and Hascall's Brigade fired massive volleys on the advancing Johnnies—joined by the now resupplied guns of Company F, 1st Ohio Battery, Wagner

---

[218] (Savage, Report of Col. John H. Savage, Sixteenth Tennessee Infantry) (Thompson, p. 11) (Patterson) (Cantrell, Vivid Experiences in Prison)

had the 15th and 57th Indiana fix bayonets and charge headlong into Adams' brigade.[219]

When word arrived at the firing line of Savage's order to withdraw, Sergeant Thompson and M. E. Adcock picked up Lieutenant Anderson by the legs and arms and rushed him to the safety of the river bank. They had just arrived as Adams' Brigade was forming for the advance. Suddenly, the two Yankee regiments of Wagner's Brigade came rushing into the woods from the right. Most of the boys had run to the bend in the river where the Sixteenth was rallying, but with the burden of a limp body, Adcock and Thompson could not make it to the turn. In minutes, the Yankee troops bore down on at least a dozen members of the Sixteenth and more than thirty members of Blythe's Regiment and forced them to surrender. From the rally point at the river bend, Savage and the Sixteenth watched as Adams' Brigade—barely formed for the advance— absorbed the massed fire from the "Round Forest" and was repulsed and routed in only minutes. The 15th and 57th Indiana regiments captured nearly eighty men of the 13th and 20th Louisiana Consolidated Regiment as they quickly gave way to the heavy fire of the Federal brigades and lost over one-hundred killed and wounded. The 16th and 25th Louisiana Consolidated lost one-hundred and ninety-six killed and wounded in the same fire that had been wrought upon the Sixteenth for three hours. Adams' Brigade sustained 544 casualties in only fifteen to twenty minutes. As the brigade became disorganized in its retreat, the right nearly broke into a rout. Many of the men from Blythe's Regiment and the 39th North Carolina found themselves swept away by this retreating force which left Colonel Savage with the Sixteenth Tennessee and only a skeleton crew of the former units he had commanded.[220]

---

[219] (Donelson, p. 712) (Savage, Report of Col. John H. Savage, Sixteenth Tennessee Infantry) (Wagner, p. 491)
[220] (Nunley) (Wagner, pp. 493-94) (The War of the Rebellion: A Compilatioin of Official Records of the Union and Confederate Armies., Vol. 20, Pt. 1, p. 678)

As Adams' men streamed to the rear, Savage collected the three companies of the 51st Tennessee and moved the Sixteenth near the river in front of and to the right of Chalmers' initial works. The regiment sat idly by here during a two hour cannonade conducted by both sides, but even here, they weren't safe. Two more of the boys were killed by spherical case shot exploding above them. By 4 p.m., a final attempt was made to take the "Round Forest" across the same ground the Sixteenth had fought on earlier in the day. This time Preston and Palmer's Brigades advanced. Preston encountered the same obstacles of the Cowan property that had retarded the other brigades' movement. His advance made it no further than the bend of the river. Darkness would soon close the contest. Although General Donelson had remained in view of the Sixteenth during the balance of the battle, he had entirely neglected the greater portion of his brigade and finally went in search of the 8th, 38th, and 51st Tennessee Regiments. Without a brigade commander present, these three regiments managed to fight their way through two Yankee brigades and push the "Round Forest" from the western approaches. Donelson soon found them east of Wilkinson Pike aligned with General Stewart's right flank on the edge of the cotton field fronting the "Round Forrest." Meanwhile, Colonel Savage located Colonel Stanton and the 84th Tennessee. He moved the two units forward to the proximity of a burnt gin house on the Cowan property as the light faded from the field. The regiment was halted here, and the colonel walked quietly on foot to the location of his first line of battle earlier in the day.[221]

At darkness, Savage sent a party to locate Captain Spurlock's body far to the front. Captain Spurlock's parents had arrived in Murfreesboro the afternoon of December 30th, and the captain had been granted a short leave from the regiment to greet his parents at the Miles' House Hotel. The Spurlock's had lost their other son in battle only two and a half months earlier at Perryville. The meeting was short and emotional. The captain's lifeless body was recovered

---

[221] (Savage, Report of Col. John H. Savage, Sixteenth Tennessee Infantry) (Donelson, p. 712)

and removed to the Miles' House that evening.[222] During the expedition to retrieve the captain's body, a Yankee captain was captured who was a little too inquisitive of the rebel losses. Later, the shredded remnants of the regimental colors were brought to Savage near midnight. At least three men had gone down while bearing them on the field, and likely even more. The flag staff had been broken and struck by balls in three places. The Sixteenth's flag was, "...literally shot to pieces."[223] During the night, Savage received orders from General Donelson to join the rest of the brigade, and the command moved through the darkness west toward the brigade's position. At darkness, Donelson had withdrawn the brigade 200 yards back into the cedars. It is unlikely the Sixteenth was formed with the rest of the command before daylight, as the field was strewn with men milling about until the wee hours of the morning.[224]

About dawn on the morning of January 1st, 1863, the regiment found itself moving into line with the rest of the brigade in rear of Stewart's and Loomis' Brigades. Throughout the day, the regiment remained in the supporting line and conducted headcounts and compiled casualty lists. The brigade remained in line of battle under occasional shelling for the next fifty-plus hours. Private W. H. White had not completely recovered from his Perryville leg wound when he left the hospital the day of the fight. Unsure of where the regiment was located, he wandered the field in rear of Chalmers' works until finally joining the regiment at their current position. Several others had left the hospital with him and missed the fight

---

[222] (Head T. A., pp. 269-70)

[223] (Savage, Report of Col. John H. Savage, Sixteenth Tennessee Infantry) Although some suggest that the regiment was carrying a Polk's Corps flag by this time, there is not sufficient evidence to warrant such. Contracts had been initiated to supply the army with more uniform flags for unit identification, but were often only supplied when a regiment's current flag was declared unserviceable or lost. As documented as this regiment is—it is more likely that the regiment fought this battle carrying the colors that had been originally presented to them at Camp Trousdale in 1861.

[224] (Savage, Report of Col. John H. Savage, Sixteenth Tennessee Infantry) (Donelson, p. 712)

attempting in vain to locate the regiment—but perhaps for the best. Parties were sent out to locate the regiment's dead and wounded on the field that had not yet been tended to. James Gribble and James Martin were two of the men detailed from the regiment that went in search of their comrades. The slain still lay as they fell in many cases. Some were missing shoes or had their pockets turned inside out. Hardin Lane was found on the spot where he had fallen the day before in the advance towards the "Round Forest." Many other wounded men who were too badly injured to leave the field were now carried back to the infirmary corps that transported them to the hospitals in the rear. Gribble and Martin were able to confirm the deaths of many of those that were thought to be missing. Others could not be confirmed as dead—their bodies were unrecognizable after losing portions of their head to shot or shell or exceptionally traumatic facial wounds. The same day, Captain Spurlock's sad parents began their journey with their son's corpse to McMinnville, "…where loving hands administered the last sad service." In the rear, R. C. Carden stole away from the regiment to walk a portion of the battlefield. He later claimed that he saw, "…more dead men to 40 or 50 yards square than I ever saw during the war." As for the dead—most of the boys were temporarily buried were they fell, but some few were lucky enough to be located by family members and taken home to family plots.[225]

Once again, the Sixteenth's loss in men was staggering. They had gone into the fight with about 400 men[226] and lost 207 killed, wounded and missing. The ranks—that had just been replenished by

---

[225] (Compiled Service Records) (Daily News Journal, 1992) (Carden, p. Apr. 19)

[226] Savage reported that he went into the fight with "about 400 officers and men." The Report of men actually engaged from the Official Records shows 24 officers and 383 men totaling 407. Thomas Head's book places the number at 360 men (enlisted). There were ten officers—not counting Savage—1 killed, 8 wounded and 1 missing. The reason for the differences in numbers of men is probably due to details for the infirmary corps—this number also reflected officers present at Murfreesboro but not able for duty. The likely total based on this estimation is 371 officers and men in the ranks that day.

nearly two-hundred fresh recruits eight weeks earlier—were once again depleted. The recruits that had wondered what their reactions in battle would be—need not wonder any longer. Colonel Savage later noted his thoughts on their conduct in his report.[227]

> The conduct of my recruits was most honorable. Many of them fell in the front rank beside the veteran soldier of the Sixteenth. It is difficult to make distinction where all act well.[228]

So it was—in two back to back battles within eleven weeks, the Sixteenth had come out of each fight with less than half the number it had gone in with. This time the brigade suffered much worse. While the Sixteenth bore the brunt of the casualties at Perryville, the fight at Murfreesboro claimed 306 members of the 474 engaged in the 8th Tennessee—including the death of their colonel. The 38th Tennessee lost 85 of their 282 men engaged, and the 51st Tennessee had 86 casualties of their 293 effective men in the ranks. Donelson's Brigade lost 700 officers and enlisted men during the fight and claimed the capture of eleven pieces of artillery and a thousand Yankee prisoners.[229]

Before dawn on the 2nd of January, Captain Carnes Battery had been ordered into position in the vicinity of the "Round Forest" where Hazen's Federal Brigade had obstinately defended the Union line, and the Sixteenth had pressed so hard to take. The Federal troops had withdrawn from the position about six hundred yards further north under cover of darkness. The guns took position on the site where Hazen's and Hascall's men had fallen in droves. In reference to the Yankees, Lieutenant L. G. Marshall related that, "…their dead still lay in the open wooded field, about the railroad, and all the way through the cotton field…" He went on to relate that even the horses were disgusted by the scene. "The place was horrible. The horses shied and snorted as they picked their way

---

227 (Donelson, p. 712)
228 (Savage, Report of Col. John H. Savage, Sixteenth Tennessee Infantry)
229 (Donelson, p. 676) (Donelson, p. 712)

among the prostrate bodies in the early morning darkness."[230]   Later that afternoon General Cheatham ordered Donelson to advance his brigade to the relief of Maney's men on the front line. The boys had heard the heavy clash of arms and booming of cannon to the east, but the result of the action was not known. Breckenridge's Division had assaulted the enemy and forced him across Stone's River at McFadden's Ford.   The victory was abruptly reversed though by massed batteries of the Yankee army that shattered the Confederate advance. That evening, Donelson's Brigade put out a strong force of pickets and skirmished with the enemy all day the following day. By the time the sun set Saturday, January 3rd, the decision to withdraw from the Federal front had been made.   Much of the army had already begun a retrograde from Murfreesboro in the afternoon. Cheatham's Division was ordered to be the rear guard of the army, and Donelson's Brigade stayed in position until about 1 a.m. Sunday morning when it began to withdraw from the front line in the direction of Shelbyville.[231]

The Battle of Murfreesboro had ended.   The Army of Tennessee's leadership had decided that—in the state the army was in—it could not risk another bloody battle that would further weaken its effectiveness. The final decision was made by Lieutenant General Braxton Bragg to withdraw in the face of the enemy—after such a hard fought battle—to rest and recuperate his army in the environs of Shelbyville and Tullahoma. A considerable distance was covered on Sunday and the army went into camp just inside the Bedford County line.   Next, the boys would have to endure months of monotony and army regulations with rumors of great victories… and of defeat.

---

[230] (Marshall, p. 817)
[231] (Cheatham, p. 708) (Donelson, p. 712)

Chapter VI

Shelbyville and the Tullahoma Campaign

5 January – 10 July 1863

While most of the boys headed south with the army, a handful of them almost immediately traveled north. On the day of the Sixteenth's big fight at the "Round Forest," Sergeant James Thompson and M. E. Adcock had been captured by Wagner's Brigade as they tended to Lieutenant R. B. Anderson on the river bank. The lieutenant was gravely wounded. Their captors allowed Thompson and Adcock to carry their wounded lieutenant to the rear. Once they were firmly in the Federals hands, Adcock was taken to the prisoner holding area while Thompson was kindly allowed to remain with his dying commander. Lieutenant Anderson lingered for about thirty-six hours and passed away on the evening of January 1st. Thompson had feelings of deep depression upon his capture—especially following his lieutenant's death, but he chose to be polite and social with his captors to make the best of the situation. His knapsack and all of his belongings had been left in camp on the 29th of December, thus he found himself wanting for any comfort items. As he was being led to the rear passing over the battlefield that was strewn with canteens, cups, and discarded gear, he scooped up a knapsack and a fat haversack and found that he had, "…two fine blankets, two or three good winter shirts, plenty of socks, etc." This find was sure to help him out in his captivity.

The Confederate prisoners were unsure of where they would be sent, but they were soon loaded aboard trains that took them through Nashville to Bowling Green, Kentucky. They then boarded steamboats that ferried them down Green River to the Ohio River and disembarked at Evansville, Indiana. Once again, they were loaded onto trains that carried them to Chicago, Illinois and the infamous Camp Douglass prison. The boys of the Sixteenth stuck together, and while there, they made the best of life. Thompson and Adcock spent their time in the "White Oak Square" portion of the prison grounds. There—they ran a breastpin shop and averaged an income of about fifty cents a day allowing them to live "extra well." The boys hoped their stay would be brief.[232]

Not all of the Confederates that were captured suffered the same fate. All of the Confederate wounded had been removed to Murfreesboro and the many hospitals established there from the commencement of the fight until the decision to retreat. The evening of the Sixteenth's fight, Captain Womack had become very feint from heavy bleeding. He was taken to the hospital at Soule College that night. When the decision to withdraw was made two days later, only the most seriously wounded were to be left behind. Trains constantly left Murfreesboro bound for towns further south that were preparing to receive mass casualties. By January 7th, newspapers were reporting the arrival of hundreds of wounded from Cheatham's Division at Winchester, Tennessee. Captain Womack fell into the seriously wounded category, but he luckily ran into two of his brothers who had been in search of him that night. His brother John B. Womack—slightly wounded only moments before the captain—had been with him since leaving the battlefield. Burgess Womack was eventually able to obtain a private house for the

---

[232] (Thompson, p. 12)

comfort of the captain and his brother John.   On January 1st, Womack's father and another brother had heard of his being wounded and came to check on him. They found him and his brother at the house of William J. Wilson on Depot Street. Like many others, they both stayed in Murfreesboro and captivity until they had recovered enough to be sent to prison camp. For John Womack it meant Camp Morton, Indiana and eventually Fort McHenry, Maryland for the captain.[233]

By the evening of January 5th, the brigade had arrived at Shelbyville, crossed the Duck River and established a camp in the bend of the river about a mile and a half southeast of the square. The regiment and brigade spent the next fifty-four days here. Resting and recuperating in camp, the boys took the time to nurse their wounds and wind down from the hell they had encountered. They found Shelbyville to be a pleasant place.[234] L. G. Marshall of Carnes' Battery noted the patriotism of the ladies in the area.

> The ladies of Tennessee knew how to flatter a soldier most exquisitely by a mere look. The young officers found delightful society in Shelbyville and on the roads in the country whenever a lady met a soldier she was able, in some subtle but positive manner, to let him know that she considered him her knight.[235]

Back in Murfreesboro on the last day of January, Captain Womack had taken all he could of the "lively jocular" Mr. Wilson. Although he admitted that he had been treated very kind by Wilson and his family the whole time, his arm wound bothered him greatly; he was "too feeble to walk alone" and "very irritable." That day he relocated to W. L. Anderson's home on Church Street.[236]

During the stay in Shelbyville, many of the boys—that had been wounded and then captured when left behind in Harrodsburg,

---

[233] (Womack, pp. 78-79) (The Charleston Mercury, 1863)
[234] (Tucker, p. 47)
[235] (Marshall, p. 818)
[236] (Womack, p. 79)

Kentucky after the Battle of Perryville—were paroled or exchanged and began to return to the regiment. Private C. H. Clark had eventually been sent to Bardstown, Kentucky to convalesce. When orders came for him to be exchanged, he was told that he was going to be sent to Louisville and then to Vicksburg for exchange. Clark took his parole, but he also decided he would probably make it to his unit more efficiently by himself. He traveled with his parole papers on foot and by rail back to middle Tennessee and found the boys encamped at Shelbyville. They returned as individuals and in groups, but the arrival of the boys—no matter how many—always warranted cheers and praise.[237]

By February, a major change had taken place in Donelson's Brigade. Donelson was being promoted and was detached from his command. Marcus J. Wright had been promoted to brigadier general in December and assumed command of the brigade on February 7th. The 28th Tennessee was transferred to Wright's Brigade from Palmer's Brigade of Breckenridge's Division on February 16th. This began a relationship that was only outlasted by the 8th Tennessee. These three regiments spent the next twenty-six months together till the very last. The 28th Tennessee had around 268 men and was under the command of Colonel Preston D. Cunningham. About the same time, Murray's 22nd Battalion Tennessee Infantry was added to the brigade. Major Thomas B. Murray—the former lieutenant colonel of the Sixteenth—was its commander. He recruited and commanded nine very under strength companies—four of which had served in the 4th Tennessee Cavalry that had disbanded in January. Murray had hoped to mount the outfit, but was unsuccessful in his attempts.[238]

On the morning of February 28th, the brigade received orders to move to Tullahoma. They reached there on March 1st and camped near the graveyard where they had back in November. On the 3rd, the brigade moved about a mile north of the town just west of the railroad. They remained at this campsite near Tullahoma for fifty-two days until April 21st. The newly promoted Major General D. S.

---

[237] (Clark, p. #16)
[238] (Civil War Centtennial Commission, pp. 166, 234)

Donelson had gone to Knoxville to assume command of the Department of East Tennessee. When Brigadier General Marcus J. Wright had taken command of the 1st Tennessee Brigade all of the men were astounded. The senior colonel of the regiment was Colonel Savage, and all eyes had looked to him to assume command. That was not the case.[239]

Colonel Savage had served faithfully and gallantly in all the Sixteenth's engagements. He was highly regarded by all of the men in the brigade. They knew his accomplishments. Naturally, they thought the vacancy would be filled by his promotion to brigadier general. Like a storm that came from nowhere, the first week of February the command was informed that Lieutenant Colonel Marcus J. Wright was appointed to brigade command—entirely skipping the rank of full colonel straight to brigadier general. In their eyes, he was a nobody. Although he had commanded the 154th

_____

[239] (Tucker, p. 47) Marcus J. Wright had been left out (not-reelected) when the army reorganized in May of 1862. He served on General Cheatham's staff through the Battle of Perryville and was then placed in command of the Conscription Bureau for Tennessee. Governor Harris was adamant in his constant letters to the President and Secretary of War attempting to have Wright promoted to brigadier general. He claimed that Wright reported thousands of new recruits to form a dozen more regiments, and that there was an unequal proportion of Tennessee generals to generals from other states. He wanted Tennesseans commanded by Tennesseans. The natural course would have been to promote Savage, but his pride would not allow him to have Savage promoted to brigade command. Instead, the boys went in to their next engagements commanded by an under qualified and undeserving brigadier general whose lack of experience was realized in Tennessean's blood. Additionally, the thousands of troops that Wright reported to form a dozen new regiments were practically nonexistent. In fact only four more regiments were organized after October 1, 1862 (at least one before Wright even assumed his position)— the 61st, 62nd, 63rd and 84th Tennessee Infantry regiments. The last was too small to operate individually and was consolidated with the 28th Tennessee. Most of these later regiments were actually comprised of previously organized commands that had been disbanded due to desertion in other regiments organized earlier in the war.

Tennessee at Shiloh, he hadn't seen a command or combat action since. The boys were stunned and confused that a junior officer with no military experience of real value would be appointed over a deserving and gallant senior colonel. Captain Dillard stated that Colonel Savage, "… was a faithful and gallant officer. He paid strict attention to the condition and welfare of his men, and had their fullest faith and confidence." He went on to explain the feeling amongst the boys of the regiment and brigade.

> …these men did not and could not comprehend why it was that the reigning powers should ignore the claims of the brigade, go outside of it, and take a stranger to it, a junior in rank, and place him in command as a Brigadier. I say these men could not see any plausible reason for such a strange, unusual course, against their wishes and merited indignity and a complete ignoring of all just claims to which meritorious service may have entitled him…[240]

Colonel Savage had good reason to believe that Governor Harris and General Donelson had been against him from the beginning. They had failed to kill him in battle, so they would use other means to be rid of him. H. H. Faulkner had once written Savage in reference to a letter that Brigadier General Donelson had read aloud from Governor Harris. In the letter, Governor Harris had stated, "…he had his foot on Savage's neck and he should never be promoted."[241] In the end, Harris got his wish much to the chagrin of the brigade. On March 6th, Colonel Savage announced his resignation and read the following speech aloud to the Sixteenth.

HEADQUARTERS SIXTEENTH REGIMENT
TENNESSEE VOLUNTEERS,
March 6, 1863.

---

[240] (Dillard, p. 344)
[241] (Savage, The Life of John H. Savage, p. 145)

Soldiers of the Sixteenth—My Friends and Companions in Arms.--Nothing but a sense of duty could have forced me to the step which I have taken. When the government selected a junior to command me, it thereby decided that I had not done well in the command of my regiment. Not tired of the war or less devoted to the cause, but it is improper that I should continue in a service where equality is denied me. It is true I did not ask the government for promotion, neither did I ask for the commanders they gave me. In the occurrence which forces me to retire may be seen the hand of a distinguished politician, who stands almost as high in public favor as Andrew Johnson once did, and whose evil offices toward me are as old as my races with Pickett and Stokes.

If selfishness or ambition controlled my conduct, I should at the beginning of the war have asked to have been made a general; but believing one good regiment worth many brigadiers, devotion to the cause, and gratitude to my old friends, induced me to take their children under my charge to protect their lives and honor, and to teach them to be soldiers.

As a regiment, I am proud of you; your friends at home are, and your State has cause so to be. If not the first, your deeds upon the field proclaim you the equal of any regiment in the service. In Virginia and South Carolina you were never off duty, and none dare say that any have done better. In the skirmishes around Corinth, you proved yourselves better soldiers and marksmen than the enemy; and when the retreat commenced, you remained three days upon the Tuscumbia, within six miles of Corinth, confronted by the enemy, and became the rear of the column, an honor that you have passed in silence, while it has been claimed in publications for several commands, brigadiers, and colonels.

On the bloody field of Perryville, far in advance of others, you began the attack on the part of Cheatham's division, which, followed up by resistless courage of our brothers of this, Stewart's, and Maney's brigades, forever dispelled the cloud of slander and detraction that had darkened the fair name of the soldiery of our State. The good people south of you never doubted the courage of Tennesseans, and henceforth cowards and miscreants will not dare assail them.

At Murfreesboro, you were the extreme right of our line of attack, and engaged the enemy's line of battle near the center, while your brigade marched to the left. Thus isolated and without protection, at a cost of more than half your numbers, you held in check for three hours the enemy's left wing, and it is believed, but for misfortune not your own, you would have maintained your ground to the last.

I mingle my tears with yours for the heroic dead, our brothers in arms, who sleep upon the fields of Perryville and Murfreesboro. We never can forget them, and they deserve to be remembered by the country.

If in my absence slander shall assail me, let no man believe that I can cease to care for your welfare or the rights of the Southern people. Character is worth more than money. Continue in the pathway of honor and duty, and if hereafter you shall meet the foe, emulate the deeds of former days, that your friends at home may still be proud of you.

My resignation having been accepted, I relinquish my command to the senior officer present, and bid you farewell, hoping that the Great Spirit may guide and protect you through the perils of the future.

JOHN H. SAVAGE

Colonel Sixteenth Tennessee.[242]

The colonel had learned of being passed over by February 7th and that Brigadier General M. J. Wright had assumed command. Upon Colonel Savage resigning and delivering his address, Colonel Donnell immediately took command with date of rank to February 20th. This was not the last they heard of the "Old man of the Mountains."

Due to losses at Perryville, Murfreesboro and illnesses, the brigade and regiments were ordered to conduct elections to fill any vacancies in command structure based on merit. The elections were no longer about popularity, but who would keep the men alive and lead them well in battle. The promotions were based on their conduct, proficiency and discipline. For the first time in the war, the leadership was selected by—for the most part—professional soldiers rather than farmers as they had been before. Over the next week, these choices were mulled over by senior commanders and approved or disapproved.

When Colonel Donnell took command of the Sixteenth, the boys were pleased. Private C. H. Clark recalled that, "He was a first class Christian gentleman and the war not the proper place for him. He made me mad, on the drill field, but I got over it and loved him all the same."[243] Thomas Head gave a shining profile of Colonel D. M. Donnell.

In private life he was a teacher by profession, and at the beginning of the war was President of Cumberland Female

---

[242] (Head T. A., p. 112)
[243] (Clark, p. #17)

College, at McMinnville, Tenn. As a soldier, he had no previous military record; as an officer, he was a strict and rigid disciplinarian, and as a gentleman, he was kind and generous. He was warmly and conscientiously devoted to the cause he had vowed to defend, and to the various duties his office imposed. He was zealously devoted to the comfort, the welfare, and efficiency of his men, and was thoroughly alive to their interests in every respect. The promotion gave satisfaction to the men of the regiment, who would have elected him to the position had opportunity offered. They had great confidence in the ability and integrity of Colonel Donnell, who now became Colonel Savage's successor, and they accorded to the new commander the same respect and obedience that had been so faithfully accorded to his illustrious predecessor.[244]

On March 7th a memorable person joined the ranks of the 8th Tennessee that affected the lives of the boys in the Sixteenth Tennessee for years to come. Neither the 8th or 16th Regiments had a permanent chaplain until that day. Officially chaplain of the Eighth Regiment, Reverend Marcus Bearden DeWitt was side by side with the boys in the brigade from that point till the end. Reverend DeWitt was only 28 years old and originally from Meridianville, Alabama. The next day he delivered his first sermon to a relatively small audience. It took some time for the boys to come around, but in due time, the chaplain had his ranks full.[245]

On March 8th, the 84th Tennessee was officially consolidated with the 28th Tennessee. An election was held to determine the field officers and company officers. Colonel Sidney S. Stanton retained his position and commanded the consolidated regiment. Four days later on the 12th of March, Captain Lucien N. Savage finally died at the age of twenty-five in a private residence in Murfreesboro. His sister, Mrs. Elizabeth Davis, had traveled straight to Murfreesboro upon learning of his wounding. She tended to his every need, but

---

[244] (Head T. A., p. 113)
[245] (DeWitt M. B., p. 1)

nothing could help the young captain. Learning of Lucien's death a few days later, Colonel Savage was devastated by the loss of his only brother. Captain Womack had learned of his death from the Captain's sister who informed him that evening. Womack stated that due to the nature of his wound, "... his suffering has been beyond description." Five days later on the 17th, Womack visited Cheatham's Division hospital in Murfreesboro. He was, "...pleased to find nearly all the remaining wounded in an advanced state of convalescence; many having died and many others gone to different camps north."[246]

Between March 17th and April 1st, the official promotions took place in the regiment. Captain D. T. Brown was promoted to Lieutenant Colonel of the regiment although he was still in captivity. Major Coffee also retained his position though he was quite ill. Adjutant and 1st Lieutenant John R. Paine resigned his commission on February 13, 1863 due to a debilitating disease. Colonel Savage had pushed Private Wright S. Hackett to assume the Adjutancy, but Wright Hackett wrote his resignation before his commission was even approved. He preferred to fight in the ranks with the other boys. Due to this, Colonel Donnell appointed Private Abner F. Claywell[247] to regimental Adjutant. The results of the company elections gave most of the boys good, veteran leadership.[248]

---

[246] (Civil War Centtennial Commission, p. 234) (Womack, pp. 80-81) (Head T. A., p. 292)

[247] **Private Abner F. Claywell** enlisted in Captain Donnell's Company on May 28, 1861. He was born in North Carolina. He served as Regimental Post Agent from November 3, 1861 until January 1, 1862 and earned 25 cents extra per day. He was wounded slightly on October 8, 1862 at Perryville, Kentucky. Claywell was appointed Adjutant to Colonel Donnell on March 25, 1863. His recommendation for promotion stated, "This man makes a fine Adjutant & deserves promotion for gallantry & good conduct." The appointment was approved by June 2, 1863 and he was given the rank 1st Lieutenant. He was 31 years old in 1863. He took a short leave of absence on February 16, 1864. Claywell was present on the Tennessee Campaign and was wounded on November 30, 1864 at Franklin. He has no further record beyond a report listing him present on November 7, 1864 at Tuscumbia, Alabama. Abner moved to Lebanon in Wilson

Company A

Captain Gideon L. Talley – promoted from 3rd Lt.

1st Lieutenant George W. Witt[249]- not present - promoted from 2nd Lt.

2nd Lieutenant W. C. Potter – promoted from Orderly Sergeant.

3rd Lieutenant Julius C. Webb[250] - promoted from 3rd Sergeant.

Company B

Captain J. H. L. Duncan – still in command.[251]

1st Lieutenant E. W. Walker – still in command.

2nd Lieutenant John K. Ensey – still in command.

3rd Lieutenant W. H. Fisher – still in command.[252]

Company C

Captain John Lucas Thompson – promoted from Bvt. 2nd Lt.

County, Tennessee after the war and married Cally Drifoos. They had at least one child named Maggie who was 2 years old in 1870.

[248] (Compiled Service Records)

[249] Witt had died of wounds received on December 31, 1862, but it was assumed he was captured. He was promoted as it was thought he was in captivity. It was learned he died in June of 1863.

[250] **Private Julius C. Webb** joined Captain Savage's Company on May 18, 1861. He was elected 3rd Sergeant on May 8, 1862 and entered upon duty on the 25th. He was elected 3rd Lieutenant on April 1, 1863. He was 20 years old in 1863. On August 17, 1862, he was promoted to 2nd Lieutenant. He is present on musters as late as April 1864. Signed a receipt dated November 26, 1864. He was probably not serving with the regiment at that time. He has no further record.

[251] He had been on detached service gathering conscripts and stragglers through most of late 1862 and in and out of hospitals ill. He returned to detached duty on January 25, 1863.

[252] He was on detached service in January with Conscript Bureau.

1st Lieutenant Charles R. Morford[253] – promoted from Private.

2nd Lieutenant C. G. Black[254] – promoted from Private.

3rd Lieutenant John Rutledge[255] – promoted from Orderly Sergeant.

Company D

Captain F. M. York – promoted from 2nd Lieutenant.

1st Lieutenant S. H. Brown – still in command.[256]

---

[253] **Private Charles R. Morford**, of Donnell's Company, enlisted May 28, 1861. He was slightly wounded at Perryville on October 8, 1862. He was elected 1st Lieutenant on March 17, 1863. He was 23 years old in July 1863. He was signing rolls as commanding the company in January and February 1864. He was captured "near Nashville" on December 16, 1864. He was sent to Louisville and on to Johnson's Island by the 22nd of December. He was released upon taking the oath of allegiance on June 17, 1865. He was 24 years old with a fair complexion and dark hair, blue eyes and 5 ft. 11 inches tall.

[254] **Private C. G. Black**, of Captain Donnell's Company, enlisted on May 28, 1861. He was detailed as assistant commissary from October 1, 1861 until November 5, 1861 and paid an additional 25 cents per day. He was elected 2nd Lieutenant on March 17, 1863. Black was 24 years old in July 1863. He was captured near Dallas, Georgia on May 27, 1864 and sent to Johnson's Island where he arrived on June 9, 1864. He took the Oath of Amnesty on May 16, 1865 and was released. He is listed at 26 years old, fair complexion, with brown hair and grey eyes at 5 ft. 6 inches tall.

[255] **Private John Rutledge**, of Captain Donnell's Company, enlisted on May 28, 1861. He was detailed as a teamster from November 20 till December 10 of 1861. He was elected to 1st Sergeant by June of 1862. He was elected 3rd Lieutenant on March 17, 1863. He was listed as 27 years old in July of 1863. He was present with the regiment on musters rolls through April of 1864. He was paid on December 6, 1864 an amount of four-hundred dollars for service from Feb. 1, '64 to June 30, '64. It is not likely he was with the regiment beyond June of 1864 as there are no receipts for clothing or other information connecting him with the regiment. He has no further record.

152

2nd Lieutenant J. P. A. Hennessee – still in command.

3rd Lieutenant Wm. H. White[257] – promoted from private.

Company E

Captain James J. Womack – still in command.[258]

1st Lieutenant Jesse Walling – still in command.[259]

2nd Lieutenant J. K. P. Webb – still in command.[260]

3rd Lieutenant Bailey Peyton Green – still in command.[261]

---

[256] Although he retained command, he had been on detached service with the conscript bureau since the summer of 1862. As his position wasn't vacant – elections weren't held for this position.

[257] **1st Corporal Wm. H. White** enlisted in Coffee's Company on May 21, 1861. En route to Virginia, he was left behind sick in Knoxville on July 26th. He rejoined the regiment while on the Cheat Mountain Campaign. He was not reelected at the reorganization and probably didn't try. When the regimental color bearer went down at Perryville, on October 8, 1862, he led the regiment with the colors and was slightly wounded in the leg by grapeshot. He was promoted to 3rd Lieutenant on March 17, 1863. He was 27 years old in 1863. On August 6, 1863, he was promoted to 1st Lieutenant. He was signing rolls as commanding the company in January and February 1864. He took a brief leave on March 24, 1864. He was commanding the company again from August 31, 1864 until his resignation on February 18, 1865 at Tupelo, Mississippi. He resigned on the grounds that he only had five men and two officers besides himself in the company. He then joined Dibrell's 3rd Tennessee Cavalry and served until the surrender. He never signed an oath or surrendered to the "damn Yankees." He rode his horse home without a parole and was never granted a pension although he had ample witnesses to his service.

[258] Recovering from wounds received on December 31, 1862.

[259] Recovering from wounds received on December 31, 1862. He resigned due to wounds on April 25, 1863—J. K. P. Webb was promoted to 1st Lt. in his place in August of that year.

[260] He was on detached service Sept. '62 thru Dec. '63 and returned in Jan. '63.

Company F

Captain John B. Vance – still in command.[262]

1st Lieutenant F. M. Amonett[263] - promoted from Private.

2nd Lieutenant J. L. Davis[264] – promoted from 2nd Sergeant.

3rd Lieutenant John F. Owen[265] – promoted from Private.

---

[261] He was temporarily serving as Brigade Commissary Sergeant.

[262] He had died of wounds in Harrodsburg, Kentucky on November 24, 1862, but the men had not yet been informed of his death.

[263] **Private F. M. Amonett** enlisted on June 9, 1861 in Captain Dillard's Company. He was absent on special duty for a time between July 1862 and February 1863. Amonett was listed as a Sergeant in January 1863. He was serving in the conscription bureau and had probably been elected to Sergeant in May of 1862. He was promoted to Bvt. 2nd Lieutenant only days before he was promoted to 1st Lieutenant on January 26, 1863 still on detached service. Amonett was 24 years old in 1863. He was present with the company by May of 1863. He was signing rolls in command of the company in July and August of 1863. He was promoted to Captain by December of 1863. He is listed as present with the company through the April, 1864 muster and signed requisitions for the company until July 31 of 1864. He may have been wounded or become a supernumerary at the reorganization. It is unlikely he participated in the Tennessee Campaign. He was captured at Macon, Georgia on April 21 or 22, 1865.

[264] **Private J. L. Davis** enlisted on June 9, 1861 in Captain Dillard's Company. He was elected 2nd Sergeant on October 1, 1862 and was on detached duty for 45 days paid at 25 cents per day. He was present by January muster. Davis was promoted to 2nd Lieutenant on March 17, 1863. He was 24 years old in July of 1863. He was promoted to 1st Lieutenant by December 1863. He took a short leave of absence on February 2, 1864. He was on musters through April of 1864. On September 29, 1864, Special Field Order No. 120 placed supernumerary officers on detached duty. He and the remainder of the detail were placed under the command of Colonel S. H. Colms of the 50th Tennessee and reported immediately to Brigadier Gen. Marcus Wright at the post in Macon, Ga. He tendered his resignation on December 26, 1864 per Special Order 305. He was paid through June 30, 1864.

154

Company G

Captain A.T. Fisher[266] – still in command – 2nd Lt. Ad Fisk- interim

1st Lieutenant W. M. Clenny – still in command – not present.[267]

2nd Lieutenant Ad. Fisk – still in command. Lt. J. R. Fisher- interim

3rd Lieutenant J. Fisher – still in command. Lawson Smith[268]- interim

Company H

Captain James M. Parks – still in command.

1st Lieutenant William G. Etter – still in command.

2nd Lieutenant Henry L. Hayes – still in command.

3rd Lieutenant John Akeman – still in command.

Company I

Captain Ben Randals – still in command.

---

[265] **Private John F. Owen** enlisted in Captain Dillard's Company on June 9, 1861. He was slightly wounded on December 31, 1862 at Murfreesboro. He was 3rd Lieutenant on March 21, 1863. He was 22 years old in July 1863. He was killed at Jonesboro, Georgia on September 1, 1864.

[266] Technically, Fisher had been ill for some time and tendered his resignation on November 19, 1862. He was not present with the unit then, and his resignation must have gone through red tape—as the company went without a captain until late July of 1863. On July 23rd, Adrian Fisk was promoted to Captain of the company.

[267] He had tendered his resignation that he was unfit in January of 1862. He was rarely present or effective for duty. His 2nd attempt at resignation was finally accepted on December 23, 1863.

[268] **Private Lawson Smith** enlisted in Captain Shields' Company on May 21, 1861. He was 25 years old in February of 1862. He was promoted to Brevet 2nd Lieutenant (3rd Lieutenant) on April 1, 1863. On December 23, 1863 he was promoted to 2nd Lieutenant. He is accounted for on muster rolls through April of 1864 and has no further record.

1st Lieutenant James Worthington – still in command.

2nd Lieutenant S. D. Mitchell – still in command.

3rd Lieutenant Denny Cummings – still in command. – Absent[269]

Company K

Captain _____ - vacant position.[270]

1st Lieutenant Wm. D. Turlington – still in command.[271]

2nd Lieutenant Wm. Lowery – still in command.[272]

3rd Lieutenant James E. Rotan – still in command.[273]

From their campground just north of Tullahoma, the boys went out on working details on a daily basis to erect fortifications and strengthen the defenses of Tullahoma. They cleared a new area free trees west and north of town that would become known as "Bragg's new ground." The area cleared of trees and shrubbery was said to be about a quarter of a mile deep. While most of the Sixteenth had been erecting breastworks in Tullahoma, Thompson and the other prisoners taken at Murfreesboro were about to be exchanged at City Point, Va. They still had to make the journey back to their regiment. Upon hearing that they were to be exchanged, Thompson purchased and filled his haversack with sausage, cheese and crackers for the trip. When they reached Baltimore, the boys were loaded aboard a large sail and steam ship for the trip to Ft. Monroe. Unfortunately for them, a heavy wind blew up and rocked the ship to and fro causing a great number of men to fall sea sick. Thompson leaned back against

---

[269] He had been wounded at Perryville and captured on October 9, 1862. He was about to be exchanged and rejoin the regiment in April.

[270] Captain D. T. Brown had been promoted to Lieutenant Colonel on February 20, 1863. Elections were not held for these positions until August 19, 1863.

[271] Promoted to Captain on August 19, 1863.

[272] Promoted to 1st Lieutenant on August 19, 1863.

[273] Promoted to 2nd Lieutenant on August 19, 1863.

156

one of the mast to help maintain his equilibrium while his comrades vomited profusely all around him. They reached City Point on the 21ˢᵗ of March and transferred to a steamboat that took them up the James River to Confederate lines. As they steamed along they saw the wreckage of the USS Cumberland and the USS Congress that had been destroyed by the CSS Merrimac on March 14ᵗʰ. Boarding trains, the boys traveled through Petersburg and felt the effects of inflation brought about by the war. The cost of one piece of fried fish and cornbread was a dollar, and their pay was still only eleven dollars a month. Finally, they arrived at Chattanooga by rail. There, a couple of the boys came down with small pox which led to all of them being quarantined. They did not receive enough rations and weren't allowed to go into the city to purchase food, so as they were camped close to the Tennessee River, they supplemented their diets by fishing. Tired of being cooped up and not being able to see their families or buddies, Thompson, M. E. Adcock and four or five others of the regiment decided to leave for home and then return to the Sixteenth. Under the guise that they were going fishing, several of the boys went to the river where they had found a number of canoes the day previous. The guards seemed unaware so the boys piled into a small canoe, but it was not big enough for all of them. Thompson had to make two trips to get them all across the swollen Tennessee River. The boys then returned home for a few days.[274]

On April 3ʳᵈ, Major Coffee resigned his commission as Major of the regiment. He had suffered from chronic diarrhea for over six months. H. H. Dillard—who had served as the first captain for Company F—was appointed Acting Major of the regiment.[275] While stationed at Tullahoma, Reverend DeWitt spent his time, "…preaching, distributing tracts, religious conversations, visiting sick, and reading, meditating, and private prayer." Meanwhile the boys in the Sixteenth found themselves falling under more strict regulations. Ammunition was in high demand and restrictions had been placed on

---

[274] (Carden, p. Apr. 19) (Thompson, p. 14)
[275] Captain Dillard was actually assigned to the Conscription Bureau, but regularly visited the boys in camp and on the march.

the use of any other than combat. Soon an order came down that soldiers were not allowed to carry their firearms out of the bivouac areas as they were wasting ammunition shooting at small game.[276]

C. H. Clark went on an illegal hunt with his buddy Mark Mitchell. Mark's brother Martin was ill and had asked him to kill a squirrel for him. Clark didn't take his gun, but Mark did. Going down to the west side of the railroad, they managed to tree a squirrel. Mark took a shot with his .577 caliber Enfield and missed the squirrel. Clark ran to the opposite side of the tree to scare it back to Mark's side, and Mark fired again missing the squirrel. In moments, the Provost Guard had heard the shooting and ran to investigate. When they arrived Mark still had a loaded gun, and the officer in charge told him to shoot off the round. Mitchell took one last aim at the squirrel but missed it again. They immediately arrested both Clark and Mitchell. The guards escorted them about a hundred yards back towards camp when Mark explained he had lost his knife under the tree where he was shooting, and he must have it. As the party turned around and got within about fifty yards of the tree, the officer in charge told Mitchell to get the knife and hurry back. As Mitchell approached the tree he dropped his rifle to 'trail arms' and ran off into the woods at a sprint. The guards offered to turn Clark loose for his buddy's name, but Clark stated, "I never run away to Alabama nor turned traitor, no sir." They delivered Clark to the guardhouse where he found another buddy—E. T. Passons and—several others of his company that had been arrested with the same charge. Fortunately, they released them all the same day without being punished.[277]

Due to casualties from previous battle, details were gathered for temporary conscription duty about this time. The men were to go back into "lost" territory to gather new recruits and enforce the Conscription Act for thirty days or more. One officer of Wright's Brigade called this a, "…hazardous and almost impractical adventure." The only ones that would join them were those that

---

[276] (Head T. A., p. 112) (DeWitt M. B., p. 2)
[277] (Clark, pp. #16-17)

already had it in their minds to join the army. As Yankee parties scoured the land, the details often had to hide away for days at a time. "Homespun Yankees" and Negroes were a wealth of information to the Yankee pursuers. The same officer related that he was, "…glad when I was released from this very dangerous and unpleasant duty imposed upon me."[278]

Those men detailed for the conscription service not only tried to entice men into joining the army, but they were also tasked with gathering up deserters or men that were absent without leave. C. H. Clark remembered three men that had run away from the army but had been arrested at home, brought back and court-martialed. The three of them were sentenced to ride a wooden horse for a few days.

A guard with their guns was kept there to see that the order was carried out. Two forks were put in the ground about 8 feet apart and a pole put in the forks which was 7 or 8 feet high. They were put astride the pole and kept there for two hours, and then taken down to rest awhile and then mounted again. This procedure went on for several days. A beef's head with horns on was fastened on the front end of the horse (or pole) and the poor fellow astride the pole in front of the other two, and near the beef's head was a preacher, and a broad slip of paper was fastened around his hat, with the following inscription, "COME ON BOYS."[279]

Upon returning to the Army of Tennessee in mid-April, Sergeant Thompson went to the Provost Marshall to report himself as an exchanged prisoner. He was then issued a pass and found the camp of the Sixteenth just north of Tullahoma – just a few days before his comrades' arrival. Thompson was raked with questions by his buddies concerning his capture and the state of the Union. The news that he passed on was far from good. He related that in his

---

[278] (Talley, p. Pt. 4)
[279] (Clark, p. #17) According to Clark, these three men were not members of the Sixteenth.

travels through the north that, "everything was prosperous and that farms and factories were in full blast."

> Ships, boats and railroads, I said, were in as fine fix as if there were no war, and the men for recruits were thick at all the cities, towns and villages. Railroad stations were often crowded with men. Then I had traveled through the heart of our own land. At the cities, towns and villages and railroad stations, I saw soldiers convalescent and wounded, but not recruits enough to make a Corporal's Guard. Our farms were idle. Just here and there a patch. Our railroads were worn out and our rolling stock done for. No stock hardly on the farms and everything so high the civilians could barely live.

His comrades were astonished by this. The thought that they were at such a disadvantage caused them to curse and state that if they believed that way, they would, "run away in twenty-four hours." Thompson quickly quieted his buddies and stated that he was still a soldier and would be with them "to the end." "But facts were facts, and all we could do was to try to overcome the disadvantages by courage and devotion to our country. The result would be with God, who rules in the affairs of men and nations."[280]

A lot of soldiers had grown, "...tired of the war and the burdens placed upon them." One of the boys had created some "meanness" in camp and was court-martialed. He was sentenced to dig up a big oak stump from the ground. Clark explained what happened next.

> Tools were furnished and the guard told him to go to digging, but he swore he would not dig up the stump. They "bucked" him awhile, loosed him and ordered him to dig, but he said "no." They "bucked and gagged" him awhile, loosed him again and ordered him to dig, but he said "no, there is no use digging up a stump out in the woods" and he never dug a lick. They

---

[280] (Thompson, p. 14)

kept up the treatment until we had to hike out from there, and he was given his gun and placed in ranks with his command.[281]

Perhaps the order that ended the punishment was received on April 21st. That day the brigade was ordered back to Shelbyville and back to Cheatham's Division on the 28th. The brigade marched to and encamped at Holt's Campground which was located on the Fayetteville Pike about five miles south of Shelbyville just off the road in, "…a fine grove." That evening, Reverend DeWitt preached to the Sixteenth at 4 p.m. per Colonel Donnell's request. The reverend called it a, "…pleasant occasion."[282]

The boys were jubilant in camp and still optimistic—at least in a joking way—despite reports from former captives such as Sergeant Thompson. They spent their downtime changing verses to old songs and creating new songs. One verse they added to "Dixie" was, "Dixe Land is a land of cotton, when a poor man dies he is soon forgotten, look away…" etc. Another song went, "Old Abe Lincoln keeps kicken up a fuss, I think he better stop it for he only makes it wuss, We will have our independence, I tell the reason why, Big pig, little pig, root hog or die." Still in their own breadbasket, the boys continued to receive food and care packages from family and friends. Times had been good enough up to then, but soon the Yankee war machine would start its engine. Federal General Rosecrans was reorganizing his army, while General Bragg concentrated on holding strategic gaps to deny the enemy's passage further south toward Chattanooga. Although urged by the Federal War Department to commence actions right away, Rosecrans deemed it necessary to perfect his plans and continue to train the large numbers of reinforcements he had been receiving. For nearly two more months, the boys constructed works in and around Shelbyville awaiting the expected Federal advance.[283]

---

[281] (Clark, p. #17)
[282] (Head T. A., p. 112) (Tucker, p. 47) (DeWitt M. B., p. 2)
[283] (Clark, p. 26)

By the end of the first week of May 1863, the Sixteenth Tennessee reported that it had 376 effective men in their ranks. The regiment had 385 Enfield Rifles on hand and 54,976 cartridges. The number of effectives had increased dramatically since January and February. This increase was directly related to wounded and captured from both of their major battles that had returned to the ranks as well as a few conscripts. Their effective total was still 30 men less than their effective total on December 31, 1862 four months earlier. The numbers would never be what they had been, and they continued to steadily decline due to desertions and casualties over the next eight months. The 51st Tennessee reported less than 250 effectives in their ranks, while the 38th Tennessee had just under 270 effective men.[284]

On the 8th of May, the 8th Tennessee had a picnic in Lincoln County only five or six miles from Holt's Campground. Many of the Eighth's boys were from Lincoln and Marshall Counties and their friends and families prepared a massive feast for them. The Sixteenth's members faired nearly as well with some of their people being less than twenty miles away in Coffee County. On May 18th, the brigade moved its camp to Shelbyville—crossed Duck River and camped in the bend, one mile southeast of the town. The town offered little for the soldiers, yet one member of Maney's Brigade thought, "…in a time of peace I would imagine it a pleasant retreat." Throughout the month the boys heard of the great victory at the Wilderness in Virginia—but with it—the death of Stonewall Jackson. They also learned of the defeat of Confederate forces at Jackson, Mississippi.[285] Their lives still mostly consisted of erecting fortifications and drilling. On May 22nd, Private George W. Etter wrote a letter to his brother Roysdson back home in Warren County—he was still recovering from wounds received at Perryville.

---

[284] (Young)
[285] (Morgan P. F., p. 1) (Tucker, p. 47) (DeWitt M. B., p. 2) (Oldham, p. May 20)

May 22, 1863 – Camp one mile from Shelbyville

Mr. R. R. Etter

Dear brother – Mr. Brown is going to go back in the morning and I thought I would drop you a note. Should have wrote to father, but had not the chance. We have moved from where we was when father was here. The health of army is good. Tho our Capt. and Mart Hayes is sick. John Bess is very low – some think he won't live. I hope Capt. and Mart will be up soon. Brother Will is well and the rest of our boys – except Andy Moore – he is some better this morning. Have you heard of the battle in Miss. I expect we got sorter whipt thare our loss three thousand – yanks four thousand.

We will hear the particulars today – I am afraid to hear from thare – All quiet in front – however our men drove in their pickets yesterday – run them clear to Murfreesboro – I do not know what we will do – tho I think we will do something pretty soon for our men is fixing to make a move of some kind. I have been out to see the boys drill – they are drilling in the Skirmish all the time – and they are drilling by the company all the time – It is very interesting but rather hard on some of the boys.[286]

George went on to urge Roysdon to not take part in any guerilla actions. George was of the opinion that most of them, "…ought to be hung."

The first week of June found Maney's Brigade on outpost duty skirmishing with Federal cavalry. Heavy rains fell on the 5th of June and distant cannon-fire could be heard. On June 8th, Wright's Brigade—formerly known as Donelson's Brigade—moved out three

---

[286] (Sullivan, pp. 172-73)

miles from Shelbyville up the Fairfield Pike to "the front." They remained encamped there for the next nineteen days. Heavy rains continued on the 10th of the month, and on June 12th, the brigade witnessed an event that not one man had ever wanted to see.[287]

> A man whose name I have forgotten ran away and carried back 2 or 3 times was court-martialed and condemned to be shot. The day of execution was set, grave dug over across the creek, west of town, and a rough box coffin made and placed at the grave. On the appointed day I went over to witness the execution. The Brigade to which he belonged was formed around to witness the scene was near where I could see the poor fellow. At the appointed hour, an officer with 6 soldiers with their guns marched the poor fellow to the grave and he sat down on his coffin.[288]

> ...the battery was ordered to form one of the three sides of a square to witness the execution... The poor fellow's infantry companions sung a hymn, Gen. Wright shook hands with him...[289]

> He appeared calm and self-possessed. Expressed his willingness to die. He was said to have been a desperate character. How severe is military law.[290]

> The officer and guard took position a few yards in front of him, and the officer gave command to the guard as follows, "Ready, aim, fire." At the word fire, all the guns fired simultaneously, and the poor fellow was dead.[291]

L. G. Marshall—of Carnes' Battery—stated that upon the volley being fired, "...the square dissolved and the parade ended. Not a

---

287 (Oldham) (Tucker, p. 47)
288 (Clark, p. #16)
289 (Marshall, p. 819)
290 (Oldham, p. June 12)
291 (Clark, p. #16)

man was present except those compelled by military authority."[292] This rigid punitive action had become too common practice by General Bragg. Most of the men and boys knew the hardships that faced the common soldiers. Some of them faced the same problems. Sick or starving children and family members back home were more than enough to make a man leave the army to aid them. General Bragg's reputation began to wane quickly throughout the army following these executions.

For the defense of Shelbyville and the most likely route of advance for the Federal army, Lieutenant General Leonidas Polk's Corps had been placed at Shelbyville and defended Guy's Gap about ten miles north of the town. General Hardee's Corps was placed in the vicinity of Wartrace and was committed to the defense of Hoover's Gap, Liberty Gap and Bell Buckle Gap. Yankee intelligence was quite accurate in the supposed location of Confederate forces. A newspaper article from *The New York Herald*—dated June 23rd and based off of week old information—laid out the position Confederate forces.

> Polk's corps, consisting of Wither's and Cheatham's divisions, are encamped at a point about four miles north of Shelbyville, upon Fall and Hurricane creek, where they cross the turnpike road from the city to Shelbyville. The First brigade of Cheatham's division, formerly Stewart's, now commanded by Colonel Strahl, Fourth Tennessee, is at Guy's Gap, ten miles north of Shelbyville. The Fifty-first Alabama mounted infantry, videtting the rebel front on the Shelbyville road, is encamped on Christmas creek and the headwaters of the Little West fork of Stone river, about eight miles from Murfreesboro... Hardee's corps, consisting of Cleburne's and Stewart's divisions are encamped at Wartrace and west of it, on the Wartrace creek.[293]

---

[292] (Marshall, p. 819)
[293] (The New York Herald, 1863)

Despite the Christian officers of Cheatham's Division protesting drill and inspections on Sundays, General Cheatham resisted their pleas, and an order was read at parade on June 15th that announced inspections would continue. Cheatham ensured that his division would be ready for the Federal advance and wouldn't let Sunday services interrupt the preparedness of his men. Nine days later—on June 23rd the same day that *The New York Herald's* article was printed—Rosecrans army advanced from Murfreesboro.[294]

The very next day Federal Colonel John T. Wilders' "Lightening Brigade" seized Hoover's Gap in an incessant rain. It was thought this would be the easiest gap to defend, but it was so lightly guarded that the speed and mobility of the Federal force, armed with repeating rifles, easily overpowered the small Confederate cavalry force there. Before word could be sent to Confederate headquarters, the gap was practically secured. Cleburne's Division had been tasked with holding Liberty Gap, but after a short contest there, his brigades gave up that gap as well. This put Polk's Corps and the Sixteenth in a precarious position. On the 25th, Confederate forces attempted to retake the gaps but were unsuccessful. General Hardee chose to withdraw towards Shelbyville and did little to slow the Federal advance which would allow the Federal Army of the Cumberland to swing into the Army of Tennessee's right and rear. Immediately, Polk was ordered to withdraw to Tullahoma. Orders came to the Sixteenth at 5 a.m. on the morning of June 27th.[295]

> The merchants of Shelbyville, like everybody else, were taken by surprise, and stood in the streets by the side of the moving column, offering their goods at any price the soldiers chose to pay; but business was light, as the medium of exchange was wanting.[296]

The Sixteenth, with the rest of Wright's Brigade, acted as rear guard for the division. As they crossed Schoefner's Bridge just

---

[294] (Oldham, p. June 15)
[295] (Potter, p. 15)
[296] (Marshall, p. 819)

southeast of Shelbyville, Cleburne's Division arrived in their rear. Apparently a wagon broke down in the long column and caused a cessation of movement. General Cleburne—concerned with the halt—rode forward to find Colonel Donnell overseeing the repair of a broken wagon wheel. The major general told him to push the wagon aside, but Donnell insisted that he was to save all the wagons per higher authority. General Cleburne immediately sent word to Lieutenant General Polk in the following dispatch.

Lieutenant–General Hardee:

> GENERAL: This road in my front is taken up with trains and troops of commands. I am making but slow progress at this moment—6:45 p.m. My rear is but 1 ½ miles south of Schoefner's Bridge. Some of General Polk's officers (Colonel Donnell for one) stop his command, and, in consequence, everything in rear of him, whenever a wagon breaks down. I ordered him to shove all wagons which were broken down out of the road, and push on. He said his orders from higher authority were to leave none of the wagons behind, and he would obey those orders. This policy will risk the safety of the army. I can hear the enemy's artillery and small arms on my flank and rear.

> P. R. CLEBURNE
> *Major-General*

Colonel Donnell had not simply made this excuse up. The higher authority would have been from his own brigade commander. Brigadier General Wright was still wet behind the ears as a brigade commander. Wright had apparently insisted that all wagons be saved which—as Cleburne stated—risked the safety of the army. Orders were immediately passed down from the commanding general himself to push all broken wagons aside and move on. Lieutenant General Polk replied to the letter he had received with the following.

In the field 5 miles from Tullahoma,

June 28—1:45 a.m.

Brigadier-General Mackall, *Chief of Staff:*

GENERAL: I am in receipt of your note of 10 p.m. of the 27th, with its inclosure. The conduct of Colonel Donnell is in the highest degree reprehensible, and entirely at variance with orders from these headquarters and the practice of this corps. From whom he has received orders I know not. The impropriety shall be stopped, and the facts investigated.

L. POLK

Lieutenant-General[297]

That evening, Wright's Brigade was pulled from the division and spent the night guarding the cross roads at Rowesville to protect the army's left-rear.[298] Shortly after dawn they marched on toward Tullahoma and arrived on the afternoon of the 28th. The next morning, they were ordered from camps at about 7:40 a.m., "...in a great hurry." They quickly moved to the Manchester Pike and formed line of battle on the left side of the road with their right flank resting on the pike.[299] The Federal troops had seized Manchester and threatened an advance from that direction. The Sixteenth and the rest of Cheatham's Division dug in the remainder of the day and prepared to defend Tullahoma against an expected Federal assault. Some of the men were almost excited at the prospect of the enemy

---

[297] Interestingly, Wright is never mentioned in the Official Records concerning this or any other event that may have cast questionable judgment upon him. But of course, General Wright was in charge of collecting the documents of the Confederate Army and determining what was relevant for the series. He would not have wanted this included if documentation was found.

[298] (OR, Ser. 1, Vol. 23, Pt. 1, p. 619-20)

[299] (Potter, p. 15)

attacking them behind defensive works. The next evening—June 30th—word came down that an evacuation of Tullahoma was taking place the following morning.[300]

On July 1st, the army moved to Allisonia and crossed Elk River. Then they passed on to Dechard and Cowan on the 2nd. The army was placed in line of battle at the foot of the mountains at Cowan, and it was originally thought they would fight there. After a council of war was held, the decision was made to have the army fall back over the mountain under the circumstances as the wagon trains had already begun crossing. On the 3rd, the division started up the mountain and camped that night on the mountaintop. The next day they resumed the march for about fifteen miles and crossed the Tennessee River at the mouth of Battle Creek on pontoon bridges. They spent the night near the crossing site that night. The boys had been short on rations during this march and were very hungry. Private Carden noticed an apple tree along the roadside that had apples about the size of a "quail's egg." He put down as many as he could. A few hours later they drew rations, but Carden was so full and tired that he didn't bother to draw any.[301]

On Sunday July 5th, the division moved on to near Shellmound and cooked rations. Sergeant Thompson came down with a severe "chill" while there, shaking for nearly three days. Doctor Mauzy administered so much opium to Thompson that he, "...could not hold my eyes open all day. But I could hear everything that went on." Many of the boys had lost their shoes on the muddy march over the mountains and were horribly foot sore. It was on the evening of the 6th when they passed Running Water Creek and stopped at White Sides Station. There, the boys were loaded onto boxcars for the last leg of their journey to Chattanooga. By the evening of the 7th, the whole of Cheatham's Division had made the journey to the city, and on the 10th, the regiment and brigade reoccupied their former camping ground of August 1862. That same day Roysdon Etter rejoined the regiment after a long convalescence

---

[300] (Potter, p. 15) (Oldham, p. June 30)
[301] (OR, Ser. 1, Vol. 23, Pt. 1, p. 619-20) (Oldham) (Carden, p. Apr. 19)

at home and in hospitals at Chattanooga. "It was a happy meeting for me and the boys." But on a sour note, they officially learned of the fall of Vicksburg and Pemberton's surrender. After nearly a full year of campaigning and two major battles, the boys found themselves back where they had started.[302]

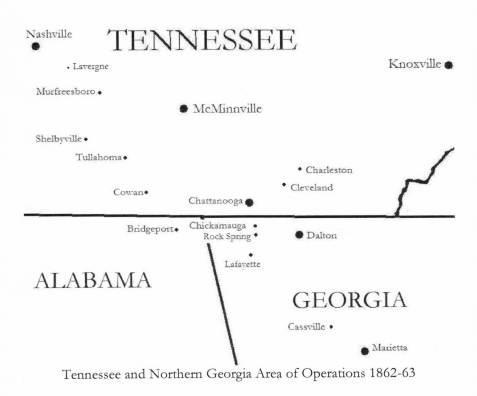

Tennessee and Northern Georgia Area of Operations 1862-63

[302] (Oldham) (Thompson, p. 15) (Carden, p. #18) (Sullivan, p. 62)

Chapter VII

Chattanooga and the Chickamauga Campaign

11 July – 18 September 1863

Roysdon Etter was excited to see his old buddies back in camp. He was—however—shocked to see so few of them. Fortunately his brothers were still there to greet him. The day after his return to the regiment, he made the following diary entry.

> I, a second time enter upon this painful struggle that has caused so much sorrow and death among us all. Our boys are yet in good spirits. Though there is many a one that was with me is with me no more. They have gone of disease and death to their long homes to return no more. I think of them often though they cannot be brought back again.[303]

That same day the newspapers reported that General Lee was falling back with the Army of Northern Virginia. Within another week, word came that Port Hudson had fallen and Lee was re-crossing the Potomac River. The boys went back to their usual work of

---

[303] (Sullivan, p. 63)

constructing fortifications to defend the city. After all the work the boys had done erecting strong fortifications at Shelbyville and Tullahoma, their motivation to build more at Chattanooga had somewhat diminished. One of Maney's Brigade wrote, "I don't think the boys like the idea of working on any more fortifications. They think they probably will have to evacuate again." Working parties were somewhat limited at first due to the lack of shoes that the men had. Only those with shoes and in good health had to go on the working parties, and it is likely that malingering became a common practice for privates that were in good health. A number began to desert the ranks finally becoming sick of the bad news and prospect of losing Tennessee once again. It seemed that July had nothing to offer but bad news for the Confederacy.[304]

By mid-July, Major Thomas B. Murray, commanding the 22nd Infantry Battalion, and a large number of his officers were assigned by General Bragg to recruiting duty. This left the unit so small that it was temporarily consolidated with the 38th Tennessee commanded by Colonel John C. Carter.[305] Within the Sixteenth after July 20th, elections were finally held for Company K to replace resigned or killed officers. A few other elections took place in the other companies for the same purpose. Due to Captain A. T. Fisher's resignation, Lieutenant Adrian Fisk was elected to Captain on July 23rd for Company G. Also, newly promoted 3rd Lieutenant William H. White was promoted to 1st Lieutenant in Company D to fill the vacancy of 1st Lieutenant S. H. Brown's resignation. Brown had served for months in the Conscription Bureau and due to an illness had resorted to drinking too often. He was charged with intoxication and unfit for duty. Charges were eventually dropped and he joined

---

[304] (Oldham)
[305] (Civil War Centtennial Commission, p. 167) This was only supposed to be a temporary consolidation, and initially the 22nd Battalion continued to file its own reports. Later, Murray and his officers found themselves practically trapped behind Federal lines. In time, this consolidation became permanent and members of the 22nd Battalion can be found paroled as members of the 38th Tennessee at the close of the war.

the cavalry. Company K's officers assumed command on August 19th. The election results follow.

Company K

Captain Wm. D. Turlington promoted from 1st Lieutenant

1st Lieutenant Wm. Lowery promoted from 2nd Lieutenant

2nd Lieutenant James E. Rotan promoted from 3rd Lieutenant

3rd Lieutenant W. G. Simms[306] promoted from Orderly Sergeant

For the majority of the boys through the remainder of July and August, they would continue to construct earthworks and suffer from poor rations. The majority of the food collected in their supply regions was either under Federal control or shipped to the Army of Northern Virginia. For the most of the boys, finding ways to occupy their free time became a major priority. The boys that weren't discouraged by the recent setbacks found ways to make light of things. R. C. Carden admitted that when he, "…didn't have any Yankees to whip – I was in some devilment."

I had a chum who was always ready for anything and when necessary I would write a pass, sign all the necessary officers' names to it and we would go to town. I had two trust comrades, Bob Tucker and John Robinson. Robinson and I

---

[306] **Private W. G. Simms** enlisted in Captain Brown's Company on June 11, 1861 at Cap Trousdale. He was 21 years old in February of 1862. He was elected 1st Sergeant on May 8, 1862. He was sent to Chattanooga Hospital on August 25, 1862 and rejoined the command on October 22, 1862. Simms was slightly wounded on December 31, 1862 at Murfreesboro. He was promoted to 3rd Lieutenant on July 24, 1863. He took a short leave of absence on March 11, 1864. Last muster roll with regiment was through April of 1864. He then has receipts for saddlebags purchased and sold in November 1864 to Captain Worthington. He probably went on detached duty to Macon with other supernumerary officers. No further record is found.

would go to town and he would borrow $10 of somebody, then we would proceed to enclose the quart. The quart cost $10. Then we would find where some citizen was selling it on the sly. I would take our canteens and go where it was kept for sale, go in and find that he had it, get my vessels full, sit down and have a big talk. About the time we got in a good way Robinson would rush in, the maddest you ever saw. He would cuss and abuse me, threaten to kick me out of the house, etc., then he would turn to the man and tell him what he would do to me when he got me back to camp, and while that was going on I would quietly walk out with the liquor. They would talk a while (to give me time to get away) then Robinson would say he must go. When the man would say that I had not paid for the whiskey, then Robinson was madder than ever. He would cuss and tear around and say he had given me the money to pay for it and he would go and bring me back. He would finally locate me out of town and as our business in town had been transacted we would go back to camp.[307]

It seemed that some of the Sixteenth's boys couldn't help but find trouble or amusement in someone else's misfortune. The next time Carden went out he took Bob Tucker. The day before he had seen a man was selling ginger cakes and had made a deal for a bunch of them. He stated that he would have to go back to camp to close the deal with his buddies. After forging more papers, the two headed back into Chattanooga and found the man very busy selling cakes. The merchant told them to go into his back room and wait – that he would be in soon. Suddenly they heard a loud commotion in the alley outside. Carden ran to the door to hold it closed while Tucker filled both of their haversacks with ginger cakes. They took advantage of the ruckus in the alley to make their escape back to camp.

A few days afterward a fellow came to camp selling pies and other things out of a wagon. I went up to where he was doing

[307] (Carden, p. Apr. 26)

business and at once saw he was in need of a clerk, as everything was going like hot cakes. I said: 'Mister, you don't seem to be able to wait on them all. I will help you if you want me to.' He said, 'All right,' so I got up in the hind end of the wagon and the way I sold truck was a sight. Robinson, my partner, and messmate wanted a whole lot of stuff and would buy only of me. He would buy 75 cents worth and give me a dollar and I would give him three or four dollars change. Now and then when Robinson was gone I would hand over what money I had to the boss. But Robinson was the best customer we had.

In the evening the fellow went to the Colonel and told him he had a load that ought to have brought him $250 or $300 and he only got about $50 out of it. I felt sorry for the fellow and never charged him a cent for helping him.[308]

The boys never missed an opportunity to poke fun at officers. On another occasion, Carden was walking down Main Street in down town Chattanooga when he saw, "...a crowd of soldiers gathered around a big fat fellow, a colonel of a Tennessee regiment, who was full as a tick."

The boys were teasing him and they got him red hot. He would cuss them with all the cuss words he could muster up and he could muster up a whole lot of them. He told them they would desert if they were not so far from home and he handed it out to them in fine style. One of the soldiers said, 'Well, old man, go on about your fishing. I hope you catch lots of fish.' He said, 'I hope I won't get a d—d bite.'[309]

Of course, as they were almost always short on rations, Carden took the time to go on a hunt of his own. As he took his mess mates' canteens to a spring to fill them, he saw three young Muscovy ducks. He, "...spread myself out like a women spreads her dress when she is

---

[308] Ibid.
[309] Ibid.

driving a hen and chicks…" and snatched them by the neck as they got near. He would pull of the head and stuff it in his shirt. By the time he had caught all three, they had flopped around so much that, "…the front of my shirt was a bloody as though a hog had been butchered…"[310]

By the end of July, the reduced strength of the Army of Tennessee was easily recognizable on inspection reports. To return the men to the ranks and increase manpower, General Bragg then issued a General Order that dropped charges against all of the men presently absent from the army. This order didn't include those already sentenced to death. Thomas Head later wrote that, "Among the beneficiaries of this Executive clemency was Private Hugh Whitehead, of Company F—a resident of Putnam County—the only culprit that was ever known from the ranks of the Sixteenth Tennessee Regiment. This man was partially demented and seemed to be utterly ignorant of the consequences of desertion."[311]

On Sunday August 2nd, a man that they supposed to be a robber or bushwacker was found hanging from a tree near Cheatham's Division camp. As death had been seen so many times on the field of battle, few men took notice of such a sight. They continued to erect more fortifications through the month of August at a feverish pace as the Federal Army crept closer toward Chattanooga. One member of Maney's Brigade recalled General Frank Cheatham passing along and checking on the boys. The general had even got into the ditches with the boys and wielded a spade. By the 21st, the Federals had appeared across the Tennessee River and commenced shelling the city. Their sharpshooters were also active along the opposite side of the river. The next day it was learned that the Federal shelling into the city had caused the death of at least two or three men and one woman. The pickets continued their skirmishing across the river through the end of August with the boys waiting for the inevitable battle, although few thought

---

[310] Ibid.
[311] (Head T. A., p. 115)

Rosecrans would be foolish enough to attack their recently constructed works.[312]

Supplies were still very limited, but as they had closed the gap toward their supply base in Chattanooga and the manufacturing heart of Georgia, they would soon find an abundance of government issued items including clothing and equipment. Their first bulk issue of clothing came in on August 31st. The Sixteenth's 350+ men were issued 351 pairs of drawers, 82 pairs of pants[313], and 182 cotton shirts including a new item—twenty-two tent flies were distributed to the regiment. On August 1st, Color Bearer W. T. Mayberry was discharged for severe wounds received at Murfreesboro. Colonel Donnell and the regimental staff had to choose a new Color bearer. About this time, 4th Sergeant James R. Thompson was called to Colonel Donnell's headquarters tent.[314]

> Knowing him to be a very strict disciplinarian, I saluted him according to military style and asked what was wanted. He informed me that he had selected me to carry his Regimental flag, and proceeded to give me such a nice compliment for my soldierly qualities that I could scarcely refuse to take it. I informed him I would take it and that I would never be the first to leave the field.[315]

Any man assuming the duties of regimental color bearer knew the death sentence that they had accepted. If the enemy could constantly drop the colors of an enemy regiment, a rout could likely ensue. Regardless, the boys in the Sixteenth were always willing to assume deadly duties in the face of a hostile enemy.

By September 7th, the Federal army was gaining ground on the city and threatening communication and supply lines to Chattanooga. That night, the Sixteenth formed part of a picket line

---

[312] (Oldham)
[313] Sixty-six of these pairs of pants were manufactured with all cotton jeans.
[314] (Compiled Service Records)
[315] (Thompson, p. 15)

that ran along the south bank of the Tennessee River to the mouth of Chickamauga Creek. Private Thomas Head got too close to the bank of the river and tumbled down the slope about fifty feet landing on a raft made of pine logs which saved him from being dunked. He worked his way back up the steep embankment pulling at "canes and brush."[316] As expected over a month earlier by the privates who were building the massive earthen fortifications to protect Chattanooga, the Army of Tennessee found itself withdrawing the following day in the direction of Crawfish Springs. At 8 a.m. on September 8th, the regiment marched thirteen miles in the direction of Rome, Georgia to Chickamauga Creek. That night while waiting for an obstacle in the road to be moved, another infamous stampede took place. A wagon team got spooked and tore full speed down the road. This sent the boys running in every direction. One of the Sixteenth implied that war itself was less frightening than a stampede. After regrouping, they marched on to at Lee & Gordon's Mill where they camped for the night.[317] The march didn't take place without loss however. That night, James Dodson, Andrew J. Moore, Harmon Willis, Solomon Baldwin, William Willis, John Stepp, Crawford McConnell and John Brown—all of Company H—left the ranks and went home. Not all of them were gone for good; some surrendered, some captured and others later returned to the ranks.[318]

On September 9th, the regiment moved out about two miles from the bridge to Crawfish Springs. Sergeant Major Thomas Benton Potter wrote that the spring was, "…one of the largest and best I ever saw…" They stayed there all day and through the night.[319] The Sixteenth remained on picket there until about 9 p.m. on September 10th. During this stay, C. H. Clark and Jim Martin went out foraging for food. Clark stated that "…when foraging had to be done, he (Martin) never failed." They dug up about a peck of Irish potatoes and had a "fine meal."[320] At about 9 p.m. they received

---

316 (Head T. A., p. 116)
317 (Clark, p. #18) (Potter, p. 18) (Sullivan, p. 64)
318 (Sullivan, p. 64)
319 (Potter, p. 18)
320 (Clark, p. #18)

orders to march, "…immediately in the direction of Lafayette, Ga." They marched about fifteen miles all night long and arrived there at 2 p.m. on the afternoon of September 11th. They immediately went out on picket about a mile from town and were relieved at darkness. That night they cooked three days of rations.[321]

The brigade moved out from Lafayette at 3 p.m. on September 13th and marched till midnight. Upon halting, they encamped at Rock Spring Church. The boys stayed here till the 16th of September when they moved about a mile and cooked more rations. Two days later on September 18th, the Wright's Brigade crossed Chickamauga Creek at Lee & Gordon's Mills and marched nearly ten miles south toward Lafayette, but upon their arrival, they were ordered to countermarch directly back to the vicinity of the Mill. That night they camped on the south side of the creek with heavy skirmishing heard in the distance.[322] The boys knew this movement and countermovement meant a fight. The question was—when? Color Sergeant James R. Thompson later wrote that although their ranks would never be as full as they once were, "…we were as full of fight as we were at the beginning, and a great deal more effective, for we had learned the lessons of war by hard experience."[323]

---

[321] (Potter, p. 18) (Etter, p. 18)
[322] (Etter, p. 18) (Clark, p. #18) (Potter, p. 19)
[323] (Thompson, p. 15)

Chapter VIII

The Battle of Chickamauga

19 – 20 September 1863

The morning of September 19th broke hot
and dry. Weeks without rain had left the ground hard and cracked,
and the roads—from the tramp of men and rumble of wagons—had
begun to resemble shallow rivers of dirt and dust that left a light
brown coat on vegetation and men alike. Lieutenant L. G. Marshall,
serving with Carnes' Battery and still supporting Wright's Brigade
recalled the morning's movements. "About nine o'clock the order
came to move to the west side of the creek, the crossing of which
was made at Hunt's Ford,[324] some two miles above Alexander's
Bridge, a march of about two miles."[325]

> On both sides of the road sat the soldiers of Longstreet's
> corps, who had just reached the ground from Dalton, where
> they arrived early that morning by rail. The soldiers of
> Longstreet's corps were splendid-looking men, healthy, clean,
> and well dressed. As the battery, accompanied by Wright's
> brigade, thundered rapidly over the rough road between the
> rows of Eastern veterans, the latter fixed a gaze of

---

[324] Hunt's Ford was also known as Dalton's Ford.
[325] (Lindsley, p. 821)

astonishment upon these the first Western Army men they had yet seen. The Virginians were excusable. The Army of Tennessee never looked worse, while at the same time it was never in better fighting order. But three weeks of maneuvering in the densest dust without washing had conferred the same uninteresting color upon everything—man, beast, and material.[326]

As the boys passed the Virginians, they probably were just as astounded as the Virginians had been. The well-fed, well-dressed, clean and well-armed men of Longstreet's command may as well have been from another country's army. There was no comparison—except in fighting spirit. By about 11 a.m., Cheatham's Division—consisting of Strahl's, Maney's, Jackson's, Smith's and Wright's Brigades—was in position and facing west in the bend of Chickamauga Creek east of the Hunt residence.

It was noon when orders came for Cheatham to advance in the direction of the heavy gunfire that was heard off to their right in the distance. The division advanced north for about a mile, and the boys finally halted in woods less than a ½ mile east of Brock field. The tremors of cannon fire and constant rattle of musketry grew and would then subside to a degree. Even in this semi-defilade position, balls could be heard snapping through the treetops or an occasional cannonball would crash through the woods smashing tree trunks or anything else in its way. The sulfuric smell of gun powder wafted through the woods and here or there personal gear would be found lying on the ground discarded by its owner. Walker's Division had just been engaged and was retiring in some disorder when Cheatham ordered the advance. Cheatham's front line consisted of Wright's, Smith's and Jackson's Brigades from left to right. In the supporting line, Strahl was on the left and Maney on the right. Wright's Brigade moved westward for the first quarter mile and maintained contact with the 29th Tennessee on the left of Preston Smith's Brigade, but as they grew nearer, the order to double quick was given. The last

---

[326] (Lindsley, p. 821)

quarter of a mile was covered at a jog while attempting to maintain alignment. This would be a difficult task when marching at quick time through woods and across rolling terrain already. The Sixteenth Tennessee was the extreme right of the brigade. Continuing to the left from the Sixteenth was the 8th Tennessee, 51st & 52nd Tennessee Consolidated, the 28th Tennessee Consolidated, and finally the 38th Tennessee on the left flank. Carnes' Battery followed through the open woods in the middle-rear of the brigade. The limbers and caissons creaked and bounced over logs and other debris as they advanced to the front. By the time the brigade had reached the southwest corner of Brock Field, Sergeant Major Potter noted that the brigade was, "...without support and wholey isolated from our lines."[327]

In Brock Field to the Sixteenth's right, Smith's Brigade had broken off and wandered to the northern extremity of the field and was only partially visible. A massive eruption of gunfire had been heard only moments earlier to the right of the brigade. It seemed that the division had advanced west, through the lines of Walker's Division, and struck an advancing Federal force diagonally. The first engaged was Jackson's Brigade on the extreme right, followed now by Preston Smith's men who were striking the enemy in force. Colonel Horace Rice, of the 29th Tennessee on Smith's extreme left, noted that his left was unsupported as, "The brigade on our left (Wright's) not moving up at the time we did, my left was for some time exposed to an enfilading fire."[328] It was then that Wright's Brigade was halted and his lines were dressed in the midst of flying minie balls and increasing shell fire passing overhead. This part of the woods was open with low ground vegetation and decent visibility for the majority of the brigade, but the Sixteenth and Eighth Tennessee regiments were on the edge of Brock's field. As they dressed the lines—now less than three hundred yards from the enemy position—Colonel Donnell shouted to the men to be careful because friendly pickets were still falling back from Walker's Division. This had just

---

[327] (Potter, p. 20)
[328] (OR, Ser. I, Pt. 2, Vol. 30, p. 114)

been adamantly impressed on him by one of General Wright's staff. Just then, Jim Martin yelled out, "There they are!" Colonel Donnell quickly snapped, "Don't shoot—they are our men!" Martin took another look as he raised his rifle and shouted, "Our men hell!" "BAM!" went his gun.[329] The Yankee force in their front was the advance of Palmers' Federal Division that was in the process of moving laterally from left to right across the brigade's front. They had not noticed the approach of Wright's Brigade, but once their men started to fall, the force fell back to the support of their artillery. As the brigade came into action so abruptly, the normal gap that should be left in the middle for Carnes' Battery to fill was not afforded to it. The battery halted in rear of the brigade and watched the fight begin to escalate in their front.[330]

The order to advance was given, and the brigade stepped off with the Sixteenth and part of the Eighth regiments clearly exposed in the open field. They had advanced nearly 300 yards and reached the opposite tree line when all hell broke loose. Federal General Cruft's Brigade had rushed back to the foot of a ridge and occupied a line at the base of the ridge in their front running from north to south. Brigadier General Wright had instructed each regiment to have skirmishers thrown forward to feel out the enemy's position, but the regiments on the left of the brigade had not been aware of the enemy so close in their front as the brigade was striking the enemy forces obliquely. The first to come under heavy fire were the Eighth and Sixteenth regiments.[331] A section of Federal cannon was on the immediate left-front of the Sixteenth, and as the 242 riflemen of the regiment advanced, the enemy battery opened a destructive fire of canister on the regiment.[332] This initial fire dropped a considerable number of men in the left wing of the regiment. One of the first to fall was the captain of Company H. Captain James M. Parks was leading his men through the woods after crossing the field

---

329 (Clark, p. #18)
330 (OR, Ser. I, Pt. 1, Vol. 30, p. 728-36) (Lindsley, p. 821)
331 (OR, Ser. I, Pt. 2, Vol. 30, p. 117-21)
332 This was a section of Standart's Battery of Cruft's Brigade.

when a shower of canister whizzed through the air and impacted the ground and trees all around him and his company. He was entirely knocked off his feet by a canister ball that punched through his frock coat, tearing into his upper left breast and passed close to his heart. The captain lay on his back wheezing his breaths away when Mark Mitchell ran up to the captain and assisted him up and to the rear. The left of the regiment—shocked by the initial blast of the masked battery—at first appeared to break, but the leadership of Acting Major H. H. Dillard and the left wing officers halted the men after dropping back about 15 paces. Surprised by this initial heavy fire, General Wright immediately retracted his order for skirmishers out, and the brigade continued to advance on the left for some distance. The right wing of the Sixteenth moved forward and to the left to get out of the corn field and took up positions behind trees for immediate cover.[333]

To the Sixteenth's left, the Eighth Tennessee had advanced to within about 200 yards of the enemy line when they received the order to halt and open fire. At first they succeeded in driving the enemy back a short distance, but with the successful placement of Cruft's Brigade at the foot of the hill, the enemy fire picked up in volume and caused the Eighth to lay prone or kneel behind trees and return fire into the smoke filled woods in the direction of the enemy. Due to the heavy canister fire that the Sixteenth's left flank had received, Colonel Anderson of the 8th Tennessee at first thought the Sixteenth had retired from the field; however, the left of the regiment had only dropped back a short distance to the rear while Anderson continued forward and found himself advanced beyond the Sixteenth.[334] To the Eighth's left, the 51st Tennessee (Consolidated) had lost contact with the Eighth. Colonel Hall was unsure whether his guide was to the right or left, a point that may not have been made clear by the brigade commander. When he came under fire from the right of the 31st Indiana and the left of the 2nd Kentucky (U.S.) and learned that the brigade commander was on the left, he

[333] (OR, Ser. I, Pt. 2, Vol. 30, p. 124-25) (Head T. A., p. 271) (Thompson, p. #19)
[334] (OR, Ser. I, Pt. 2, Vol. 30, p. 122-24)

decided to maintain contact with the 28th and 38th Tennessee regiments to his left. This led Colonel Anderson to believe the 51st Tennessee had retired also, and he was standing fast on his own.[335] A short distance to the rear while positioned in the approximate middle of the brigade's line of battle, three cannoneers of Carnes' Battery were killed in the initial bursts of rifle and cannon fire. Owing to the immediate action in front, the regiments were either never ordered to make room for their battery or General Wright failed to consider them in the initial actions that afternoon.[336]

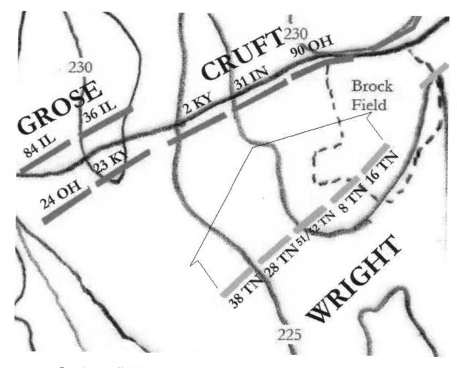

See Appendix III for Primary Area of Operations on USGS Map.

The 28th Tennessee, under Colonel Stanton, had advanced to the left of the 51st Tennessee and bumped into the Federal force only

---

[335] (OR, Ser. I, Pt. 2, Vol. 30, p. 129-30)
[336] (Lindsley, p. 821)

100 yards to their front. This regiment found itself confronting the 2nd Kentucky (U.S.). The Federals blasted a volley of fire into the ranks of the 28th Tennessee that caused them to stagger, but they pressed forward a few more yards and dropped to the ground to return fire. To the left of the 28th Tennessee, the 38th Tennessee had halted about 150 yards from the enemy lines when they commenced firing. This regiment primarily found itself engaged with the extreme left of Grose's Federal Brigade. Colonel John C. Carter had been informed by General Wright that Maney's Brigade would support his left and he halted his men and ordered them to commence firing. The regiment in their front was apparently the 23rd Kentucky (U.S.) and part of the 24th Ohio. The fire grew in ferocity all along the brigade front. Colonel Hall, with the 51st Tennessee, was in a very vulnerable position. His regiment had now become completely detached from the Eighth Tennessee to his right. The Fifty-first found itself in a sort of "open glade" that was mostly level. There was little cover for the regiment in the form of trees or underbrush. Colonel Hall knew the position was hardly tenable, but without orders to withdraw he held his position as Federal rounds continued to find their mark in his ranks.[337]

By now, Colonel Anderson and the 8th Tennessee had been under heavy fire for a considerable time. He knew the position of the Sixteenth Tennessee was to his right and still had contact with them, but he saw no sign of the 51st Tennessee to his left. Under the circumstances, Colonel Anderson immediately dispatched an officer to find the brigade commander for orders. Several minutes later, he sent another officer to locate the brigade commander in the event the first officer couldn't get through. The minutes continued to pass, and with them, the casualties grew. Finally, after a considerable amount of time he sent a third messenger to the general. All of the messengers eventually returned, but they all came back with the same response. General Wright could not be found. Colonel Anderson felt compelled to hold his position, but sent an officer off to his left to see if any force was in fact supporting him. Several minutes later

---

[337] (OR, Ser. I, Pt. 2, Vol. 30, p. 125-30)

the officer returned with bad news. There were no friendly force on the Eighth's left, but there were strong enemy forces there. The colonel made the decision to hold his position since the enemy to his left was not yet threatening him.[338]

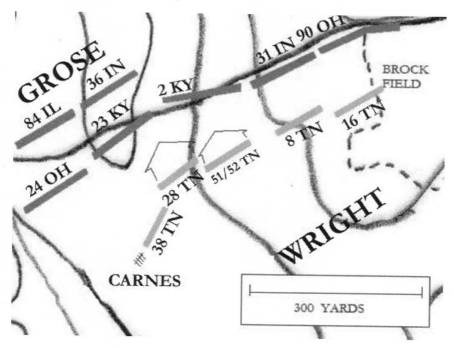

Colonel Stanton's 28th Tennessee had come under a murderous fire by the enemy in his front—primarily the 2nd Kentucky (U.S.) on the right flank of Cruft's Brigade. This had eventually forced his men back about fifty yards. With canister flying thick through the air and minie balls riddling the trees in their midst, Colonel Stanton briskly walked in front of his regiment and tried to seize the colors from the color bearer Frank Arnold, but he refused to release them. Showing cool bravery and unsurpassable gallantry, Colonel Stanton and Ensign Arnold advanced with the regiment loading and firing and regained their lost ground and nearly seventy-

---

[338] (OR, Ser. I, Pt. 2, Vol. 30, p. 122-24)

five additional yards.[339] This forced the 2nd Kentucky back alongside the 23rd Kentucky—the left regiment of Grose's Federal Brigade. The official report of the commanding officer of the 23rd Kentucky stated that he was of the belief that the Confederates had been reinforced; however, it was the sheer will power and fighting prowess of the 28th Tennessee that pushed the 2nd Kentucky back. Colonel Carter's 38th Tennessee had advanced to the left of Stanton and started to press the 24th Ohio in conjunction with Stanton. By now, Wright's Brigade had been in action no less than an hour.[340]

Finally, either by Captain Carnes' own initiative or by order—as Wright claimed—the battery was ordered to the extreme left of the brigade to take position. General Wright stated that he still expected Strahl's—and or Maney's—brigade to move to the left of the division and to his support. Maney was eventually sent in to support Jackson, and Strahl was soon to support Smith's Brigade. Thus, the intended support was never to arrive. Captain Carnes moved his battery by the left flank and to a slight elevation on the extreme left of the brigade. As Carnes wheeled his guns into action on the left of the 38th Tennessee to unlimber, they came under a murderous fire from the Federal infantry forces in their front consisting of the 24th Ohio. Within only a matter of minutes, the situation grew extremely desperate. Federal General Van Cleve's Brigade was just beginning to arrive on the field from the vicinity of Lee & Gordon's Mills.[341] Captain Carnes was in the act of wheeling his guns into position. Lieutenant L. G. Marshall recalled the scene vividly.

> The limber-chest standing open, and the team not having been reversed, the white pine of the unclosed cover raised vertically attracted hundreds of hostile infantry shots, which, passing through the wood and puncturing the outside tin, made the chest resemble a huge grater. Three or four men were endeavoring to loosen the ammunition at the same time with their heads over the chest, but strangely enough not one of

---

[339] (Lindsley, p. 431)
[340] (OR, Ser. I, Pt. 2, Vol. 30, p. 125-27)(OR, Ser. I, Pt. 1, Vol. 30, p. 792-93)
[341] (OR, Ser. I, Pt. 2, Vol. 30, p. 118) (Lindsley, p. 821)(OR, Ser. I, Pt. I, p. 821)

them was then hit. All the horses of the piece, however, except the wheel-team, were killed before the gun was discharged. The wheel-team were hit, and, springing over the roots of a large tree, turned the limber bottom upward, scattering the ammunition on the ground like a load of apples. ... Four times a minute for the first three or four minutes, at least, each gun was discharged at very short range, probably two hundred yards; but the battery was a target for the concentrated fire of both the adverse artillery and infantry...[342]

With Wright's Brigade practically split in half, and all of his regiments hunkering against the ground and around trees firing into the smoke filled woods to their front, their casualties continued to mount. Colonel Carter had lost track of the 28th Tennessee that had advanced a considerable distance to his front and right. He also noticed the reinforcements of Van Cleve's men arriving. The colonel felt compelled to warn Captain Carnes of the impending threat; and in the storm of missiles that were flying thickly through the woods, Colonel Carter, "...came walking into the battery as if for a social visit. His lavish display of coolness and his intrepidity were indeed admirable."[343]

General Wright had been in rear of the brigade since the commencement of the action. By now, he had practically lost control of the brigade. Not one regimental commander was given a direct order in person by the brigade commander. Although it was reported that General Wright had his horse shot from under him, Wright wasn't seen on the field by any of the regimental commanders, and the few orders that were delivered was done so by his staff. Unaware of the true disposition of his brigade and certain that they were hard pressed, Wright finally gave orders for the brigade to retire about a quarter mile to a hillside in their rear. At least at one point an order was sent to the 28th Tennessee to shift to the left. It had been made clear that the enemy was approaching the brigade and battery's left flank. Whether this order came from

[342] (Lindsley, pp. 821-22)
[343] Ibid.

General Wright—or Colonel Carter made contact with Colonel Stanton—is not clear, but the 28th Tennessee began to move by the left flank. This brought the regiment under a very heavy fire and more men fell killed and wounded. Now, in a hopeless situation, Wright sent messengers to the regiments to fall back to prevent being completely flanked by Van Cleve's men. Each of the regimental commanders received this message, but Colonel Carter was of the belief that he was the last to receive it, although it is likely that he had simply found himself detached alongside Carnes' Battery. The left wing of the brigade, including the 51st Consolidated likely received the order before the right wing comprised of the Eighth and Sixteenth regiments.

When the order reached Colonel Hall's 51st Tennessee, he ordered the regiment to retire to the rear. The regiment had successfully held their position for two long hours using what cover and concealment they could, but now, the nature of the movement exposed them once again to heavy fire. Colonel Hall related the retrograde in his report.

> When the order to fall back was being complied with, Color Bearer W. M. Bland, who distinguished himself at Murfreesboro for his coolness and bravery, was shot through the head and killed. The colors were immediately seized by Sergeant Troborough, but almost simultaneously with his receiving them he received a wound from one of the enemy's shots which caused him to relinquish the colors to Private Rivers, who was also wounded and assisted from the field, and the colors left.[344]

About the same time, Colonel Stanton's 28th Tennessee had received the order to move to his left flank to "meet the enemy." As they commenced this action they suddenly felt the effects of the enveloping force to the brigade's left. Beatty's Brigade—comprised of the 79th Indiana on its left—pressed relentlessly forward with a sustained fire into the front and left flank of the 28th Tennessee that

---

[344] (OR, Ser. I, Pt. 2, Vol. 30, p. 129)

190

was now standing and conducting the movement to the left. Only moments after he had commenced this movement, he received the order to withdraw. The colonel then ordered the regiment back, and they retired about 150 yards to the rear. There, they reformed and prepared for more sustained combat.[345] When the order to retire was given, the messenger requested Major Smith, of the 28th Tennessee, to deliver the order to the 8th and 16th Tennessee regiments. Wright and his entire staff had by now become dismounted and apparently Major Smith was one of the only officers of the brigade still mounted. Finally, Colonel Carter got the order to withdraw his 38th Tennessee, but not before his arrival on foot at Carnes' Battery.

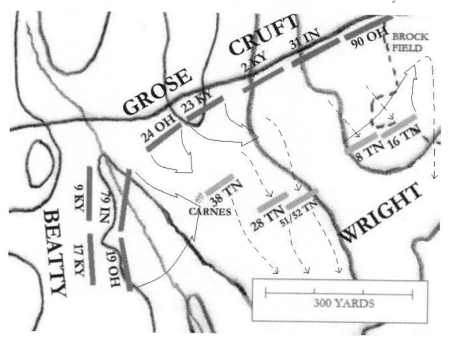

Colonel Carter had just arrived at Carnes' Battery and requested Captain Carnes to turn all his guns toward the enemy that was now plainly visible on the battery's left flank. Colonel Carter was of the opinion that, "the infantry would attend to the enemy in

---

[345] (OR, Ser. I, Pt. 2, Vol. 30, p. 125-17)

front."[346] Lieutenant Marshall recalled the situation on the left of the battery.

> The enemy, easily perceiving the odd exposure of the artillery, jumped over their works, ran behind a large fallen tree, about a hundred yards farther to the left, lying at right angles to the line of the guns, and, resting their muskets on the fallen tree, poured a heavy fire right across the battery from flank to flank. The left piece under the direction of the Captain, wheeled and gave them several shots, mainly to cover the retreat of the battery men not killed, for it was now evident that the place was untenable. Lieut. Cockrill was serving the guns of his section effectively, though only two or three men remained to each detachment. The right section was playing squarely to the front under command of Lieut. Marshall, who was on foot assisting, for by this time only two of the detachment of the right piece had escaped death or severe wounds. ... Nineteen of the men were killed dead in their places, and upward of twenty men were wounded, most of whom never resumed service in the artillery. Forty-nine horses were killed in harness.[347]

Just then, orders arrived from General Wright to fall back. Colonel Carter had—at the same time—seen that the situation was helpless.

> The situation was held about ten minutes after the infantry left us. ... When all the horses had fallen except one of the teams of the right section, the Captain gave orders to limber up the right piece and get away. The team came forward under the gallant drivers in the midst of a storm of all sorts of shot, but the six horses fell in a heap, the lead-team with their heads on the trail of the piece they were going to save. The Captain then said: "We can't save the battery; let the men leave as quick as possible." The guns were now silent. The men were all now lying on the ground, whether dead, wounded or unhurt, and

---

[346] (OR, Ser. I, Pt. 2, Vol. 30, p. 127-28)
[347] (Lindsley, p. 822)

occupying as little space as possible. Marshall called to his section to rise and follow, when he mounted his horse, which stood near hitched to a swinging limb. He mounted not very hastily, for the act seemed to challenge the enemy's fire. The latter, however, were intent on killing at first all the artillery-horses they could, and beside they were at the moment extending their flanking enterprise, and were now somewhat in rear of the battery. These two circumstances probably saved the survivors, for it was at that time quite in the power of the enemy, without danger, to pick off every one of the battery men who left the place. Thirty-five men only followed the Captain and Lieutenants from the terrible spot. The little party, instead of going to the rear, had to travel for two hundred yards across the line of the enemy's fire, as the battery was nearly surrounded before they started.[348]

On the extreme right, the Sixteenth and Eighth had found themselves in a non-stop static firefight for over two hours at this point. The 90th Ohio confronted the Sixteenth, and their force exceeded the numbers of the Sixteenth by nearly one hundred men. They lay prone or kneeling and exchanged fire continuously with the regiment. The enemy's artillery prevented an advance, but the marksmanship of the regiment paid off in the end by inflicting a few more casualties than they received.[349] To the Sixteenth's left, the Eighth confronted the 31st Indiana. They continuously held their ground exchanging shots side by side with the Sixteenth. To the right of the Sixteenth, it was now clear that Preston Smith's Brigade was in trouble. The fight had raged horribly in that direction beyond the support of Wright's Brigade. As Sergeant Clark loaded and fired, an enemy ball clipped his canteen strap which loosed his canteen and caused it to fall to the ground. He quickly reached down, grabbed it, and stuffed it into his haversack. It seemed the missiles would never

---

[348] (Lindsley, pp. 822-23)

[349] The Sixteenth suffered 68 total casualties while the 90th Ohio had 84 for both days. The Sixteenth also suffered from the effects of Standart's Battery of Cruft's Brigade.

stop. "The boys were falling killed & wounded all around. A grape shot struck a tree a little way from me and a piece of bark struck my nose a glancing lick, tearing off a lot of hide…"[350]

Private Carden was kneeling among his company when a ball tore across his cheek only a half inch from his right eye. Bleeding profusely, and unsure of the nature of the wound, Carden retired from the field to the rear. As he was in route to the infirmary corps, he heard a loud "crack!" overhead, and paused for a brief moment. Just then, a large limb fell directly in front of him from the top of a huge pine tree he was walking beneath that missed crushing him by a single step.[351] Private J. P. Smartt was struck two times during the action, but he failed to leave the field.[352] The boys had been nearly deafened by the constant roar of battle. Occasionally, Sergeant Clark would glance to his left or right to see if the line was still in position. On one glance to his left, a few steps away, "…stood Bill Payne banging away & a load of grape shot from a cannon struck the ground in front of us & flew by us like a drove of pheasants."[353]

Colonel Anderson's 8th Tennessee had held their position as long as they could, but with the arrival of heavy Federal reinforcements on their left and owing to the fact that they were basically detached from the rest of the brigade, the regiment finally found itself having to retire about 150 yards. The Sixteenth followed this movement. About that time, Colonel Donnell observed the advance of Strahl's Brigade. As neither the Eighth nor Sixteenth had received any orders after the commencement of the action, Donnell decided to move with Strahl's Brigade and informed Colonel Anderson of the same. They had just commenced their advance and only gone about 20 yards or so when Major Smith arrived on his wounded horse (struck 13 times) with the order from General Wright to retire. It is almost certain that this wing of the brigade received the order to retire last. They were ordered to move to the rear,

---

[350] (Clark, p. #19)
[351] (Carden, p. Apr. 26)
[352] (Confederate Veteran, Vol. 22, p. 517)
[353] (Clark, p. #19)

194

"...about a mile and join the balance of the brigade" to resupply their ammunition. The boys picked up and fell back after a nearly three hour hard combat.[354]

On the left of the brigade, Wright had the regiments fall back about a half mile. He had noticed the advance of Stewart's Division to his left rear. Colonel Carter ran up to Brigadier General Clayton—commanding the lead brigade—to warn him of the impending danger. Clayton's advance was more northerly than westerly, and the colonel impressed upon him the importance of changing his front. Clayton marched his men by the left flank and then filed them to the left. Wright informed Stewart of the loss of his guns, and within two more hours, thanks to Stewart and Clayton, Carnes' guns as well as the abandoned flag of the 51st Tennessee were recaptured.[355] Wright's Brigade continued for the rest of the battle without any artillery support. After resupplying their ammunition at about 5 p.m., they were ordered to move to the north, about 400 yards to the right of where they had been engaged earlier in the day. They were placed on the left of Smith's Brigade that was positioned to the left of Cleburne's command.[356] That evening at about 6:30 p.m., Smith's Brigade and Cleburne's Division made a direct assault on Federal positions to the north. Although the assault was partially successful, it resulted in the death of Brigadier General Preston Smith and large numbers of casualties in both commands.

The Sixteenth rested in place that evening and was ordered to bivouac were they were by about 7 p.m. Sergeant Clark remembered, "Night came on & we lay in line all night. ... The moans & cries of the wounded on the field between our lines during the night were terrible & pitiful, but dangerous to go to their rescue."[357] Color Sergeant J. R. Thompson recalled the silence in their front that was regularly broken by a wounded man that continued to call for "John"

---

[354] (OR, Ser. I, Pt. 2, Vol. 30, p. 123 & 124)
[355] (OR, Ser. I, Pt. 2, Vol. 30, p. 120 & 401)
[356] (OR, Ser. I, Pt. 2, Vol. 30, p. 120)
[357] (Clark, p. #19)

in their front. Eventually his cries faded away.[358] The day's fight had resulted in 68 casualties or 29% of the men engaged on the official casualty report for the Sixteenth. This number was unquestionably under reported, as had been the case for all of their engagements thus far. Colonel Donnell was among the number wounded but had failed to retire from the field either. The brigade as a whole sustained a loss about 475 casualties that afternoon. Forty-four were killed dead on the field, forty-three missing and almost four-hundred wounded—some of whom were destined to later die of their wounds or from gangrene incurred at the hospitals.[359] This battle had presented a different and unique aspect to it for the Eighth and Sixteenth regiments. The other two large fights that they had participated in took place in either open fields or light underbrush with a scattering of trees. Also, they had previously experienced a fair amount of maneuver in the other engagements. Here, at Chickamauga, they had largely fought in dense woods with heavy underbrush, favorable to defender and attacker alike. In fact after becoming engaged in their combat, neither side—Federal or Confederate—had attempted much maneuver, thus the right wing of Wright's Brigade was afforded long term cover during the contest. This was fortunate for both the Eighth and Sixteenth regiments as they had suffered more casualties than their fair share in the two previous major fights.

The exhausted boys quickly fell off into deep sleeps that were intermittently broken by the cries of wounded in their front. 1st Lieutenant White had fallen asleep under a massive oak tree located with the rest of his company. He had received a slight arm wound in the battle, but it was not serious enough to seek medical aid. He laid under the tree peering up at the half moon that began to slowly drop off to the west wondering what lay in store for tomorrow. Only yards away, Sergeant Thompson quickly fell into his slumber. That night he had a vivid dream.

I fell asleep and dreamed of being out on a lake of clear water in a round bottomed canoe which had four stanchions up, two

---

[358] (Thompson, p. 17)
[359] (OR, Ser. I, Pt. 2, Vol. 30, p. 121 & 125)

196

at each end on opposite sides and some very thin plank thrown on them. A storm arose and the waves began to roll. I decided I would climb one of the stanchions and get on the plank, but my canoe turned over and I was thrown into the lake. I began to swim very slowly and look for a place to land, but there was not a twig in sight. Presently I began to see very clearly. The water was getting shallower and finally I reached a sandbar, all safe and sound.[360]

When the boys were awoken the next morning, Thompson told of his dream to his buddies. He interpreted the dream to mean that he would survive the day's battle and come out safely. The boys made their breakfast and waited in position there until about noon when an order came for the brigade to move to the north to support Breckenridge's command.

By 1 p.m., Cheatham's Division was in position.[361] They remained prone and in line of battle for most of the afternoon. Stray shots still found their mark through the woods on an occasional basis. One man was hit while in this reserve position that afternoon. Private Gardner Green was only a few paces away from Sergeant C. H. Clark when a solid shot tore through the trees and swept away Green's leg.[362] He was quickly attended to by the litter bearers and taken to the rear. The incessant roar of artillery and musketry to their front would grow and diminish throughout the day. They waited in anxious anticipation until just about sunset. At nearly 6 p.m., two brigades of Cheatham's Division were ordered to charge the fortified line that the Confederates had failed to break all day. Maney's and Wright's Brigades gained their feet and with their wild rebel yells charged forward over the ground that Breckenridge, Walker and Cleburne's commands had pummeled away at all afternoon. The sight of a fresh, highly motivated force rushing their position caused the Federal troops under Starkweather and Baldwin to break and run to the rear. General Wright wrote that, "The men were in the highest

---

[360] (Thompson, p. 17)
[361] (OR, Ser. I, Pt. 2, Vol. 30, p. 121)
[362] (Clark, p. #19)

spirits, and moved forward with an animation that I have never seen surpassed."[363]   Only the 38th Tennessee had a few men that discharged their weapons as the enemy evacuated under the tremendous pressure so quickly. The 28th Tennessee only had three men wounded. One man—Private William Hodges of Company F—was killed and none were wounded in this final charge by the Sixteenth.[364]

After seizing the Federal breastworks, the boys were halted and reformed. Within an hour and just after sunset, they were given instructions, "…to stack arms, amid the dead and dying…"[365] Here, Captain Dillard—acting Major for the Sixteenth—recorded the scene.

Here indeed was witnessed all the dreadful "horrors of war." "Water, water!" seemed to be the universal cry of the wounded. The gray and blue were indiscriminately mixed up everywhere on the ground, and our men furnished them all alike with all the water they had, and filled canteens and kept them supplied as much as possible. From exhaustion and loss of blood they complained much of being cold. A great many fires were built all along the line, and the suffering were brought to them by the soldiers, friend and foe alike. Some that were clad in blue expressed their earnest thanks for such attention. The scene was sad indeed and pitiable. Some talked of their loved wives and children, others were calling for their mothers. Some were praying, some were dying; while the rough, stern soldiers, with hands and faces all black with powder, pitying, stood in groups about them. It was a moonlight night. I rambled about a good deal over the field where we were, and the havoc was frightful. The woods were full of branches and tops of trees, like a heavy storm had just passed through. Some trees more than a foot through were cut down by cannon balls. The underbrush was shorn off to the ground. One man was squatted by the side of

---

[363] (OR, Ser. I, Vol. 30, Pt. 2, p. 121)
[364] (Head T. A., p. 121)
[365] (Dillard, p. 342)

198

a tree with his gun up, resting against it, cocked and aiming toward the log breastworks about fifty yards off. His head was leaning forward; he was shot through about the heart. He was a Confederate. Another was lying on his face with one hand grasping his gun just below the muzzle and the rammer in his other hand. Another lay on his back with both hands clinched in his long, black, whiskers, all clotted with blood. He was shot in the mouth, and I think a federal lieutenant. About five feet off was another, with his head gone. I came across a soldier leaning down over one that was dead, and as I approached him he was in the act of spreading a handkerchief over his face. He looked up at me, and said: "This is my Captain, and a good one too. I want to send him home if I can." I think he was a Georgian. I saw a good many looking over the dead for a comrade, and when identified would straighten him out, put a knapsack or chunk under his head, and lay a hat on his face; then perhaps cast their eyes up and around for some peculiar tree or cliff or hill by which to identify the spot in coming back. Here you might see a caisson with the ammunition box nearly or quite empty, there a gun with its carriage torn to pieces, here a field horse dead with saddle on; and in one pile I counted sixteen horses literally piled up together, some in their death plunges having jumped astride of those dead. They belonged to the artillery, and were in full harness, having been loosed from the guns during the action. In another place twelve were in a pile, and so on. … I turned and went back, lay down under a tree and fell asleep, listening to the humming, dull roar that pervaded the heavens everywhere above our camping victorious army.[366]

That night after stacking arms and conducting head counts, Sergeant Thompson and E. L. Atnip went in search of water. They were able to find their way quite easily to Chickamauga Creek and filled several canteens with cold water. Upon filling the last of the canteens, they turned back to find the regiment which proved to be much harder

---

[366] (Dillard, pp. 342-43)

than locating the water. After wandering much of the battlefield and becoming completely disoriented, the two finally lay down to rest their weary bodies. They stopped at a light breastwork that had been constructed and set afire by the bursting of a shell. The night had turned quite cold, and the two lay down next to the burning log to fall asleep.[367]

---

[367] (Thompson, p. 18)

Chapter IX

Aftermath of Battle and Detached to Charleston

21 September – 23 November 1863

The night wore slowly by. Eventually, the fire that Atnip and Thompson had fallen asleep by burned itself out. Exhausted and nearly freezing, the semi-conscious Atnip pulled a blanket onto his body and dozed off under the stars. At the first sign of light, Private Atnip woke to a heavy frost that had covered the ground. He and Sergeant Thompson had spent the night alone after becoming disoriented the night before. Atnip thought they were alone anyway, until he woke to find the blanket that he had pulled onto himself during the night was actually covering a dead Yankee. The two found that they had wandered to the southern end of the battlefield. They quickly set off to the north to locate the regiment and found the boys by about 8 a.m. Their travels took them nearly the length of the battlefield, and Thompson recalled that, "Dead men, horses, and artillery wagons broken by cannon shot, timber cut and scarred, and general destruction marked everything."[368] The army stayed in position until about 2 p.m. that afternoon, and then Cheatham's Division took the advance. That night the division camped in the vicinity of the Mission House. On the morning of the

---

[368] (Thompson, pp. 16-17)

22nd, the division reached Missionary Ridge by about 10 a.m., and Maney's Brigade and Smith's old brigade—now commanded by A. J. Vaughn—pushed back the Federal forces in a brief exchange of fire. That afternoon the Federal troops withdrew into the breastworks that the boys had so diligently constructed only weeks before. The regiment and brigade arrived at the western foot of Missionary Ridge in sight of Chattanooga and traveled about five and a half miles up the ridge by the end of the day. Arriving in the vicinity of Shallow Ford, they stayed on picket until the morning of the 3rd of October.[369]

After a ten day stretch on picket duty, the boys were relieved to get a break from the front lines. Word had made it to the regiment on the 24th of September that Captain Parks had died of his wounds. Many of the men in the regiment were disappointed to learn that he had passed—especially those from Company H. Quarter Master Sergeant Roysdon Etter entered into his diary, "We mourn his loss and his place canot be filled with a better man."[370] Thomas Head also recorded his recollections of James Parks.

...Captain Parks was much respected for his upright, exemplary life, and for his many sterling qualities, both as a gentleman and a soldier. ... Captain Parks was in every respect a worthy young man. Kind and respectful to all, he won the good will and respect of all who knew him. His daily walk and conversation was without spot or blemish. Upright, circumspect, and conscientious in all things, he possessed the respect and confidence of his superiors, as well as those who were under his command. ... When he entered the army, those Christian graces which he cherished with so much prayerful care in his previous life never yielded to the temptations of army life.[371]

---

[369] (Evans E. G., p. 111) (Clark, p. #19) (Sullivan, p. 103)
[370] (Etter, p. 22)
[371] (Head T. A., p. 271)

Captain Parks was buried near the field hospital not far from where he was wounded at Brock Field.[372] Oddly only one man had been killed in action—on the second day of battle nonetheless. A few others would not recover from their wounds. James M. Cope and Gardner Green of Company K soon found themselves occupying beds alongside one another in a hospital near Cassville, Georgia. Green had lost his leg to a cannon ball, while Cope lost his leg by surgical amputation due to a gunshot wound to the left thigh.[373]

Private R. C. Carden had gone to the hospital on the first day of battle after being wounded in the face. A facial wound could be frightening in itself. He was just a young man – unmarried. A Confederate soldier of Longstreet's command with a foot wound painted a vivid picture of the field hospital scene witnessed by every soldier that was slightly wounded or worse.

> When I arrived at the field infirmary it was dark and there was straw for bedding. I was put in about fifty feet from the operating table, with a few others between me and it. I lay there all night, bleeding slowly, as my wound was not of a nature that required immediate attention. Near the table, but not in line, was a stout young man who was shot through the head. From the sides the brain could be seen oozing out. He seemed to be suffering greatly and would rise, make a step or two, and fall. He repeated this time and time again for quite a while after daylight. I don't know what hour he was brought in, but I thought how brutal human custom was in this particular, and wondered if it was handed down from barbarism and why it was that doctor or friend could not end one's misery, even if done with the best method at hand and that was only a rock or a club.[374]

---

[372] After the war, his father—Carroll Parks—removed his body from the battlefield and his remains were reinterred at Hebron in Warren County.
[373] (Compiled Service Records)
[374] (Fletcher, pp. 100-101)

Carden and the others at the field hospital had certainly witnessed similar scenes. After a few days in the hospital, Carden complained that he felt the authorities there tried to starve the soldiers so they would want to go back to their regiments. It was during his stay that he decided to leave the hospital in search of food.

> I sauntered out to where some citizens were selling things that a hungry soldier likes and there I did one of the meanest tricks I was guilty of during the war. I never have felt just right about it to this good day. While I was standing around seeing others buying and eating I saw a woman selling half moon pies. She had an old horse and buggy and I walked up to her and said, "Madam, do you see that man walking off there?" pointing to a fellow about twenty steps away. She said she did and I said, "That fellow stole a lot of your pies." She went after him, and as soon as she started I commenced to pile half moon pies into my bosom. I stored away my goods and by the time she got through with the fellow I had business somewhere else..."[375]

Others were a lot more fortunate. Hamilton M. Hennessee of Company D had been wounded two times in his left leg on the first day of the battle. After a brief stop at the field hospital, he went by rail to Dalton, Georgia where he had an aunt that carefully nursed him back to health with food plentiful.[376] On September 26th, Carden was released from the hospital and returned to the Sixteenth. The next day he returned to the battlefield as he was still unfit for full duty. As he walked along, he was astonished to see that they Yankee soldiers had still not been buried. "The bodies were swollen so one could hardly see that they were men. They were actually as large as a horse." As large as a horse may have been exaggerating, but as the bodies decomposed and the gases in their bodies continued to build, the skin blackened and eventually the corpse would leak away the fluids or in some cases literally pop open spraying the area around them with decomposed flesh and fluids. The stench was unfathomable and unforgettable. One of the most bothersome

---

[375] (Carden, p. May 3)
[376] (Confederate Pension Applications)

things to Carden was the stacks of rifles that had been gathered after the battle. All of the weapons lost to killed and wounded men of both sides were, "...stacked up like cord wood." He didn't measure the length of the stacks but estimated them to be seventy-five yards each.[377]

On September 30th, the eight week long drought was broken by a steady rain that continued through October 1st. When the boys came in from picket on the 3rd, they were still filthy from the hard marching and fighting over a week earlier. The Sixteenth stayed in position here until the afternoon of October 16th. On the 4th of October, Quartermaster Sergeant Roysdon Etter visited his Aunt Polly who lived on Lookout Mountain. From that vantage, he was able to take in the whole scene. He could easily distinguish their breastworks and forts and found them to be very strongly fortified. Of course, many of these works had been started by the rebels themselves. On October 6th there was a heavy frost, and the next day the rain commenced again until the 8th. Two days later, the regiment returned from picket duty and was ordered to wash their clothing in preparation for the arrival of the President of the Confederate States of America. Rumors of foreign intervention had abounded since the victory at Chickamauga, and most of the army was enthusiastic.[378]

It was about this time that Colonel Savage made a visit to Marietta, Georgia. He learned that the army had been positioned atop Missionary Ridge and spoke in harsh terms of Bragg's competence to command the army. He felt very strongly that the position was untenable in the event the enemy tried to force them from the ridge. As he had stated in West Virginia, Savage was certain that the army would have to expose themselves to the enemy in order to shoot as they advanced up the ridgeline and silhouette themselves against the skyline. He believed in the concept of dominating key terrain but not the defense of such from its apex. When he learned that Jefferson Davis was visiting the army, he was sure that the Commander in Chief would advise the commanding general to

---

[377] (Carden, p. May 3)
[378] (Sullivan, p. 103) (Head T. A., p. 122)

relocate the position of his forces to a more advantageous defensive position.[379]

After delivering a stirring speech to that portion of the army that could be pulled from the lines on the evening of October 11th, the President returned to Richmond. The position of the army was left unchanged, and this furthermore added to Savage's belief that they were fighting a war that could not be won under the current leadership. The next day a steady rain began and continued until the 16th. On the 15th, the bridge over Chickamauga Creek had washed away and separated the regiment from the supply wagons of the brigade. The water rose so high, that the brigade wagon train had to be moved about a mile the same day. The roads had turned to mush and wagon passage was nearly impossible. It rained at least two more times in the next week on the 18th and the 23rd. The boys had begun constructing breastworks once again; only this time they confronted Chattanooga.[380]

They awoke to a heavy frost on the morning of the 19th. That same day, the Federal army heavily shelled the point of Lookout Mountain. Etter distributed a small amount of clothing to the regiment on the 22nd of October, and the following day, General Wright received orders from army headquarters to move his brigade to Charleston, Tennessee. The brigade marched to Tyner's Station that afternoon and boarded trains for the trek. They arrived in Charleston that afternoon. The brigade ambulances and wagon trains remained behind until the 29th when they moved out to Cleveland, Tennessee about eleven miles southwest of Charleston. The next day they continued on to Charleston and arrived there by 7 a.m. The brigade was tasked with rebuilding the bridge over the Hiawassee River and guarding the line of communication between Knoxville and Chattanooga. The time spent at Charleston was quite leisure. The boys had little to do other than forage for food and provide the security that they had been posted there for.

---

[379] (Savage, The Life of John H. Savage, pp. 146-47)
[380] (Savage, The Life of John H. Savage, p. 147) (Etter, p. 19)

Colonel Donnell had been wounded at Chickamauga and had also suffered from poor health throughout several of the last few months. Often, he was too ill to retain command, and regularly, Captain Ben Randals would assume command of the regiment in his absence. Although Lt. Col. D. T. Brown was second in command, he too suffered from ailments that often kept him bedridden. Captain Dillard had acted in the capacity of regimental major at Chickamauga but had now returned to the Conscription Bureau. Ben Randals was up to the task. He managed the regiment regularly for the next few months and learned the role of a regimental commander and his responsibilities to the boys of the regiment. Now was the time when he made an impression on them that enabled him to lead them with confidence and efficiency when the time came. By November 6th, nearly all of the more slightly wounded from the battle of Chickamauga were returning to the ranks. That day, Sergeant Major Tom Potter was released from the hospital at Cassville, Georgia. He arrived in Charleston on the 8th.[381]

Since the brigade was operating by itself about thirty-five miles from Chattanooga and the rest of the army, it was left to forage for food on its own. Many of the boys often went to foraging for themselves by roaming the countryside and killing hogs, sheep and chickens without owners' consent. After Captain Randals had received several complaints from nearby families, he began to regularly send guards to protect their private property. 3rd Sergeant C. H. Clark was asked to guard the home of Mrs. Bates who lived nearby. Over the next few weeks he made a close association with the family and they treated him very nicely.[382] Official foraging parties would scour the land and pay for the sustenance that they obtained from nearby farmers. On November 6th while on one of these expeditions in this mostly Unionist section of the country, one of the men of the foraging party was shot and killed by a Unionist bushwhacker. Although the parties went out armed, it was random

---

[381] (Compiled Service Records) (Potter, p. 3)
[382] (Clark, p. #20)

ambushes that inflicted the most damage on men and morale.[383] One afternoon in early November, Sergeant Thompson got a pass for himself and W. L. Ludkin—a messmate of his—to go to the country and get some milk.

> We came to a good gristmill owned by a man named Cleveland. Two cavalrymen were ready to take the man's fine team of oxen... I asked them by whose authority they proposed to take the team. They said by their own authority. I answered them, "By your authority, you cannot take them." Then they said by order of the Quartermaster. I answered and told him to show his written order and I had not one word to say. They had no order. I saved his team, and he gave us a splendid dinner.[384]

The remainder of the time spent at Charleston was consumed by picket duty and drill. Doubtless, the regiment and brigade had by now heard of the rumors of the resignation of their beloved division commander—Frank Cheatham. When the War Department failed to accept his resignation, General Bragg reorganized his division to contain only the Tennessee regiments of Wright's Brigade and it was temporarily under the command of the Georgian, John K. Jackson. Additionally, their corps commander—the much loved Leonidas Polk—had been transferred and they now fell under the command of Lieutenant General Hardee. The esprit de corps so long experienced by the Tennesseans since May of 1862 had now been fractured. By November 17th, more constant cannonading was heard in the direction of Chattanooga. Only six days later on October 23rd, the Federal army—now under the command of Ulysses S. Grant—advanced from their positions at Chattanooga and seized Orchard Knob in front of Missionary Ridge. That afternoon, orders were received from the commanding general by General Wright to return with the balance of his command to Missionary Ridge.[385]

---

383 (Etter, p. 20)
384 (Thompson, p. 18)
385 (Losson, p. 118 & 121) (Etter, p. 20)(OR, Ser. I, Pt. 2, Vol. 31, p. 706)

The brigade immediately broke camp and loaded their camp equipage into the wagon trains. The infantry was marched to the depot at Charleston to await the train that would transport them back to Chickamauga Station while the wagon train waited for morning to commence the movement. Wright was also ordered to retain one regiment at the Hiawassee Bridge. Colonel Carter's 38th Tennessee was chosen for the task of securing the bridge in the event Longstreet's command—that had been sent to Knoxville in early November—returned to the Army of Tennessee.[386] The boys prepared themselves for expected combat once again with high hopes of ending the war, but the blunders of their commanding general would once again affect the outcome of an important battle.

---

[386] (Civil War Centtennial Commission, p. 258)

Chapter X

Action at Chickamauga Creek and Missionary Ridge

24 – 26 November 1863

By mid-morning, the Eighth, Sixteenth, Twenty-Eighth Consolidated and Fifty-first Consolidated Tennessee regiments had boarded the train bound for Chickamauga Station. The progress was relatively slow and the train arrived at the station by about noon.[387] Although Wright's Brigade fell under the divisional command of Brigadier General John K. Jackson, the rest of the division and its commander had been placed in position for the defense of Lookout Mountain. The urgency of the situation called for immediate action on the right of the Confederate line that was the most lightly secured. Initially, the brigade acted under orders from the commanding general himself, but by the end of the day, the brigade was indirectly under the command of Major General Patrick R. Cleburne and directly under Brigadier General Lucius Polk.

Immediately upon their arrival, the brigade had been ordered to "proceed at once" to the mouth of the Chickamauga "to resist any

---

[387] (Potter)

attempt the enemy might make at crossing the Tennessee River at that point."[388] Colonel Donnell was not completely well, but he was intent on leading his men into any potential fight. None of the field officers of the brigade were mounted except for General Wright as the remaining horses of the brigade were still being transported from Charleston. Wright informed his regimental commanders of the orders, and at about 2 p.m., they commenced the advance toward the Harrison Road on the north side of Chickamauga Creek and toward its mouth that emptied into the Tennessee River. He was ordered to leave one regiment to guard the railroad bridge and Shallow Ford about a mile and a half northwest of the station. This task was given to the 51st & 52nd Tennessee Consolidated. The remaining three regiments marched down the north side of the creek with the 8th Tennessee in the lead, followed by the Sixteenth and finally the 28th Tennessee.[389]

General Bragg had already informed General Cleburne—who was moving into position at Tunnel Hill—that the Federal army already had a division on an eminence in his front. General Wright had received the same information and his route would take him alongside and perhaps beyond the Federal force now known to be on the south side of the creek. By about 3:30 p.m., the brigade was marching up the Harrison Road less than two and a half miles from the mouth of the creek.

I came into a road running parallel and adjacent to the Chickamauga on the margin of open fields, which gently sloped up toward a line of precipitous hills on the right. It was a very exposed position, but the road passing through this space was the only one practicable for artillery in the direction of the mouth of the creek. Capt. R. F. Kolb, with his battery, had reported to me at the railroad bridge for duty and was with my command.[390]

---

388 (OR, Ser. I, Pt. 2, Vol. 31, p. 706-08)
389 (OR, Ser I, Pt. 2, Vol. 31, p. 711, 715-16)
390 (OR, Ser. I, Pt. 2, Vol. 31, p. 706-08)

The column of regiments was marching four men abreast up the road with little knowledge of the enemy situation when a few random shots were fired from their left less than a hundred yards away. Next—within seconds—a terrific fire was opened with rifles followed by the blast of a masked battery of artillery that was hidden in defilade behind a railroad embankment on the opposite side of the creek. Inexplicably, General Wright had either forgotten to order the regiments to load their rifles or had just expected them to do so without orders. The brigade had suddenly found itself in the midst of an ambush.[391]

At least one unidentified member of the brigade recalled that, "We were marched right along into close contact with the enemy without heed to repeated warnings which were given to our commander."[392] General Wright referred to this as, "...a galling fire" from the opposite side of the creek. The Federal infantry had hidden in the underbrush along the south side of the creek and allowed the whole column to come into range before revealing their position.[393] In the initial burst of rifle fire, nine members of the Sixteenth were struck. Lafayette Clark was instantly killed while eight others were wounded—four seriously. The regiments quickly faced to the left and loaded as they advanced to a staked and rider fence. Private Henry Tate was on the color guard with Color Sergeant J. R. Thompson. Thompson saw that Tate was shocked by the sudden excitement and showed signs of breaking. Tate, "...jumped up and his eyes were spread as if he were excited. I took him by the arm and shook him, and said to him, 'Nobody scared here but you, Henry.' It calmed him at once." Some of the boys had hopped over a fence just on the right side of the road for cover and commenced firing. The fence was strangled with briers that added to the annoyance of the situation.[394] The whole of the brigade returned fire long enough to force the enemy infantry from the brush and to the cover of their

---

[391] (Thompson, p. 18)
[392] (Confederate Veteran, Vol. 1, p. 377)
[393] (OR, Ser. I, Pt. 2, Vol. 31, p. 706-08)
[394] (Thompson, pp. 18-19)

railroad embankment. But not without the Eighth and Twenty-Eighth regiments losing three men wounded—each.

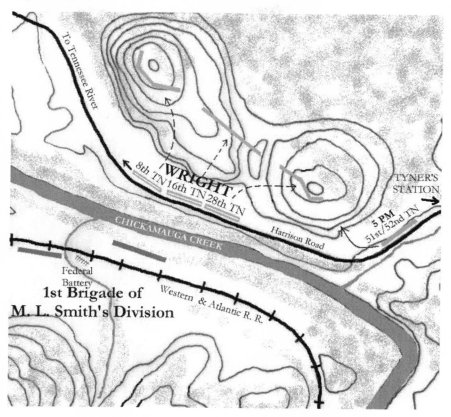

General Wright turned his horse away from the front of the column, and while passing to the rear, he told Colonel Anderson and the Eighth Tennessee to retire by the left flank—back up the road from where they had just advanced. He then galloped off to the rear towards Kolb's Battery. Colonel Anderson was puzzled at the general's order. If they retreated back up the road from which they came, they would continue to be under the fire of the enemy guns for four to five hundred yards. Anderson then took the initiative. Only two hundred or so yards to their rear (or north of their position) two dominant hills could afford protection and observation for the brigade. He immediately ordered the regiments to retire to the rear by the right of companies which was done without artillery fire being concentrated on them.   General Wright—had indeed—gone to Kolb's Battery and instructed them to open fire. They unlimbered at least one gun and got off two shots before Wright had him limber up and rejoin the remainder of the brigade that had sought the protection of the hills north of their position.   There, a section of Kolb's guns unlimbered and continued a brisk duel with a section of the enemy's 3" rifled guns firing seventeen more rounds.[395]

As Wright had apparently retired some distance to the left rear of the brigade, he was approached by Colonel Grigsby, commanding a cavalry detachment, and informed that Federal cavalry had already crossed the Tennessee River above the mouth of Chickamauga Creek.   The colonel believed their destination to be Tyner's Station. Wright was already apprehensive at the detachment of two of his regiments. Apparently—General Wright—still the only officer mounted in the brigade—left his command to order up the 51st Tennessee.   Whether he actually went to the rear to order the command up to the rest of the brigade is uncertain, but when he reached the vicinity of Shallow Ford he saw that Lucius Polk's Brigade was guarding the ford and bridge. He immediately sent the 51st Tennessee forward, and they approached the extreme left of the brigade just after sunset. Apparently, Wright stayed at or near the ford and bridge.[396]

As the light faded, the Fifty-First advanced up the lane that the brigade had moved along earlier in the day.   The Federal forces saw the approach of the lone regiment, and a spattering of gunfire was sent in their direction inflicting no harm. By the time the Fifty-First arrived, Grigsby's Cavalry detachment was supporting the right of the brigade and Colonel Anderson was currently in command of the brigade. They occupied two hills with the 8th Tennessee on the right, the Sixteenth in the saddle between the hills and the 28th Tennessee on the left nearest the creek. Spencer Talley, of the 28th Tennessee, sat on the elevation and observed the scene in his front.

---

[395] (OR, Ser. I, Pt. 2, Vol. 31, p. 706-08, 712, 716)
[396] (OR, Ser. I, Vol. 31, Pt. 2, p. 715)

No attack was made on our position, and we had nothing to do but watch the contending forces on both sides from our splendid view point. It was the first and only battle I ever had the privilege of witnessing the maneuver of both sides. We could see the Yanks with solid columns marching on our one little long spun line reaching from the river to Lookout Mountain.[397]

The brigade rested atop the hills until after nightfall. At about 9 p.m., the commanding general sent orders to General Wright to move to Chickamauga Station. General Wright was quite ill by this time and whether he was present with the brigade at this time or not is uncertain. The brigade received the order and commenced the movement arriving at the station around 10:30 p.m. Word had arrived that a potential cavalry raid may take place. General Wright was advised to position his brigade for the defense of the station. He found three batteries of artillery and had them put in position for an effective defense.[398]

By 2 a.m. the morning of November 25th, an order arrived for the brigade to move to the railroad bridge a mile north. Now, General Wright—suffering from a severe chill—had apparently become completely incapable of performing his duty. He officially relinquished the brigade command to Colonel Anderson. Anderson quickly relayed the orders and the brigade stepped off in the moonlight toward the bridge. When they arrived near the bridge, Colonel Anderson reported to General Lucius Polk for duty. The general instructed him to form the brigade on the crest of a hill 200 yards below the bridge. He was also instructed to detach one regiment to a commanding hill 300 yards further downstream. The 28th Tennessee was detached to the distant hilltop while the remainder of the brigade deployed onto the nearby hill. The boys tripped their way through the moonlit woods and moved into position. They were additionally instructed to fortify their positions, and they quickly went to work constructing breastworks. By 5 a.m.,

---

[397] (Talley, Pt. 4)
[398] (OR, Ser. I, Pt. 2, Vol. 31, p. 708)

the boys had managed to erect ample defenses. Finally, the boys were able to get a short period of rest. They sat in this location through the hazy morning and could only hear the sounds of actions beginning to develop in Cleburne's front about a mile west of their position.[399]

Quarter Master Sergeant Roysdon Etter had left Charleston early on the morning of the 24th with the brigade wagon train. They made fairly good time considering the condition of the roads and were able to travel until 9 p.m. owing to a full moon that had risen that evening. The train stopped for the night just north of Ooltewah after having traveled over 20 miles in the course of the day. The wagon masters were fast asleep when they were awoken with urgent information at 2 a.m. on the morning of the 25th. Yankee cavalry was reported to be very nearby. At 3 a.m., the whole train moved out, and by about 7:30 a.m., they had crossed a very steep ridge and descended to Ooltewah. Initially they were traveling toward Tyner's Station, but reports had come in that Yankee cavalry had already raided that place. The brigade quartermaster decided to detour the wagon train south on to the Ringgold Road. At 8 a.m., another report came that Yankee cavalry was very near at hand, and the wagon masters whipped the mules to move at a frenzied pace. The roads had been good enough up to this point, but shortly after turning south onto the Ringgold Road, they found it to be a quagmire of mud. Just south of Ooltewah, some of the lead wagons began to bog down in the mud. Etter found himself near the end of the column and had to halt awaiting the movement of the wagons in his front. As wagon masters hopped down to push the wagons out of the mud, "…the Yankees came in full sail – sword in hand." The 3rd Ohio Cavalry of Long's Federal Brigade had swooped down on the column. There was a small detachment of armed guards for the wagon train, but all knew it would be a futile attempt to try and save it. Within moments, the wagon masters and guards had run into the woods that blanketed both sides of the road. Many of them were run down and captured, but a large number were able to make their

---

[399] (OR, Ser. I, Pt. 2, Vol. 31, p. 710, 714)

escape. Etter ran into the woods and hid in a pine thicket. He lay there helplessly watching the Federal troopers plunder the personal clothing and equipage of the entire brigade. They raided General Wright's personal baggage and took one of his dress frock coats adorned with lace and gold gilt. They additionally located the flag of Company E's "Warren Guards" and took it as a trophy. Once they had gathered all they wanted, they set fire to the wagon train and galloped away. Etter waited about an hour or so after their departure and then sauntered out to the wreckage. In all—52 wagons were destroyed with all the documents and equipment of the entire brigade. He picked through the wreckage and took the few items not destroyed by the fire including some cooking utensils and walked to the nearest house. It was the home of a Mr. Blackburn; he allowed Etter to stay the night.[400]

Back at Missionary Ridge by 11 a.m., the boys heard the start of heavy fighting on Tunnel Hill in their front. They were anxious as to what the outcome might be. About two hours later, General Polk ordered the brigade to advance down the creek about a half mile below the bridge. There, they occupied a range of hills perpendicular to the creek and became a prolongation of the left of Polk's Brigade. The 28th Tennessee was on the left—their left resting on the creek—followed by the 51st Tennessee and Scoggins' Battery on an eminence in the center then the Eighth and Sixteenth on the right. During and after their movement to the ridge, they could hear and see some of the heavy fighting taking place on Tunnel Hill between Sherman's Divisions and Cleburne's command. At 4 p.m., an order from the commanding general came to Colonel Anderson that instructed him to leave one regiment to occupy the most dominant hill and move immediately to the bridge at Shallow Ford some two miles away. Unknown to the boys in the brigade, the Confederate center on Missionary Ridge had given way. The 28th Tennessee was designated to stay behind. Anderson was instructed to, "…resist the enemy to the last extremity, and hold the position until I was satisfied that all

---

[400] (Etter, p. 20) (Crofts, p. 122)

the troops had passed over, and then to effectually destroy the bridge and bring up the rear."[401]

The brigade moved rapidly to the bridge at Shallow Ford. As soon as Colonel Anderson arrived two batteries of artillery reported to him. He placed them both in commanding positions half-way between the bridge and the ford. The three regiments under his immediate control were displaced according to topography to resist any attempt by the enemy to gain the position. The rout of Confederate positions at Missionary Ridge had commenced. When they arrived, many troops were already streaming to the rear, but the realization of the situation sank deeply in as they watched unorganized mobs of weary soldiers passing to the rear for hours on end. The 51st Tennessee had been placed in position to command the ford, while the 8th and 16th Tennessee regiments held positions near the bridge. As darkness fell, Colonel Anderson dispatched a small force across the creek to observe enemy movements and gather straggling soldiers. The day had proven a disaster except for on the extreme Confederate right flank.[402]

By midnight, the last of Cleburne's command crossed the bridge and Colonel Anderson ordered the bridge to be fired, but the timbers were too green to burn. He quickly ordered up axes that the boys put to good use by chopping the timbers down. The process took fully two hours. At 2 a.m., orders came to destroy the bridge if it hadn't already been done and move to Chickamauga Station to rejoin the division one and a half miles away. So as it was, the brigade was the absolute rear guard of the army and provided security at the crossing of the bridge until the last of the effective forces of Cleburne's command had crossed over. It was now November 26th and the boys had worked almost nonstop for nearly fifty-six hours. By 3 a.m., they had arrived at the station and fell back under the command of their broken division. The Sixteenth and the rest of the brigade moved on toward Dalton throughout the remainder of the day and bivouacked that night in the vicinity of Ringgold Gap. At

---

[401] (OR, Ser. I, Pt. 2, Vol. 31, p. 710-11)
[402] (OR, Ser. I, Pt. 2, Vol. 31, p. 715)

sunset on the 25th, Etter had left the safety of Mr. Blackburn's house and set off on foot toward Ringgold. About the same time that the Sixteenth was destroying the bridge at Shallow Ford, Etter met up with Colonel Benjamin Hill's 35th Tennessee near Catoosa Springs— just east of Ringgold. Cleburne's Division continued to bring up the rear of the army and halted to camp on the west bank of East Chickamauga Creek at about 10 p.m. that night.[403]

---

[403] (OR, Ser. I, Pt. 2, Vol. 31, p. 715) (Etter, pp. 20-21)

Chapter XI

Dalton

27 November – 31 December 1863

On November 27th, the brigade arrived at Dalton. Cleburne's Division defended Ringgold Gap from a vastly superior force at Taylor's Ridge in an engagement that had started early in the morning. The army and its trains were now safe, and the Federal army showed no signs of renewing offensive actions. That night was cold and stormy. The boys found it nearly impossible to even light a fire. At 9 p.m. that night, Etter finally found the regiment. They spent a miserable night contemplating the loss of Tennessee once again. The next day the division's camp site was selected, and the regiment was located about three miles southeast of Dalton. Within days, it had become clear that the Federal army had chosen to rest for the winter and likewise the Confederates. They had no tents, were low on supplies and many of the boys were shoeless. In the first week of December word came down that General Bragg had resigned his position and General Joseph E. Johnston was taking command of the Army of Tennessee. One member of the 28th Tennessee remarked, "This change was pleasing and gratifying to the Southern army. The boys thought, "...what "Old Joe" didn't know about handling an army wasn't worth much." By December 7th, they were ordered to establish winter quarters, and they began erecting cabins for their stay at Dalton. The next day orders came to move their campsite, and after clearing the ground, they moved on the 9th of December. They chopped down trees and constructed logs cabins, "…daubed with mud & made chimneys of wood and clay."[404]

> Comest the chimney work all day hard. At night we have us a nice hous everything is complet everything looks nice. Our bed is composed of some chestnut that we have made – we have raised it up off of the ground coverd it over with sage grass. We have got a big fire – took our seet before it and feel with great obligation to our Heavenly father for giving us the comfortable dweling that I now sit in. Those that enjoy the cabin with is Bill – A D. Ware – David Miller – W. H. Russel[405]

It took Etter and his pards three days to finish construction of their home. The whole army was lacking in sustenance at this time. A few days earlier, Etter had purchased mutton for the boys to eat at the inflated cost of ten dollars, but it was still the cheapest price they had paid. They still suffered from inadequate rations through the majority of December.

R. C. Carden had twice been promoted to corporal, but owing to his adolescent antics, he had twice been reduced to private. Now, he was promoted to 3rd corporal once again. One night he was placed on guard with a half dozen privates. He was instructed to see that nothing was disturbed at the army's wood shed and water tank at the Dalton depot. As they pulled duty, Carden noticed a soldier that was waiting for the train to pull in to collect a jug of whiskey that he had ordered. One of the privates spied a bottle of whiskey that the fellow had in his pocket and informed Carden. The man eventually dozed off next to a fire, and when he started snoring, one of the boys tried to ease it out of his pocket. Unsuccessful, Carden then tried his hand at it. Soon, the bottle was freed and they "…went out in the

---

[404] (Clark, p. #20) (Etter, p. 21) (Talley, p. Pt. 4)
[405] (Etter, p. 21)

dark and tanked up on it." The same night, he managed to haul off a sack of apples that a citizen had entrusted him with.[406]

On December 14th, the brigade was still reported under the command of Colonel Anderson. Since Wright's illness on the 26th of November, the general had not returned to his command. One of the brigade's members later wrote, "The next we heard of him he was commanding the Post at Atlanta, a post we were willing he should fill, as it gave us a brigade commander."[407] Now, the Sixteenth was reported under the command of Captain Randals, and Colonel Donnell's failing health was certain to become an issue. The regiment reported 918 men present and absent[408] with 212 men actually present for duty. However, the regiment only had 157 serviceable rifles which limited their effective total to 157 men ready for action. This left 55 men to act in the capacity of regimental wagon masters, infirmary corps, ordinance and any other regimental responsibility. Although no reports were filed for 'captured' following the retreat from Missionary Ridge, a considerable number of men had been uninformed of the withdraw on the night of the 25th of November. This led to a no less than 56 men being captured that belonged to the Sixteenth. The boys that had not been captured with the wagon train were captured where they had been left to guard various fords in the vicinity of Chickamauga Creek.[409]

Owing to the losses incurred at both Chickamauga and Missionary Ridge, elections were held on December 23rd to fill vacancies.[410] At least one officer position was vacant and several

---

[406] (Etter, p. 21) (Carden, p. May 10)

[407] (Confederate Veteran, Vol. I, p. 377)

[408] The number of Present and Absent included all men who were in the hospital sick or wounded, all men recovering at home from wounds, all men absent without leave, all men still reported to be prisoners of war, and all men on any special or detached duty. This number did not reflect any men who had been killed in battle or died of wounds or disease.

[409] (OR, Ser. I, Pt. 3, Vol. 31, p. 823)

[410] (Compiled Service Records) 2nd Lieutenant James R. Fisher was promoted to 1st Lieutenant in Company G.

noncommissioned officer positions. About this time, Captain Randals was informed by his superiors that soldiers were once again raiding the countryside stealing chickens, hogs and other livestock to feed themselves and messmates. In response, orders were issued to place guards at nearby residences for the protection of their property. C. H. Clark was posted as a guard at the home of A. C. Leeks on the Conasauga River for such protection. The family treated him well and he made the acquaintance of all the family members. Mr. Leek was "quite well to do" and owned a big farm. One morning, Clark went out to inspect the barn lot and noticed that, "...5 or 6 geese were missing, and I knew had been taken by soldiers, but did not know what part of the army had taken them, whether Tennesseans or Georgians or from other states." Later that afternoon, Clark returned to camp to check on the boys and, "I found to my surprise, Mrs. Leek's geese snugly quartered in my regiment being stuffed with dough." When Clark made mention of the matter, several of the boys quickly snapped that he ought, "keep my mouth shut." Clark decided that it was probably in his best interest to leave the matter alone.[411]

On December 25th, 1863, the boys found themselves spending their third Christmas away from home. Carden and his comrades were on the prowl again. Being Christmas day and all, Carden, G. J. "Gabe" Newman and John W. Robinson, "...put ourselves to thinking." They didn't want standard rations for the holiday and wanted to make something special of the occasion. Gabe drove a commissary wagon, and on Christmas Eve, he had carted in a barrel of whiskey for the officers. He quickly informed Corporal Carden of the arrival of the libation. Just after darkness, Robinson took a water bucket and filled it with whiskey from the barrel. They then filled their canteens and whatever else they could find to store the spirits in. Just before dawn on Christmas Day, Gabe went over to Carden's mess and asked Robinson to go to Dalton with him to get more rations. Carden was sure they would have a "hummer" of a

---

[411] (Clark, p. #20)

Christmas dinner after Robinson, "...filled up from a canteen before he left."

> When Robinson and the teamster got to the depot at Dalton Robinson went in and saw a box that he thought would suit him, so he carried it out and put it in the wagon, then went back and got a side of bacon and loaded it. When they arrived in camp Robinson brought the box and meat to our mess and when we opened the box the stuff was there sure enough. The box had been sent from somewhere down in Georgia to some of their folks who were camped around Dalton but they never received it. The contents consisted of sugar, pies, eggs and plenty of other good things too numerous to mention. We invited our company officers and some of the regimental officers to take dinner with us. They inquired where all the good things came from but they never found out. Besides having plenty of good things to eat we had plenty of good old fashioned eggnog. It was a Christmas long to be remembered. We had good times at Dalton as there were no Yankees near to cause us any uneasiness.[412]

That night Roysdon Etter recorded in his diary, "This is Christmas – the boys have got some whiskey and some are tite and others feel there liqor. It is very nice day." He probably wished he had been in Company B's mess that night; his mess dined on potato soup.[413]

By December 27th, a steady rain began that only lapsed on the 29th and continued until New Years Eve. The weather continued to turn colder and the army settled snugly into their cabins to batten down for the winter. The Sixteenth Tennessee and the Army of Tennessee had braved four major battles and trying campaigns in the last sixteen months. Now—with a new army commander, their hopes began to look up as they were to soon again feel the esprit de

---

[412] (Carden, p. May 10)
[413] (Etter, p. 22)

corps and comradeship that their new commander was certain to instill in a dispirited, veteran army.[414]

---

[414] (Ibid.)

Postscript

Writing "No hope of getting out alive" was more rewarding than I ever could have thought. Just as I thought I knew the battles, I knew there was more to learn. Additional research along the way has helped me to see the participation of this regiment in each battle in wholly new dimensions.

Only thirty-eight days into the writing of this volume, I realized that I couldn't tell the story of this regiment at Perryville without first addressing the inaccuracies that historians have been repeating for the last thirty-plus years. For that reason, I took a break from this volume to write what I thought would be a brief pamphlet about the regiment at that battle. I soon learned that their story—that had been told unmolested since the battle and gradually forgotten—had been changed so dramatically and become so entrenched in the civil war community—primarily due the work of Kenneth Hafendorfer's "Perryville: Battle for Kentucky"—that it would be no easy task to overturn his ideas. His work was unquestionably needed, as the fight at Perryville had been long neglected, and in the piles of research that he had certainly accumulated, he eventually came to his own personal conclusion as to the footsteps that the regiment took there. Upon publication of his book which became a sort of bible for those trying to understand Perryville, his understanding of where the Sixteenth went and what they did at that battle became scripture. The Sixteenth Tennessee's true role and their participation in the battle was forever changed—until now hopefully.

His book suggested that the Sixteenth Tennessee and Donelson's Brigade assaulted straight up the gut into the center of the Federal lines using Harris' Battery as a target more or less. His idea was probably solidified with the fact that many soldiers in the Sixteenth mention cabins that they were in the vicinity of and fighting around. Savage was—himself—wounded while standing between two of them. Since few structures of the civil war era were still standing by the time he wrote his book, it would seem most likely that the cabins referred to belonged to the Widow Gibson. A lot of the concept would seem to fit his interpretation of their role there—if you haven't studied the battle for thirty-plus years.

When I published "The Battle of Perryville and the Sixteenth Tennessee Infantry Regiment: A Re-evaluation" in December of 2011, I attempted to address the different interpretations that the regiment had been given in the last thirty years. I tried to challenge all of them. The one thing that continued to haunt my interpretation was the lack of cabins where I felt the regiment attacked. In the end—without an archeological dig to verify my supposed cabin locations, my hypothesis will hang in limbo without the hard evidence. But eyewitness evidence was plentiful. The men's accounts, officer's reports and chronology of the battle favor my supposition far better than current interpretations. At any rate, the telling of the role of the Sixteenth there had been changed so dramatically that my 'pamphlet' turned into a book that was one-eighth longer than my first volume on the regiment. Of the 216 pages, only 74 pages relate my actual re-evaluation or new interpretation of what they did there. The majority of the remaining pages (142 of them) provide hard evidence in black and white that support this new 'theory'—a term that seems goofy to use in light of the overwhelming evidence.

I have gotten positive feedback from a few that have an open mind. Others tend to rely on their bible and stick to the scripture. Maybe we can just call this a new religion?

At any rate, if you have enjoyed the second volume of this regiment's history, the third and final volume entitled "Lions at Bay" will be published in 2013. It will cover the final one-third of the war and cover the Atlanta Campaign, Tennessee Campaign and the North Carolina Campaign.

If you missed the first volume of the series (We were spoiling for a fight.), it included the formation and organization of the regiment at its beginning, the Western Virginia Campaign, Coastal Duty in South Carolina, Reorganization at Corinth and the campaign for that place.

Any inaccuracies or omissions of pertinent information are strictly the author's fault. If you have additional information regarding this regiment, such as war time photographs, letters, diaries or other memoirs not mentioned in this work *or corrections*, PLEASE contact me at gunnyjgillum@yahoo.com.

Appendix I

Command Organization

September 1862 – December 1863

SEPTEMBER 1862 – DECEMBER 1862

ARMY OF TENNESSEE
Lieutenant General Braxton Bragg

POLK'S I CORPS
Lieutenant General Leonidas Polk

CHEATHAM'S DIVISION
Major General Benjamin Franklin Cheatham

DONELSON'S BRIGADE
Brigadier General Daniel Smith Donelson

Eighth Regiment Tennessee Volunteers

Fifteenth Regiment Tennessee Volunteers

Sixteenth Regiment Tennessee Volunteers

Thirty-Eighth Regiment Tennessee Volunteers

Fifty-First Consolidated Regiment Tennessee Volunteers

Captain W. W. Carnes' Battery

DECEMBER 1862 – FEBRUARY 1863

ARMY OF TENNESSEE
Lieutenant General Braxton Bragg

POLK'S I CORPS
Lieutenant General Leonidas Polk

CHEATHAM'S DIVISION
Major General Benjamin Franklin Cheatham

DONELSON'S BRIGADE
Brigadier General Daniel Smith Donelson

Eighth Regiment Tennessee Volunteers

Sixteenth Regiment Tennessee Volunteers

Thirty-Eighth Regiment Tennessee Volunteers

Fifty-First Consolidated Regiment Tennessee Volunteers

Eighty-Fourth Regiment Tennessee Volunteers

Captain W. W. Carnes' Battery

FEBRUARY 1863 – MARCH 1863

ARMY OF TENNESSEE
Lieutenant General Braxton Bragg

POLK'S I CORPS
Lieutenant General Leonidas Polk

CHEATHAM'S DIVISION
Major General Benjamin Franklin Cheatham

WRIGHT'S BRIGADE
Brigadier General Marcus J. Wright

Murray's Twenty-Second Battalion Tennessee Volunteers

Eighth Regiment Tennessee Volunteers

Sixteenth Regiment Tennessee Volunteers

Twenty-Eight Regiment Tennessee Volunteers

Thirty-Eighth Regiment Tennessee Volunteers

Fifty-First & Fifty-Second Regiment Tennessee Volunteers[415]

Eighty-Fourth Regiment Tennessee Volunteers

Captain W. W. Carnes' Battery

---

[415] Originally consolidated in April of 1862, Congress declared it illegal. The portion of the 51st Tennessee that had been captured at Ft. Donelson rejoined the regiment in April of 1863 and the 52nd Tennessee rejoined them in a field consolidation maintaining separate rolls for the remainder of the war.

MARCH 1863 – DECEMBER 1863

ARMY OF TENNESSEE
Lieutenant General Braxton Bragg

POLK'S I CORPS
Lieutenant General Leonidas Polk

CHEATHAM'S DIVISION
Major General Benjamin Franklin Cheatham

WRIGHT'S BRIGADE
Brigadier General Marcus J. Wright

Eighth Regiment Tennessee Volunteers

Sixteenth Regiment Tennessee Volunteers

Twenty-Eight Consolidated Regiment Tennessee Volunteers[416]

Thirty-Eighth Regiment Tennessee Volunteers[417]

Fifty-First & Fifty-Second Regiment Tennessee Volunteers

Captain W. W. Carnes' Battery[418]

---

[416] On March 8, 1863, the 84th Tennessee was officially consolidated with the 28th Tennessee Infantry. Colonel S. S. Stanton, of the 84th Tennessee, was elected colonel of the consolidated regiment.

[417] In July of 1863, Murray's 22nd Infantry Battalion was temporarily consolidated with the 38th Tennessee. Although this was not meant to be a permanent consolidation, the 22nd Battalion's members are found in the roster of the 38th Tennessee at the final surrender in Greensboro, North Carolina.

[418] Carnes' Battery was annihilated at Chickamauga and afterwards, artillery battalions were established for each division. Thus, after September of 1863, batteries were only temporarily assigned to support individual brigades.

232

Appendix II

CLOTHING, ARMS & EQUIPMENT

SEPTEMBER 1862 – DECEMBER 1863

KENTUCKY

Although no requisitions were received in Kentucky during the 1862 Kentucky Campaign other than food rations for men and animals, a considerable number of men did benefit from the use of captured blankets and sack coats.[419]

TENNESSEE

November 1862 – Upon the army's arrival back to Tennessee, the government was still unable to distribute substantial amounts of clothing its soldiers. The last week of October and first week of November details were sent back to the counties of origin to gather clothing produced by families and relief societies. This consisted of jackets, pants and coats with a scattering of scarves and knit mittens. Owing to the issue of Enfield Rifles at Chattanooga in August, only one new firearm was issued to the Sixteenth. A Whitworth Rifle was awarded to Private J. D. Phillips who had won a marksmanship competition at Tullahoma prior to the movement to Murfreesboro.

2 fine English flannel shirts on Nov. 21, 1862 – Lt. Col. Donnell

---

[419] (Biggs, p. 142) "…we got a lot of good, warm blankets and comfortable blue suits in this fight." Davis Biggs, 38th Tennessee, Donelson's Brigade

February 1863 – Following the Battle of Murfreesboro, the army settled into positions about Tullahoma and Shelbyville where they continued to receive clothing from relief societies and family over the next five months. It appears that there was at least an effort to standardize the uniform of the officers in the army.

Shelbyville, TN – Feb. 7, 1863 issued 16 Overcoats by regimental QM

Shelbyville, TN – May 7, 1863 – Capt. Parks of Co. H buys 2 yards grey cloth for $14.00

Shelbyville, TN – May 7, 1863 – Capt. Thompson of Co. C buys 2 yards of grey cloth for $14.00

Shelbyville, TN – May 7, 1863 – Adjutant A. F. Claywell, 1st Lt. W. D. Turlington (Co. K) and 1st Lt. E. W. Walker (Co. B) buy six yards of grey cloth for $42.00

August 1863 – With the retrograde of the army to Chattanooga and due to the proximity of government manufactories in northern Georgia, the government was finally able to begin a serious effort at supplying the army. Regular requisitions consisting of drawers, pants, shirts, tent flies, and camp equipage began to be filled on a nearly monthly basis.

Aug. 31, 1863 – **Regimental Requisition totals**: 351 pr drawers, 16 pr pants, 66 pr duck pants, 182 cotton shirts, 18 mess pans, 17 tent flies, 2 camp kettles, 2 quiver F. O. paper, 11 quiver letter paper, 1 pot ink, 100 envelopes, 70 pr shoes, 1 case, 4 mule collars, 1 two horse wagon, 5 wagon prov., 137 ½ bush corn, 150 lbs Bran, 11,226 lbs hay, 1,675 lbs oats (Ritchey, 16th Regt)

Aug. 31, 1863 – 2 pr pants, 20 pr duck (or buck?) pants, 28 shirts, 51 pr drawers, 17 pr shoes, 3 tent flies, 2 mess pans, 1 camp kettle (Talley, Co. A)

Aug. 31, 63 – 1 pr pants, 11 pr duck (or buck) pants, 12 shirts, 20 pr drawers, 5 pr shoes, 2 tent flies, 2 mess pans (E W Walker, Co. B)

Aug. 31, 63 – 2 pr pants, 2 pr duck pants, 20 shirts, 35 pr drawers, 6 pr shoes, 3 tent flies, 2 mess pans, 1 camp kettle (CR Morford, Co. C)

Aug. 31, 1863 – 1 pr pants, 3 pr duck pants, 17 shirts, 17 pr drawers, 3 pr shoes, 2 mess pans, 2 tent flies (FM York, Co. D)

Aug. 31, 1863 – 2 pr pants, 15 shirts, 34 pr drawers, 2 pr shoes, 2 mess pans, 2 tent flies (Webb, Co. E)

Aug. 31, 1863 – 1 pr pants, 5 pr duck pants, 17 shirts, 42 pr drawers, 8 pr shoes, 1 mess pan, 2 tent flies (Amonett, Co. F)

Aug. 31, 1863 – 1 pr pants, 12 pr duck pants, 20 shirts, 46 pr drawers, 6 pr shoes, 2 mess pans, 2 tent flies (Fisk, Co. G)

Aug. 31, 1863 – 2 pr pants, 6 pr duck pants, 18 shirts, 30 pr drawers, 7 pr shoes, 1 mess pan, 2 tent flies (Parks, Co. H)

Aug 31, 1862 – 2 pr pants, 2 pr duck pants, 16 shirts, 38 pr drawers, 8 pr shoes, 2 mess pans, 2 tent flies (B Randals, Co. I)

Aug 31, 1863 – 2 pr pants, 1 pr duck pants, 18 shirts, 39 pr drawers, 9 pr shoes, 2 mess pans, 2 tent flies (WL Turlington, Co K)

September 1863 – Regular requisitions were still filled on a supply basis. Only specific items were available for issue. The month of September allowed for only drawers and shoes.

Sept. 30, 1863 – 10 pr drawers, 15 pr shoes (JC Webb, Co. A)

Sept. 30, 1863 – 1 pr drawers, 5 pr shoes (EW Walker, Co. B)

Sept. 30, 1863 – 6 pr drawers, 9 pr shoes (JL Thompson, Co. C)

Sept. 30, 1863 – 6 pr drawers, 11 pr shoes (FM York, Co. D)

Sept. 30, 1863 – 14 pr shoes (Webb, Co. E)

Sept. 30, 1863 – 2 pr drawers, 5 pr shoes (Amonett, Co. F)

Sept. 30, 1863 – 5 pr drawers, 12 pr shoes (Fisk, Co. G)

Sept. 30, 1863 – 5 pr drawers, 10 pr shoes (WG Etter, Co. H) at Chickamauga

Sept. 30, 1863 – 6 pr shoes (B Randals, Co. I)

October and November 1863 – The regiment and brigade were on detached duty at Charleston, Tennessee over 30 miles from the army and not afforded the ability to receive regular army issues.

GEORGIA

December 1863 – Having returned to the army and following the Battle of Missionary Ridge, the regiment settled at Dalton, Georgia. All of the regimental officers had special requisitions for themselves on December 12, 1863 consisting of shirts, drawers, shoes and jackets. This was likely an effort by General J. E. Johnston to instill pride and uniformity back within the officer ranks. Company requisitions were again filled for the men of the regiment. This issue consisted of caps (rather than hats), jackets, pants, drawers, shirts, blankets, socks, shoes and more camp equipage.

Dec. 31, 1863 – 1 cap, 17 jackets, 41 pr pants, 43 pr drawers, 45 shirts, 10 blankets, 4 pr socks, 14 pr shoes, 5 camp kettles, 7 mess pans, 146 lbs castings, 1 tin cup, 1 water bucket, 1 axe, 1 axe handle (JC Webb, Co. A)

Dec. 31, 1863 – 3 caps, 4 jackets, 11 pr pants, 10 pr drawers, 13 shirts, 1 blanket, 2 pr socks, 8 pr shoes, 2 camp kettles, 4 mess pans, 97 lbs castings, 1 tin cup, 1 water bucket (EW Walker, Co. B)

Dec. 31, 1863 – 1 cap, 11 jackets, 14 pr pants, 17 pr drawers, 15 shirts, 3 blankets, 2 pr socks, 7 pr shoes, 3 camp kettles, 5 mess pans, 97 lbs castings, 1 tin cup, 2 water buckets, 1 axe, 1 axe helve (FM York, Co. D)

Dec. 31, 1863 – 6 jackets, 14 pr pants, 15 shirts, 4 blankets, 2 pr socks, 7 pr shoes, 3 camp kettles, 5 mess pans, 113 lbs castings, 1 tin cup, 1 water bucket (Webb, Co. E)

Dec. 31, 1863 – 1 cap, 9 jackets, 15 pr pants, 11 pr drawers, 17 shirts, 4 blankets, 3 pr socks, 9 pr shoes, 3 camp kettles, 4 mess pans, 98 lbs castings, 1 tin cup, 1 water bucket (Amonett, Co. F)

Dec. 31, 1863 – 13 jackets, 17 pr pants, 27 pr drawers, 27 shirts, 7 blankets, 3 pr socks, 10 pr shoes, 3 camp kettles, 5 mess pans, 129 lbs castings, 1 tin cup, 1 water bucket, 1 axe, 1 axe helve (Fisk, Co. G)

Dec. 31, 1863 – 5 jackets, 17 pr pants, 20 pr drawers, 16 shirts, 6 blankets, 4 pr socks, 9 pr shoes, 3 camp kettles, 5 mess pans, 98 lbs castings, 1 tin cup, 1 water bucket (WG Etter, Co. H)

Dec. 31, 1863 – 2 caps, 9 jackets, 31 pr pants, 24 pr drawers, 22 shirts, 11 blankets, 3 pr socks, 11 pr shoes, 3 camp kettles, 8 mess pans, 129 lbs castings, 1 tin cup, 1 water bucket, 1 axe, 1 axe helve (Worthington, Co. I)

Dec 31, 1863 – 3 caps, 10 jackets, 19 pr pants, 30 pr drawers, 37 shirts, 7 blankets, 5 pr socks, 5 pr shoes, 3 camp kettles, 5 mess pans, 140 lbs castings, 1 tin cup , 1 water bucket (WL Turlington, Co K)

In Summary, the regiment received little other than commutation clothing up until August of 1863. There had been an attempt to make the appearance of the officers more uniform in February at Shelbyville, but the vast majority of men in the ranks still relied on home-made coarse or fine jeans materials that consisted of standard cut shell jackets in varying shades of gray or brown with little or no trim, 6-7 button front and standing collar. Pants were home-made as well as socks and drawers. Since the regiment's flag was as so much destroyed at Murfreesboro, they most likely received a new Polk's Corp pattern flag to replace their tattered banner during the lull at Tullahoma, although there is not documentation to prove such. Much of their clothing was in poor shape by the time the army arrived at Chattanooga, and many men were shoeless. Upon arriving there, stores of all sorts began to be distributed on an as needed basis. Cotton "duck" pants and "tent flies" were introduced to the army in August. With their detachment to Charleston, they missed two issues of clothing from the army and their garments became heavily worn. All of the regiment's baggage was lost on the 25th of November by capture. The regiment remained armed with 1853 Enfield rifles. A whole new lot of camp equipage was issued in December, and at least eleven kepis (as opposed to hats) may have been an attempt to uniform the officer corps of the regiment.

APPENDIX III

CASUALTIES BY BATTLE

The Battle of Perryville, KY – October 8, 1862

(National Archives)

Col. John H. Savage	F&S	Wounded
Sgt. Maj. T. B. Potter	"	"
Capt. L. N. Savage	Co. A	Wounded Slightly
Lt. G. L. Tally	"	"
Private Ben A. Atnip	"	Killed
Private A. M. Hooper	"	"
Private F. E. P. Kennedy	"	"
Private Robert Rowland	"	"
Sergt. W. E. Moore	"	Wounded Severely
Private L. G. Bing	"	"
Private R. M. Banks	"	"
Private G. P. Cantrell	"	"
Private B. M. Cantrell	"	"
Private J. M. Cantrell	"	"
Private M. L. Cantrell	"	"
Private C. B. Davis	"	"
Private R. Jones	"	"
Private Jno. LaFevre	"	"
Private R. M. Magness	"	"
Private S. M. Phillips	"	"
Private H. D. Seawell	"	"
Private F. Turner	"	"
Private P. G. Webb	"	"
Private D. W. Cantrell	"	"
Copl. W. Wilmoth	"	Wounded Slightly
Private L. Cantrell	"	"
Private J. W. Caldwell	"	"
Private J. Driver	"	"
Private T. R. Hooper	"	"
Private J. W. Johnson	"	"
Private B. C. Wilkinson	"	"
Private A. C. Taylor	"	"
Sgt. W. R. D. Wiser	Co. B	Killed
Private Isaiah Wiser	"	"
Private J. A. Walker	"	Wounded Severely
Private L. B. Campbell	"	"
Private Ezekiel Smart	"	Missing
Private P. W. Vaughn	"	"
Lieut. Cicero Spurlock	Co. C	Killed
Lieut. E. C. Read	"	Wounded Severely

Private W. H. Wooten	"	Killed
Corp. H. S. Thompson	"	Wounded Mortally
Private T. W. Grier	"	"
Private W. P. Woods	"	"
Private Reese Bruster	"	Wounded Severely
Private Horatio Marbury	"	"
Private Alex Smith Jr.	"	"
Corpl. J. B. Biles	"	Wounded Slightly
Private Chas. Allred	"	"
Private A. Blackburn	"	"
Private E. A. Braxton	"	"
Private A. F. Claywell	"	"
Private J. L. Cunningham	"	"
Private W. S. Hill	"	"
Private L. C. Harp	"	"
Private C. R. Munford	"	"
Private A. J. Paine	"	"
Private L. D. Mercer	"	"
Private Wm. Ray	"	"
Private E. B. Wilson	"	"
Capt. J. G. Lamberth	Co. D	Killed
Private J. A. Wheeler	"	"
Private J. M. Summers	"	"
Private J. S. B. Blanks	"	Wounded Severely
Private J. L. Davis	"	"
Private W. W. Williamson	"	"
Private R. A. Ware	"	"
Sgt. T. J. Martin	"	Wounded Slightly
Sgt. Gribble	"	"
Private Jno. Duncan	"	"
Private J. England	"	"
Private H. Edwards	"	"
Private A. Higginbothan	"	"
Private W. H. White	"	"
Private J. D. Lusk	"	"
Private W. A. Miller	"	"
Private W. E. Quick	"	"
Private B. G. Webb	"	"
Private Joseph W. Green	"	Missing
Private Wm. Bue	Co. E	Wounded Mortally

Private J. M Christian	"	"
Sgt. R. W. Ware	"	"
Copl. A. B. Womack	"	Wounded Severely
Private Jno. Boren	"	"
Private Enoch Cooksey	"	"
Private L. Keiff	"	"
Private A. D. Mason	"	"
Private J. L. Medley	"	"
Private G. H. McNeely	"	"
Private J. L. McGregor	"	"
Private W. T. Moore	"	"
Private G. Nunnelly	"	"
Private W. D. Wood	"	"
Private F. G. Womack	"	"
Private R. R. Womack	"	"
Sgt. W. N. Lowry	"	Wounded Slightly
Copl. H. L. Moffitt	"	"
Private R. P. Burks	"	"
Private W. W. Evans	"	"
Private W. E. Jones	"	"
Private Arch Nunnelly	"	"
Private J. S. Turner	"	"
Private Jno. Vanhooser	"	"
Private J. P. Green	"	"
Capt. J. B. Vance	Co. F	Wounded Mortally
Lieut. Pointer	"	Killed
Lieut. Baldwin	"	Wounded Slightly
Sgt. Bullington	"	Killed
Private M. M. Anderson	"	"
Private B. F. Scudders	"	"
Private T. C. Thompson	"	"
Private J. J. Richardson	"	Wounded Mortally
Sgt. Mayberry	"	Wounded Severely
Private Sam Benson	"	"
Private W. F. Grimsley	"	"
Private H. J. Hughes	"	"
Private M. J. Nichols	"	"
Private J. T. Addison*	"	"
Private P. M. Wassom	"	"
Sgt. (H.L.C.) Pearson	"	Wounded Slightly

ed| Private L. H. Stockton | " | Wounded Mortally |
Private F. M. Wright	"	"
Corpl. J. S. Roberts	"	Wounded Severely
Private M. Blount	"	"
Private W. A. Cotton	"	"
Private Lawson Knowles	"	"
Private L. M. Pettit	"	"
Private J. L. Brittian	"	Wounded Slightly
Private W. W. Gleeson	"	"
Private W. F. Roberts	"	"
Private H. L. T. Sanders	"	"
Private Adolphus Wiggins	"	"
Private Lawson Fisher	"	"
Lieut. W. G. Etter	Co. H	"
Lieut. H. L. Hayes	"	"
Sergt. R. B. Hayes	"	Killed
Sergt. W. H. Rhea	"	"
Private W. M. Hennessee	"	Wounded Mortally
Private Jno. Countiss	"	"
Private Obadiah Hennessee	"	"
Private J. N. Smith	"	Wounded Severely
Private R. R. Etter	"	"
Private J. M. Parks	"	"
Private Jerome Safely	"	"

Corpl. Jacob Curtis	"	Wounded Slightly
Private J. V. Brown	"	"
Private G. T. Brown	"	"
Private R. L. Brown	"	"
Private Martin Curtis	"	"
Private W. F. Hennessee	"	"
Private Isaac Cunningham	"	Missing
Lieut. D. Cummings	Co. I	Wounded Mortally
Lieut. S. D. Mitchell	"	Wounded Slightly
Sgt. W. G. Jones	"	Killed
Corpl. J. J. Steakley	"	"
Private Levi Johnson	"	"
Private G. W. Sparkman	"	"
Private Peter Shockley	"	"
Private James Moore	"	"
Private W. B. Haston	"	"
Private J. C. Steakley	"	"
Private James Parker[420]	"	"
Sgt. W. B. Wood	"	Wounded Severely
Private Jno. Smaller	"	"
Private Simeon Phillips*[421]	"	"
Sgt. C. H. Clark	"	Wounded Slightly
Private W. T. Thurman	"	"
Private W. J. Underwood	"	"
Private T. A. Priest	"	"
Private J. E. York	"	Missing
Capt. D. T. Brown	Co. K	Wounded Severely
Lieut. J. E. Rotan	"	Wounded Slightly
Private Simm Baker	"	Killed
Private James Clark	"	"
Private Jasper Knowles	"	Wounded Severely
Private J. W. McConnell	"	"
Private Alex Oaks	"	"
Sgt. James Brown	"	Wounded Slightly
Private R. D. Baker	"	"
Private W. W. England	"	"

---

[420] Believed to be Samuel T. Parker of Company I – Killed at Perryville.
[421] No service record exists, but he is listed in Head's book. He died of wounds received.

Private H. L. Gracy   "   "

Recapitulation:
Killed: 41
Wounded: 151
Missing: 7
Total: 199[422]

Company	Killed	MorW	SevW	SliW	Missing	Total
F&S			2			2
A	4		16	10		30
B	2		2		2	6
C	2	3	4	13		22
D	3		4	11	1	19
E		3	13	9		25
F	5	2	7	5		19
G	12	2	5	7		26
H	2	3	4	8	1	18
I	9	1	3	5	1	19
K	2		4	5		11
Totals:	41	14	62	75	5	197[423]

The companies of the regiment went into battle in the following order in line from left to right with corresponding casualty rates below:[424]

---

[422] Official Total reported by Cheatham's Inspection Report. The soldiers reported as casualties were only those that had to receive hospital treatment. It is certain that those who received a bandage for minor wounds at the regimental aid station were numbered in the dozens and were never reported as a casualty. Many of the men had already received very slight wounds prior to more severe ones that caused them to retire to the rear in search of the hospitals.

[423] Total as reflected by actual report.

[424] Note the casualties from the right wing of the regiment number 119 while the left wing suffers only 76. This is indicative of the 15th Tennessee's presence to their left and the lack of support on their right and proximity of Parsons' battery until the arrival of Maney's Brigade.

B	C	H	I	K	G	F	E	D	A
6	22	18	19	11	26	19	25	19	30

% of Brigade

Casualties	Killed	Wounded	Missing	Total	% of Brigade
8th Tennessee	4	29	-	33	9.5%
15th Tennessee	9	25	-	34	9.7%
16th Tennessee	41	151	7	199	57.3%
38th Tennessee	5	38	-	43	12.3%
51st Tennessee	9	25	-	34	9.7%
Donelson's Brigade	68	272	7	347	

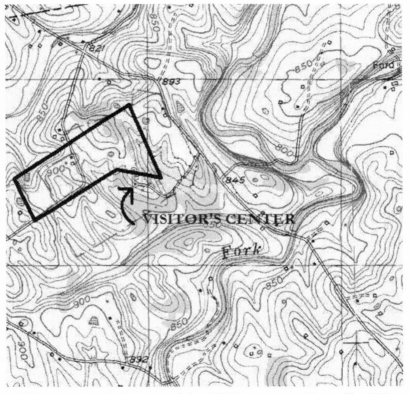

Primary engagement area of the 16th Tennessee at Perryville, KY
(From USGS Map)

The Battle of Murfreesboro, TN – December 31, 1862

(National Archives)

Sergt. J. H. Warren	Co. A	Killed
Private E. Leauge	"	"
Private F. G. Kersey	"	"
Private Lee Patterson	"	"
Corpl. J. A. Moore	"	Slight Wound
Corpl. R. M. Martin	"	"
Private S. Anderson	"	"
Private J. A. Briggs	"	"
Private I. Cantrell	"	Severe Wound
Private A. J. Kersey	"	"
Private Peter Cantrell	"	"
Private T. Parsley	"	"
Lieut. G. W. Witt	"	Missing
Sergt. J. R. Thompson	"	"
Private M. E. Adcock	"	"
Private John Cantrell	"	"
Private T. C. Harper	"	"
Private T. M. Hooper	"	"
Private E. Lockhart	"	"
Private F. M. Church	Co. B	Severe Wound
Private T. H. Douglas	"	Slight Wound
Private James Fuller	"	"
Private W. B. Campbell	"	"
Private L. P. Campbell	"	"
Private W. C. King	"	"
Capt. D. C. Spurlock	Co. C	Killed
Private B. D. Bybee	"	Severe Wound
Private F. M. Bonner	"	"
Private J. K. P. Martin	"	"
Private S. H. Alexander	"	Slight Wound
Private R. N. Henderson	"	"
Private D. W. King	"	"
Private M. D. Smith	"	"
Private J. J. Hensley	"	"
Private J. W. Smith	"	"
Private James Hobbs	"	"
Private R. W. Morrow	"	"
Private W. L. Edwards	Co. D	Killed
Private A. P. Gribble	"	"
Private Samuel Gribble	"	"

Private A. J. Gribble	"	"
Private W. Perry	"	"
Private James Rowland	"	"
Private W. F. Smith	"	"
Private Hardeman Lane	"	"
Private Walter Cope	"	Severe Wound
Private J. P. Douglass	"	"
Private J. J. Higginbotham	"	"
Private Thomas Hutson	"	"
Private J. L. McGee	"	"
Private Richmond McGregor	"	"
Private J. K. P. Nichols	"	"
Private B. M. Rowland	"	"
Private L. Smith	"	"
Private W. Templeton	"	"
Private W. J. Ware	"	"
Private T. F. West	"	"
Lieut. J. P. Hennessee	"	Slight Wound
Lieut. F. M. York	"	"
Sergt. T. J. Martin	"	"
Private W. B. Christian	"	"
Private Sam C. Gribble	"	"
Private J. A. Gribble	"	"
Private A. Higginbotham	"	"
Private J. D. Lusk	"	"
Private John McGregor	"	"
Private R. G. Martin	"	"
Private W. M. Moulder	"	"
Private W. T. Perry	"	"
Private John Quick	"	"
Private G. W. Summers	"	"
Private J. B. Smith	"	"
Private J. M. Summers	"	"
Private J. T. Molder	"	Missing
Private J. Templeton	"	Slight Wound
Private W. H. Edwards	"	Missing
Private John White	"	"
Sergt. M. Mauzy	Co. E	Killed
Private David Bonner	"	"
Private Elias Womack	"	"

Private A. Douglas	"	Severe Wound
Corpl. Van Hooser	"	"
Corpl. Jas. Kirby	"	"
Capt. J. J. Womack	"	"
Lieut. J. Walling	"	"
Sergt. Mayberry	"	"
Private G. N. Clark	"	"
Sergt. J. B. Womack	"	Slight Wound
Private A. M. Mason	"	"
Private Luke Purser	"	"
Private Isah Moffit	"	"
Private G. M. Wallace	"	"
Private A. J. Vanhooser	"	"
Private J. S. Womack	"	"
Private Jno. Green	"	"
Private Randolph Lawrence	"	"
Private William Lawrence	"	"
Private Lawrence Cantrell	"	"
Sergt. Jacob Choate	Co. F	Killed
Corpl. Jno. Laycock	"	"
Private Jas. Murray	"	"
Private Jno. Brown	"	"
Private Jas. Noe	"	"
Private Jno. Choate	"	"
Private J. Y. Ballard	"	"
Lieut. W. W. Wallace	"	Severe Wound
Sergt. J. H. Nichols	"	"
Private J. Y. Crowell	"	"
Sergt. T. C. Bledsoe	"	Slight Wound
Corpl. C. N. Ballard	"	"
Private Jas. Pleasant	"	"
Private William Webb	"	"
Private Jno. Haggard	"	"
Private R. F. Owens	"	"
Private J. F. Owens	"	"
Private W. N. Caruthers	"	"
Private Jas. Mathis	"	"
Corpl. Benj. Hutchins	Co. G	Killed
Private J. P. Cantrell	"	"
Private R. P. Moore	"	"

Private Jno. Fisher	"	Severe Wound
Private T. L. Hodges	"	"
Private P. B. Franks	"	"
Private W. Hasty	"	"
Private J. B. Moore	"	"
Lt. A. Fisk	"	Slight Wound
Lt. Jno. Fisher	"	"
Corpl. Jno. Meggerson	"	"
Corpl. A. Perry	"	"
Private Jno. Atnip	"	"
Private T. A. Cotton	"	"
Private M. L. Fisher	"	"
Private E. M. Greenfield	"	"
Private A. Hutchins	"	"
Private R. B. Love	"	"
Private James Hasty	"	"
Private J. M. Pollard	"	"
Private Jno. Stricklin	"	"
Private T. Wiggins	"	"
Private J. W. Wright	"	"
Private A. J. Youngblood	"	Missing
Private J. L. Britton	"	"
Corpl. I. R. Jones	Co. H	Killed
Private Jno. Etter	"	"
Private Henry Pennington	"	"
Private Frank Smith	"	"
Private Wm. Tallent	"	"
Sergt. Jno. Hughes	"	Severe Wound
Private T. J. Davis	"	"
Private Jas. Jones	"	"
Capt. Jas. M. Parks	"	Slight Wound
Private Jno. Brown	"	"
Private J. N. Clendenen	"	"
Private Joe Ferrin	"	"
Private W. P. Hughs	"	"
Private A. Hughs	"	"
Private A. J. Jordon	"	"
Private Ed Pursley	"	"
Private W. N. Russell	"	"
Private W. S. Bullin	"	"

Name	Company	Status
Private Jno. Davis	"	Missing
Private Henderson Rhodes	Co. I	Killed
Private Peter Baker	"	"
Private Marion Priest	"	"
Private I. C. Moore	"	Severe Wound
Private I. Hollinsworth	"	"
Private W. J. Underwood	"	"
Sergt. N. B. Hambrick	"	"
Sergt. S. R. York	"	"
Private Thos. Rawlins	"	"
Private Sam. Porter	"	"
Private W. T. Worthington	"	"
Sergt. S. Worthington	"	Slight Wound
Sergt. W. R. Paine	"	"
Private S. M. Fleming	"	"
Private C. H. Worthington	"	"
Private Sol. Porter	"	"
Private G. W. Stipe	"	"
Private J. M. Thomasin	"	"
Private Joshua Worley	"	"
Private Shelby Walling	"	"
Private Elisha Martin	Co. K	Killed
Private Martin Cope	"	"
Private John Hardley	"	Serious Wound
Private Jno. Casteel	"	"
Private T. J. Templeton	"	"
Lieut. Wm. Lowry	"	"
Private A. D. Nash	"	"
Private S. Humphries	"	"
Private Jas. Carlin	"	"
Sergt. W. G. Simms	"	Slight Wound
Sergt. J. N. Wilson	"	"
Sergt. D. L. Hensley	"	"
Corpl. S. M. Snodgrass	"	"
Corpl. Ben. Lack	"	"
Private Bryce Parsley	"	"
Private Jno. Bothirs	"	"
Private G. Green	"	"
Private Elbert Cope	"	"
Private Wm. Hodges	"	Missing

Official

Recapitulation: Killed: 36   Wounded: 156   Missing: 16   Total: 207

Actual

Recapitulation: Killed: 36   Wounded: 150   Missing: 14   Total: 200

Corresponding casualty rates by company, killed, wounded and missing.

	B	C	H	I	K	G	F	E	D	A
K:	-	1	5	3	2	3	7	3	8	4
W:	6	11	13	17	16	20	12	18	29	8
M:	-	-	1	-	1	2	-	-	3	7
T:	6	12	19	20	19	25	19	21	40	19

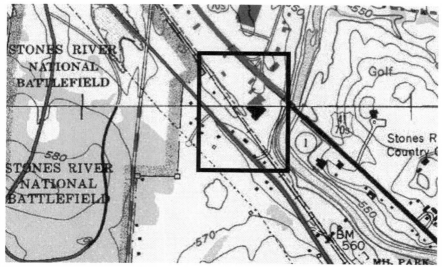

Primary engagement area for the Sixteenth Tennessee at Murfreesboro.
(From USGS Map)

Battle of Chickamauga, GA Sept 19 & 20, 1863

The Sixteenth Tennessee officially reported 68 men wounded.

*Incomplete – 38 of the 68 total casualties

Colonel D. M. Donnell	F&S	Wounded
1st Lt. W. C. Potter	Co. A	Wounded
Daniel W. Cantrell	Co. A	Wounded (arm)
Capt. Gideon L. Talley	Co. A	Wounded
Perry G. Cantrell	Co. A	Overheated
R. C. Carden	Co. B	Wounded slightly (face)
4th Cpl. T. J. Wiser	Co. B	Wounded
Capt. J. L. Thompson	Co. C	Wounded
L. C. Harp	Co. C	Wounded
Robert W. Morrow	Co. C	Wounded
James P. Smartt	Co. C	Wounded (twice)
A. J. Rayburn	Co. C	Wounded (twice – once in hip)
Hamilton M. Hennessee	Co. D	Wounded (two places in left leg)
Thomas J. Martin	Co. D	Wounded
W. R. Nunneley	Co. E	Wounded (right hip by shell fragment)
Elias T. Taylor	Co. E	Wounded
J. C. Watson	Co. E	Wounded
Thomas Laycock	Co. F	Wounded
Bvt. 2nd Lt. John F. Owen	Co. F	Wounded
Hugh Whitehead	Co. F	Wounded (both hands – lost finger)
1st Lt. James Fisher	Co. G	Wounded
Nathan Troglin	Co. G	Wounded
Capt. James M. Parks	Co. H	Wounded mortally (chest – died on Sept 20)
1st Lt. W. G. Etter	Co. H	Wounded
W. H. Russell	Co. H	Wounded (exploding shell)
2nd Sgt. Charles M. Rutledge	Co. H	Wounded
1st Lt. James Worthington	Co. I	Wounded
Pvt. Andrew J. Agent	Co. I	Wounded
Joseph Cummings	Co. I	Wounded
T. J. Mooneyham	Co. I	Wounded (gunshot through thigh)

Capt. Wm. D. Turlington	Co. K	Wounded
James A. Boyd	Co. K	Wounded (exploding shell – left hip)
James Madison Cope	Co. K	Wounded (left thigh – leg amputated)
Hosea Gist	Co. K	Wounded
Gardner Green	Co. K	Wounded (lost leg to cannon ball)
Pvt. J. A. Herd	Co. K	Wounded
Thomas J. Templeton	Co. K	Wounded (gunshot to left hand)
Pvt. William L. Hodges	Co. K	Killed (Sept 20)

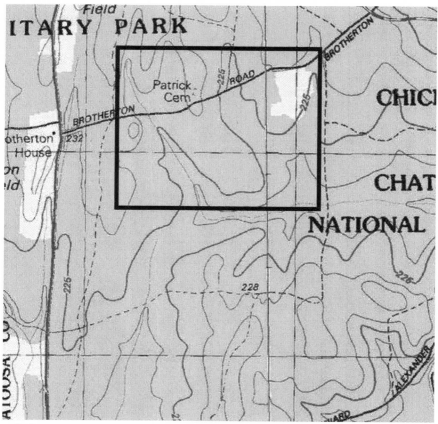

Primary engagement area for Wright's Brigade on September 19, 1863.
(From USGS map)

Engagement at Missionary Ridge, TN – Nov 24, 1863

Nine casualties were reported.

Pvt. Tennessee M. Hooper	Co. A	Wounded (shell fragment)
Garrison Taylor	Co. A	Wounded
J. D. Hicks	Co. A	Wounded
Dallas Hicks	Co. A	Wounded slightly
Henry D. Blanks	Co. D	Wounded (right elbow)
Lafayette Clark	Co. D	Killed
3rd Lt. William C. Womack	Co. E	Wounded seriously (thigh)
A. J. Hawkins	Co. E	Wounded seriously (left breast)
E. M. Irwin	Co. K	Wounded seriously (arm)

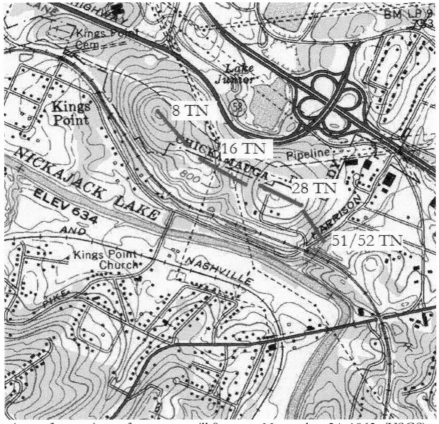

Area of operations afternoon untill 9 p.m. – November 24, 1863. (USGS)

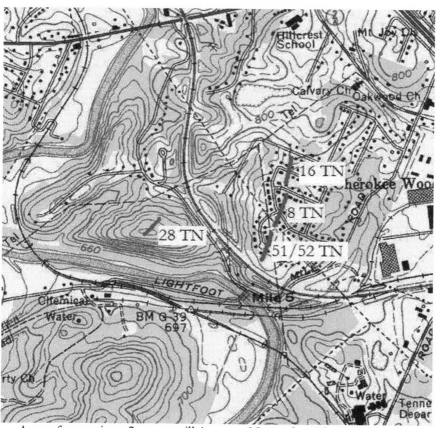

Area of operations 2 a.m. untill 1 p.m. – November 25, 1863 (USGS)

Area of operations from 2 p.m. untill 4 p.m. — November 25, 1863. (USGS)

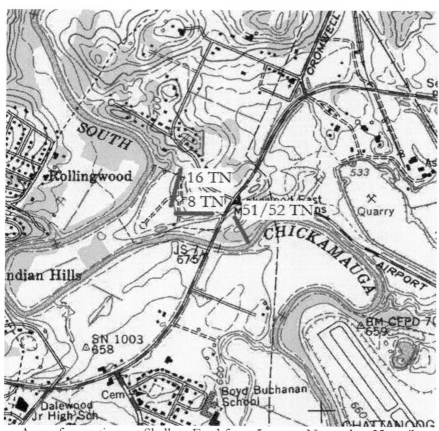

Area of operations at Shallow Ford from 5 p.m. – November 25 until
2 a.m. November 26.
(USGS Map)

Captured as wagon masters / wagon guards south of Ootewah, Tennessee and pickets that had not been informed of the withdrawal of Confederate forces from fords and bridges on Chickamauga Creek.

Nov 25 – 27, 1863

All of the men listed below were sent to Rock Island Prison in Illinois. A small number volunteered for frontier service in the U. S. Army, and a few were finally sent for exchange in February and March 1865. Most remained in prison until the close of the war.

W. H. Bing	Co. A	Captured (Cleveland, TN)
Peter H. Cantrell	Co. A	Captured (Chattanooga)
Leonard Cantrell	Co. A	Captured (Graysville, GA)
Pvt. James B. Fisher	Co. A	Captured (Missionary Ridge)
John Lafevre	Co. A	Captured (Missionary Ridge)
B. C. Wilkinson	Co. A	Captured (Ringgold, GA)
J. B. Wilkinson	Co. A	Captured (Ringgold, GA)
James J. Harney	Co. A	Captured (Ringgold, GA)
John Womack	Co. A	Captured (Ringgold, GA)
2nd Cpl. Russell Brewer	Co. B	Captured (Morrison's Ferry)
George W. Kennedy	Co. B	Captured (Dowdy's Ferry)
C. G. Lance	Co. B	Captured (Dowdy's Ferry)
Robert E. Garrett	Co. B	Captured (Harrison's Ferry)
Jacob A. Walker	Co. B	Captured (Ooltewah, TN)
Michael Blackburn	Co. C	Captured (Dowdy's Ferry)
J. W. Bybee	Co. C	Captured (Missionary Ridge)
James Lytle	Co. C	Captured (Missionary Ridge)
Thomas C. Wheeler	Co. C	Captured (Missionary Ridge)
John M. Perry	Co. C	Captured (Missionary Ridge)
H. J. Thaxton	Co. C	Captured (Missionary Ridge)
John B. Reynolds	Co. D	Captured (Ringgold, GA)
James Sullivan	Co. D	Captured (Graysville, GA)
George W. Summers	Co. D	Captured (Missionary Ridge)
William J. Ware	Co. D	Captured (Missionary Ridge)
Charles Ware (SLAVE)	Co. D	Captured (Missionary Ridge)

Gillam N. Clark	Co. E	Captured (Graysville, GA)
Arnold Moss Mason	Co. E	Captured (Graysville, GA)
J. N. Fuston	Co. E	Captured (Missionary Ridge)
A. M. Womack	Co. E	Captured Cleveland, TN)
Wm. J. Fuston	Co. E	Captured (Missionary Ridge)
Elias H. Green	Co. E	Captured (Charleston, TN)
Moses A. Messick	Co. E	Captured (Harrison's Landing)
Hugh Whitehead	Co. F	Captured (Harrison's Landing)
1st Cpl. Wm. E. Braswell	Co. F	Captured (Ringgold, GA)
James Lewis Ollison	Co. F	Captured (Cleveland, TN)
D. L. Dunham	Co. G	Captured (Missionary Ridge)
Joseph W. Gilbert	Co. G	Captured (Missionary Ridge)
James Mullins	Co. G	Captured (Ringgold, GA)
Pvt. James Millum	Co. G	Captured (Ringgold, GA)
Rueben Hampton	Co. H	Captured (Chattanooga)
William Hughes	Co. H	Captured (Ringgold, GA)
William Martin	Co. H	Captured (Ringgold, GA)
Mark Mitchell	Co. I	Captured (Missionary Ridge)
John Bothirs	Co. K	Captured (Missionary Ridge)
Pvt. Robert L. Bronson	Co. K	Captured (Ooltewah, TN)
John Downey	Co. K	Captured (Ooltewah, TN)
Allen Nash	Co. K	Captured (Ooltewah, TN)
James Lack	Co. K	Captured (Missionary Ridge)
John B. Sherer	Co. K	Captured (Missionary Ridge)
3rd Sgt. Stephen S. Williams	Co. K	Captured (Ringgold, GA)

Captured at Charleston, TN

Charles W. Mooneyham	Co. I	Captured (Nov 28)
Miles Moore	Co. I	Captured (Nov 28)
Jerome B. Smith	Co. D	Captured (Dec 3)
Henry Harpole	Co. F	Captured (Sequatchie Valley – Dec 7)
Thomas J. Davis	Co. H	Captured (Dec 12 – on detached duty – made escape and returned home)
R. W. Ferguson	Co. F	Captured (played deserter – Took oath at Nashville on Dec. 24,

1863 but returned to army in
January 1864)

Total Casualties from September 1, 1862 thru December 31, 1863

	Killed	Wounded	Captured
Perryville, KY – Oct. 8, 1862	41	151	7
Murfreesboro, TN – Dec. 31, 1862	36	150	14
Chickamauga, GA – Sept. 19-20, 1863	1	68	-
Chickamauga Creek, TN –Nov. 24, 1863	1	8	-
Chattanooga – Ooltewah – Cleveland Charleston – Nov. 25-Dec. 12, 1863	-	-	56
TOTAL:	79	377	77

KILLED	79[425]
WOUNDED	377[426]
CAPTURED	77[427]
DESERTED	30(+)[428]
TOTAL	562[429]

---

[425] This number represented men killed dead on the field, not counting those who died within a day or two of their wounding.

[426] Many of those wounded later died of their injuries. All of the official casualty lists were inaccurate and underreported the actual wounded. It may be safe to say that a calculation of 15% of the total casualties per battle could be added to any given casualty list to achieve a more accurate number that reflected self treated or minor wounds.

[427] This number was certainly much higher than the reported totals that did not reflect men on detached service that were captured on duty or trapped and captured behind enemy lines.

[428] The number of desertions is impossible to determine but most took place during the retreat to Chattanooga.

[429] This number is an approximate value.

Bibliography

(1863, January 13). *The Charleston Mercury* , p. 1.

(1863, June 23). *The New York Herald* , p. 1.

(1992, February 1). *Daily News Journal* . Murfreesboro, TN, USA.

Anonymous. (1861, October 2). Letter Written from Camp Sewell Mountain, V. W. V. A. *The Union and American Newspaper* , *Box 11 (Folder 45)* . (M. Division, Ed.) Nashville, TN, USA: TSLA.

Biggs, D. (n.d.). Incidents in the Battle of Perryville, KY. *Confederate Veteran* , *33*, p. 1412.

Blackburn, J. K. (n.d.). *Online Archive of Terry's Texas Rangers*. Retrieved from
http://www.terrystexasrangers.org/histories/southwestern_historical _quarterly/blackburn1.html

Blake, W. H. (1887). Report of Col. William H. Blake, January 6, 1863. In *War of the Rebellion: Official Records of the Union and Confederate Armies* (Vols. Series I, Part I, Vol. 20, pp. 551-54). Washington D. C., USA: War Department.

Buell, G. P. (1887). Near Murfreesborough, Tenn., January 5, 1863. In *War of the Rebellion: Official Records of the Union and Confederate Armies* (Vols. Series I, Vol. 20, Pt. I, p. 481). Washington D. C., USA: War Department.

C. K. Barrow, J. H. (1995). Forgotten Confederates; An Anthology about Black Southerners. (J. H. C. K. Barrow, Ed.) *Journal of Confederate History Series , 14.*

Cantrell, A. J. (n.d.). Vivid Experiences in Prison. *Confederate Veteran , 16,* p. 216.

Carden, R. C. (1912). Three Years, Seven Months and Twenty-seven Days in the C. S. A. in the War Between the States. *The Independent .* Boone, Iowa, USA.

Cheatham, B. F. (1887). Report of Murfreesboro. In *War of the Rebellion: Official Records of the Union and Confederate Armies* (Vols. Series I, Vol. 20, Pt. I, pp. 704-08). Washington D. C., USA: War Department.

Civil War Centtennial Commission. (1964). *Tennesseans in the Civil War - A Military History of Confederate and Union Units with Available Rosters of Personnel Part I.* Nashville, TN: Civil War Centennial Commission.

Clark, C. H. (n.d.). My Grandfather's Diary of the Civil War/Carrol H. Clark, Co. I Sixteenth Regiment Tennessee Volunteers, C.S.A. McMinnVille, TN, USA: C. W. Clark Jr.

Compiled Service Records. (n.d.). TSLA.

Confederate Pension Applications.

Confederate Veteran. (n.d.). *Confederate Veteran , 22,* p. 517.

Crofts, T. (1910). *History of the Service of the Third Ohio Veteran Volunteer Cavalry.* Columbus: The Stoneman Press.

Cross, R. J. (1864). *Papers from the Portfolio of an Army Chaplain.* Macon, Ga.: Burke, Boykin & Company.

Davis, J. L. (1862, October). *Denny-Loftis Geneology*. Retrieved May 2012, from http://www.ajlambert.com/thompson/stry_cwl.pdf

DeWitt, M. B. (n.d.). Some Memories and Facts. *Confederate Veteran* , 7, p. 299.

DeWitt, M. B. (1863-1865). War Diary. Confederate Collection, Box 6, Folder 6. Nashville, TN, USA: TSLA.

Dillard, H. H. (1886). Sixteenth Tennessee Infantry. In J. Lindsley, *Military Annals of Tennessee* (Vol. 1, pp. 335-47). Nashville: J. M. Lindsley & Co. Publishers.

Donelson, D. S. (1887). Report of Brig. Gen. Daniel S. Donelson, C. S. Army commanding First Brigade. In *War of the Rebellion: Official Records of the Union and Confederate Armies* (Vols. Series I, Vol.20, Pt. I, pp. 710-714). Washington D. C., USA: Government Printing Office.

Editors of Time-Life. (1991). *Arms and Equipment of the Confederacy*. Alexandria, VA: Time-Life Books.

Etter, R. R. (n.d.). Resinor Etter Diary. TN, USA.

Evans, C. A. (Ed.). (1899). *Confederate Military History* (Vol. 10). Confederate Publishing Company.

Evans, E. G. (1899). *Confederate Military History Extended Edition, Vol. X, Tennessee*. Confederate Publishing Company.

Finley, L. W. (1902). The Battle of Perryville. In *Southern Historical Society Papers* (Vol. 30, p. 248).

Fletcher, W. A. (1908). *Rebel Private: Front and Rear*. Beaumont, TX, USA: Press of the Greer print.

Hale, W. T. (n.d.). The Cantrells of Tennessee. *Confederate Veteran* , *22*, p. 476.

Hampton, H. (1864). *Cheatham's Corps Returns for Dec. 13, 1864.* Number of men present, Carter House Archives, Franklin.

Head, T. A. (1885). *Campaigns and Battles of the Sixteenth Regiment Tennessee Volunteers.* Nashville, TN, USA: Cumberland Presbyterian Publishing house.

Head, T. A. (n.d.). Insert on Wounded at Perryville. *Confederate Veteran* , *5*, p. 435.

Hooper, T. R. (n.d.). Diary of Thomas R. Hooper, Co. A, 16th Tennessee Infantry Regiment. Murfreesboro, TN: Stones River National Battlefield.

Jr., M. H. (1864). A Soldier of the Cumberland: Memoir of Mead Holmes Jr. *American Tract Society* , pp. 92-96.

Kearny, W. H. (n.d.). Concerning the Battle of Nashville. *Confederate Veteran* , *13*, p. 68.

Kirbey, J. C. In *Tennessee Civil War Veteran Questionnaires* (pp. 1299-300). Nashville.

Lawson Smith. *Confederate Veteran.*

Lindsley, J. B. (1886). *The Military Annals of Tennessee* (Vol. 1). Nashville, TN, USA: J. M. Lindsley & Co. Publishers.

Losson, C. (1989). *Tennessee's Forgotten Warriors: Frank Cheatham and His Confederate Division.* Knoxville: University of Tennessee Press.

Marshall, L. G. (1886). Jackson's Battery-Carnes' Battery-Marshall's Battery. In J. B. Lindsley, *The Military Annals of Tennessee* (Vol. 2, pp. 805-44). Nashville, Tenn., USA: J. M. Lindsley & Co. Publishers.

Mason, A. M. (n.d.). Sgt. Arnold Moss Mason Diary / Co. E, 16th Tennessee. *Box 7 , Folder 4*. (M. Division, Ed.) Nashville, TN, USA: TSLA.

McMurry, R. M. (1989). *Two Great Rebel Armies*. USA: Universtiy of North Carolina Press.

M'Neilly, J. H. (n.d.). The Retreat from Tennessee. *Confederate Veteran , 36*, p. 306.

Morgan, J. M. (n.d.). Secession in Putnam County, Tenn. *Confederate Veteran , 17*, p. 170.

Morgan, P. F. (1864). P. F. Morgan Diary. In C. C. 7/4a (Ed.). Nashville, TN: TSLA.

N. B. Forrest Camp, U. C. (n.d.). James Polk Smartt. *Confederate Veteran , 22*, p. 517.

Noe, K. W. (2001). *Perryville: This Grand Havoc of Battle*. Lexington: The University Press of Kentucky.

Nunley, J. E. (1988). *Grundy County History*. Retrieved 2011, from http://grundycountyhistory.org/06_GenCh/RC5/Nunley,%20William%20Carroll%2005.pdf

Oldershaw, P. (n.d.). Battle of Perryville Report. *OR* .

Oldham, V. B. (1998). *Civil War Diary of Van Buren Oldham: 9th Tennessee Infantry Regiment*. (D. Ullrich, Ed.) Retrieved 2010, from http://www.utm.edu/departments/acadpro/library/departments/special_collections/wc_hist/vboldham.htm

Parks, G. W. (n.d.). A Fatihful Watch and its History. *Confederate Veteran* , *17*, p. 604.

Patterson, L. (n.d.). Retrieved May 2011, from www.ajlambert.com.

Potter, T. B. (1861-1865). Memo Books. In T. P. II (Ed.), *Diary*.

Savage, J. H. Report of Col. John H. Savage, Sixteenth Tennessee Infantry. In *War of the Rebellion: Official Records of the Union and Confederate Armies* (Vols. Series I, Vol. 20, Pt. I, pp. 717-718). Washington D. C., USA: War Department.

Savage, J. H. (1903). *The Life of John H. Savage*. Nashville: J. H. Savage.

Sullivan, D. C. (2010). *The Civil War Diaries of a Confederate Soldier*. (D. C. Sullivan, Ed.) USA: Dena Croft Sullivan.

Talley, S. B. (n.d.). Civil War Memoirs of Lt. Spencer B. Talley, 28th Tennessee. (D. Harris, Ed.)

Tennessee Veteran Questionaires (Vol. 5). TN, USA.

The Louisville Daily Journal. (1862, October 14). Retrieved from http://search.proquest.com/civilwar/docview/506125605/133D993 75CC14410CF0/19?accountid=14351

The War of the Rebellion: A Compilatioin of Official Records of the Union and Confederate Armies. (Vols. 20, Pt. 1). (1887). Washington, D. C.: Government Printing Office.

Thompson, J. R. (1966). Hear the Wax Fry. McMinnville, TN, USA: Nellie Boyd.

Tolley, W. P. (n.d.). Capt. W. P. Tolley of Winchester, Tenn. writes:. *Confederate Veteran* , *9*, p. 356.

Tucker, O. P. (1977). Oliver P. Tucker's Notebook. *Coffee County Historical Quarterly* , *3* (1).

Unknown. (n.d.). Second Hand Pictures for Silly Southerners. *Confederate Veteran* , *1*, p. 377.

Visit to Camp Trousdale and its Incidents. (1861, July 7). *Nashville Patriot* . Nashville, TN.

Wagner, G. D. (1887). Report of Col. George D. Wagner, Jan. 6, 1863. In *War of the Rebellion: Official Recrods of the Union and Confederate Armies* (Vols. Series I, Vol. 20, Pt. I, pp. 492-495). Washington D. C., USA.

Winchester, G. W. (1862-63). *Diary of George W. Winchester, Quartermaster, Donelson's Brigade.* TSLA, Nashville, TN: Winchester Papers, Confederate Collection, Manuscript Division, #1117, MF 793.

Womack, J. J. (1961). *The Civil War Diary of Capt. J. J. Womack.* McMinnville, TN: Womack Printing Company.

Young, C. (Ed.). (1863, May 6-9). Report of Inspection for Polk's Corps.

Index

Confederate Units listed numerically

38th Tennessee	31, 35-37, 40, 53, 63-66, 68, 69, 71, 101, 120, 138, 162, 172, 182, 185, 186, 188, 191, 198, 209
39th North Carolina	129, 130, 134
41st Georgia	55-57, 62
51st Alabama Mounted Inf.	165
51st & 52nd Tennessee	31, 73, 101, 120, 122, 124, 130, 131, 135, 138, 162, 182, 184-186, 190, 195, 210, 211, 214, 217, 218
84th Tennessee	120, 135, 149
154th Tennessee	144

Federal Units listed numerically

Bush's Battery	34, 36, 38, 39, 43, 45, 46, 64, 66, 68, 70, 88
Garrard's Detachment	50, 54, 66, 67
1st Ohio, Battery F	130, 133
1st Wisconsin	64, 66, 74
2nd Kentucky	184, 186-188
3rd Ohio Cavalry	216
9th Indiana	124, 127
10th Indiana Battery	132, 133
15th Indiana	130, 132, 134
21st Wisconsin	63-66
23rd Kentucky	186, 188
24th Illinois	68, 71, 74
24th Ohio	186, 188
31st Indiana	184, 193
33rd Ohio	33
40th Indiana	127, 132

Alphabetical Index

Made in the USA
Charleston, SC
09 December 2012